Discover Your *Dream* House...

Discover Your *Dream* House...

IT COULD BE THE HOUSE YOU'RE LIVING IN NOW!

John S.M. Hamilton

BETTERWAY PUBLICATIONS, INC.
WHITE HALL, VIRGINIA

Published by Betterway Publications, Inc.
Box 219
Crozet, VA 22932

Book design and cover by Deborah B. Chappell
Text illustrations by James R. Schnirel
Photographs by Mark Boisclair, Dave Davis, and the author

Every precaution has been taken in *Discover Your Dream House* to make your home remodeling project as satisfying as possible. However, neither the author nor Betterway Publicatons, Inc. assumes any responsibility for any problems, damages, or losses incurred in conjunction with the use of this manual

---

Library of Congress Cataloging in Publication Data

Hamilton, John S. M.
Discover Your Dream house.
Includes index.
1. Dwellings—Remodeling—Amateurs' manuals.
I. Title.
TH4816.H288 1988 643'.7 88-2850
ISBN 0-932620-90-6

Printed in the United States of America
9 8 7 6 5 4 3 2 1

To Sue,
who brightens every space she enters

Several chapters were reviewed by Bob Hurt, whose thoughtful commentary was very helpful. I am grateful to him.

Special thanks to Sue Hamilton whose encouragement and positive comment was always on time and on target.

Jim Schnirel, my old friend, came through like a champion, producing the illustrations for this book on a tight schedule.

My appreciation goes to Trisha Morgan for typing — and retyping — and for being able to read my writing.

And thanks to all of you who believe that the effort made to improve your environment is worth the doing.

Table of Contents

Introduction: Help Is On The Way 11
1. Getting Started 13
2. Kitchen and Dining 29
3. Family Room and Living Space 53
4. Hobby and Recreation 75
5. Bedroom and Bath 87
6. Storage and Utility Spaces 105
7. Lighting — Natural and Artificial 121
8. Special Purpose Spaces 155
9. Additions 167
10. Exterior Improvements and Landscaping 191
11. Furnishings 203
12. The Budget 219
13. Working With An Architect 223
14. Getting It Done 227
Glossary 261
Index 267

Introduction
Help Is On The Way

Maybe you *can* afford your dream house! With the right alterations, it might be the one you're living in right now.

Two basic options are available to those whose lifestyle and needs have outgrown their existing home: (1) Buy or build another house, confronting the high cost of land, construction, and moving, or (2) Renovate your existing home into the one you always wanted.

Too often the mention of remodeling conjures up visions of confusion, wasted money or a driveway leading to a family room that was converted from a garage. It doesn't have to be that way. With good direction, you can decide where to start, what to do, and how to get the most for your money.

The remodeling process can be exciting and satisfying. A home alteration should increase the *pleasure, use* and *value* of your home. I will present methods to help you accomplish these goals.

This is a *what-to-do* book. "How to" is of little help if you can't apply it in the right direction. I want to help you to know *what to* build.

Most of my home remodel clients already have read magazines and "how-to" literature, but they voice a common complaint: the ideas presented do not apply to *their own* situation. In other words, pictures are pretty, but it's not enough to see solutions to someone else's problems. I'll show you a better way.

My success in home remodeling centers on working with homeowners to reveal the nuts and bolts of specific remodeling *needs*. I will show you how this method can apply to *your* situation.

In Chapter 1, I describe the approach used to help you get the most from the rest of the book. Read it before skipping to other chapters.

The rest of the book provides you step-by-step, room-by-room guidelines. The check list sheets with each chapter will help you to know your home, your habits, and your desires.

We will work together to identify the problems and find solutions. Priorities will be established, decisions made, and materials selected.

So let's get started. Working together, we will transform remodeling from a chore into an adventure.

1

Getting Started

The Right Approach

Good design, in home remodeling, brings new pleasure to your life. A well-designed home suits the needs and lifestyle of the owners, *and* provides a good measure of aesthetic delight.

To improve your home, *first get to know how you live within it.* You may be surprised what you learn. To accomplish this, you must study your needs, living habits, likes and dislikes, and budget.

What to Do

"I know what I want. I just don't know what to do." I have heard that so often. Knowing what to do, in home remodeling, is usually a process of elimination — arriving at the *highest priorities* among all your needs and desires. This book gives you a method to name those priorities and open your eyes to your home's potential.

Most home alterations require only that you explore the problem area and those areas affected by it. So, the job is not complicated and this book will make it even easier.

KNOW THE PROBLEM

Much remodeling money is wasted by people who don't know the problem before trying to solve it. *Do not begin any remodeling* before developing what I refer to as a *design program.* A design program starts by examining rooms, spaces and situations in your home and how well they satisfy your needs, wants, and living habits. The "*program*" then becomes a list of must haves, wants, and options for remodeling. From this list you will make your final choices about *what* to do.

Specific Needs

Perhaps you have isolated your remodeling needs to just one space or function — redoing the kitchen, for instance, or the bathrooms. Or, maybe, you want to create a special-purpose space in an unused room, or add a garage and more storage. If so, concentrate on those chapters that relate to your specific needs.

General Needs

Your remodeling needs may be general rather than specific. You might have a long list of complaints, such as: an odd traffic problem, poorly-lit rooms, a small master bedroom, a shabby yard, too little storage, not enough bathrooms, etc.

In this case, you need to read more chapters. So, use the book to meet your needs.

It's meant to help you.

In other words, use this book for guidelines, reference, ideas, and motivation. Concentrate on the chapters that will help you *now*.

As time goes by, your needs might change. Then come back to the book. It still will be helpful. Even technical and product changes happen slowly in the building industry. Guidelines given here will be applicable for a long time.

Developing the Design Program

In the following chapters, I provide you with check list sheets relating to the various areas of your home. Either copy them or cut them out for handy reference.

Creating your design program becomes simple if you use these check lists. They are easy to use and will identify the kind of changes needed in your home. I explain how to use them later in this chapter.

Whether your alterations involve one room, or the entire house, final decisions should not be made until you complete the design program. For instance, the check list results might indicate that simply redoing an unused room, or maybe adding a room, will solve everything. Not only will the check list help you decide what to do, you can proceed knowing it's the logical way to spend your money. Your *improvements will be cost effective.*

The Preconception Trap

For now, try to erase preconceived design solutions from your mind. It's possible to become attached to an idea that won't be best for your *overall* project. In the early planning phase, your mind should be free of concern about *final* choices and solutions. Let your mind expand and explore. Be receptive to what develops.

The Habit Trap

Study the habit patterns in your daily living. Habit is not necessarily based on natural desire, but often on the fact that you have been shoe-horned into your existing as-is house. You have adapted to fit the house, and habit behavior, which becomes involuntary, can cloud your thinking about remodeling capabilities. Being aware of those "shoe-horn" habits helps to create an objective, fresh approach.

Habit traps often result from bad design in a house. For instance, kitchen work takes too long because of a poor layout. You may be missing a gorgeous view, because the builder did not include a window in the right place. A poorly-planned entry can rob a room of needed privacy. You may be tolerating wasted space, such as an unused dining room or formal living room. Many examples will arise as you go through the following chapters and their check lists. *Write them down.*

Habit inhibits creative thinking. Knowing that should help you break the mold and develop new thoughts and ideas.

Write it Down

As you get into the swing of it, you will think about your remodeling at various times of the day. If you think of something worth remembering, *write it down.* Keep a file system. Don't try to remember everything. Also, the file will be valuable if you later consult a professional. This is all part of the system of "getting the most for the money"!

The Overimprovement Scare

Yes, it *is* possible to overimprove. In the traditional sense, to overimprove means spending more money on improvements than you can recover when selling the house. If you plan to sell your home soon, overimprovement is a concern. This book, however, is written for homeowners who plan to stay awhile and want to increase the use and pleasure of their house. So, certainly keep overimprovement in mind, but don't let it restrict your thoughts in the early planning stages.

Improvements that return the highest percentage of money invested are those basic to lifestyle. They include kitchen remodeling, a bathroom addition, or an effective change, such as adding a family room.

As you develop your design program, continue to *list all of your very special desires.* Don't let concern about overimprovements prevent you from considering that one unique feature you always wanted. When you review the check lists and establish priorities, that will be the time to compromise, if necessary. Remember, getting the "most for the money" is not just adding space, but includes the benefit to your lifestyle and pleasure derived from your home.

LOCAL MARKET VALUES

When overimprovement concern won't go away, spend time checking market values in your area. Consult real estate brokers and combine their input with your own research. Also, your tax assessor should have information on house sales in every neighborhood.

Overimprovement usually occurs in the subdivision-type of community. The same rules normally don't apply to urban and rural areas. In rural areas, with low density housing, the market value of your house may not be affected by the next house down the road.

Urban housing requires more study. The trend in inner-city areas to rehabilitate old neighborhoods has offered opportunities for creative home remodeling. However, research is required. What is the history of the neighborhood? Can you predict its future? To recapture costs from your remodeling investment, give your urban neighborhood careful study.

BUSINESS OR PLEASURE

Always ask yourself this question: Is your house strictly an economic venture, or is it your personal sanctuary? In today's transient society, it's often some of each. Only you can decide how much weight to place in each area.

How long will you live in your home? Your home is probably your most important environment. You spend much time there, and ingredients that help create your total environment become very important. *The total worth to you should be greater than the economic value alone.*

DESIGN HELP REQUIRED

Overimprovement is, on occasion, the result of poor design. With clever use of spaces, a good designer often can achieve your goals within budget limitations. The help of a consultant may be necessary.

Input to the Consultant

An architect, involved with remodeling design, can study your home and come up with a unique and beautiful remodeling scheme *without even talking to you.* But, done this way, there is a fair chance the finished product will not meet your personal desires and living requirements. The point again is that developing the design program is the first important step. The more information you give the designer regarding your taste, requirements, and priorities, the better the chance to use your money well for a successful end product.

The Value of Drawings

You will ultimately need complete drawings. Beginning sketches can be rough.

But, going to construction from a paper napkin sketch can result in more grief than satisfaction. For a project of any size, the results of careful planning should be spelled out in a set of plans and specifications.

CONSTRUCTION ON PAPER

Complete drawings, in effect, equate to first constructing your project on paper. Here you develop the work, refine ideas and make changes. Changes made during actual construction can be expensive! *Avoid construction "extras"*!

KNOWING THE COST

With complete plans (Note: the words *drawings* and *plans* are used interchangeably here) a contractor can bid the work and estimate the project cost. Without them, he may prefer to *work on a "cost plus" basis.*

"Cost plus" means that you pay the contractor for labor and materials as costs occur, plus a fee. With this open-ended agreement, you won't know the final cost until it arrives. It may or may not be a nice surprise.

Chapter 14, GETTING IT DONE, covers this subject in more detail.

THE DO-IT-YOURSELF PROJECT

Drawings and specifications are also necessary for the do-it-yourself project. Experienced builders know the how, what, and when of construction. You don't have that advantage, and without drawings to guide you, much time and money can be lost.

Your Existing Floor Plan

One of the most helpful tools in overall planning is the existing, or "as is", floor plan of your house. It reveals at a glance, exactly where spaces are in relation to other spaces. Planning will be easier. You will save time.

If you have the original drawings, they should show you construction materials, material sizes, and bearing walls. If complete, they will locate pipes and duct work inside the floor, walls, and ceilings. Check the drawings against your room layout and dimensions. Sometimes changes made during construction are not then noted on the original drawings.

OBTAINING THE PLAN

If you do not have the plans, possibly you can obtain prints (blueprints) from the builder or your local city building department. If not, two choices remain: (1) Hire someone to produce them, or (2) Draw them yourself.

HIRE A DRAFTSMAN

"As built" floor plans can be produced by a competent architectural draftsman. Normally, such work is done relative to an hourly rate.

DRAW IT YOURSELF

Drawing the existing floor plan of your house is not that difficult. Take it *one step at a time* and it will go together sooner than you think. Start with an 18-inch by 24-inch sheet of graph tracing paper with a ¼-inch square grid. *(See ILLUSTRATIONS Chapter 14)*

Use a separate sheet of paper for each floor. You may want to use two sheets for each floor . . . one for the first rough sketch and one for the finished drawing. Tracing paper is handy to lay one sheet over the other and see through.

You may be one of those people who say, "I couldn't draw a straight line if my life depended on it!" Forget it. You don't have to draw straight lines. Draw crooked lines. You still will benefit from the drawing.

The basic procedure is to measure the house and transfer those measurements to the paper. The drawing must be done to

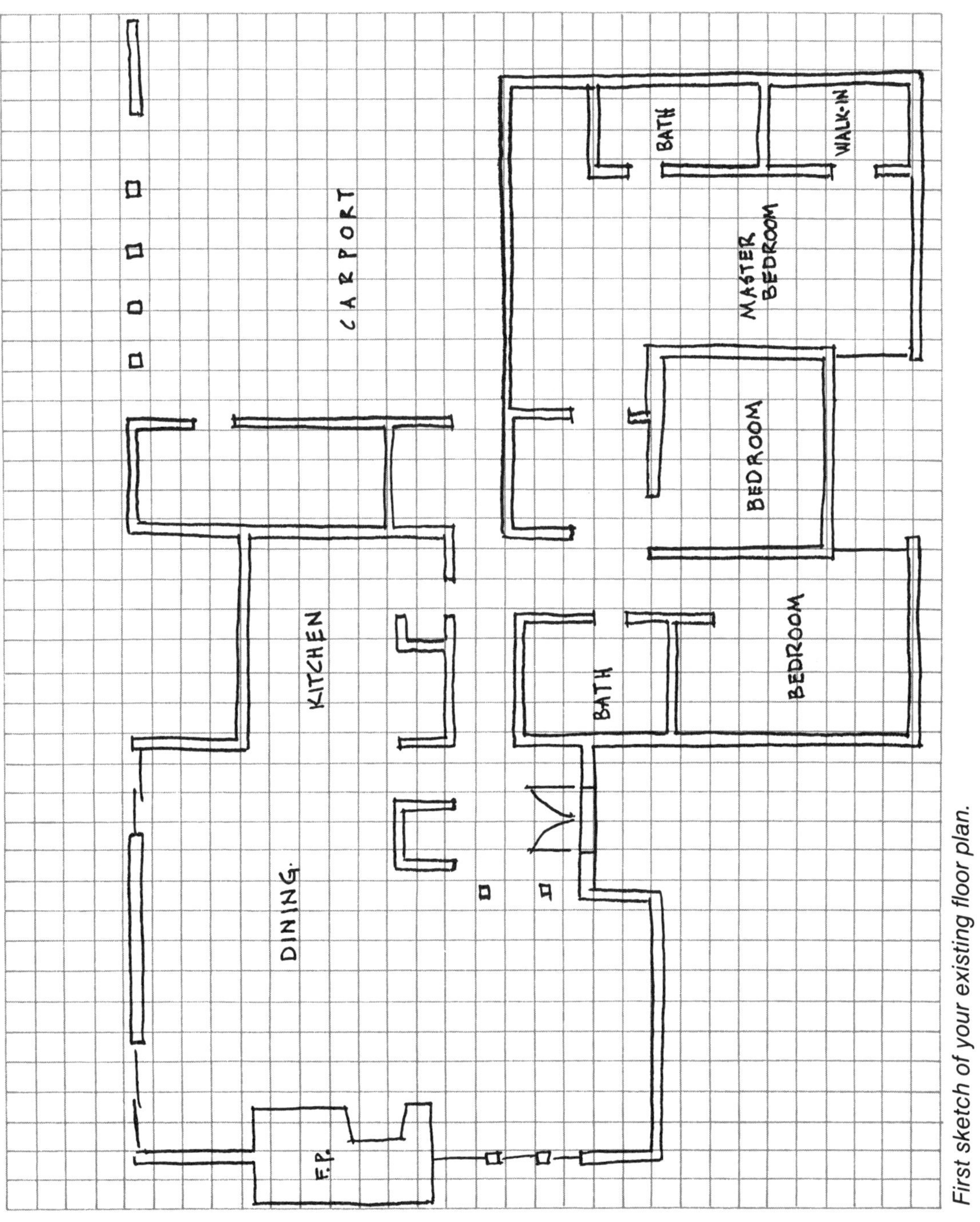

First sketch of your existing floor plan.

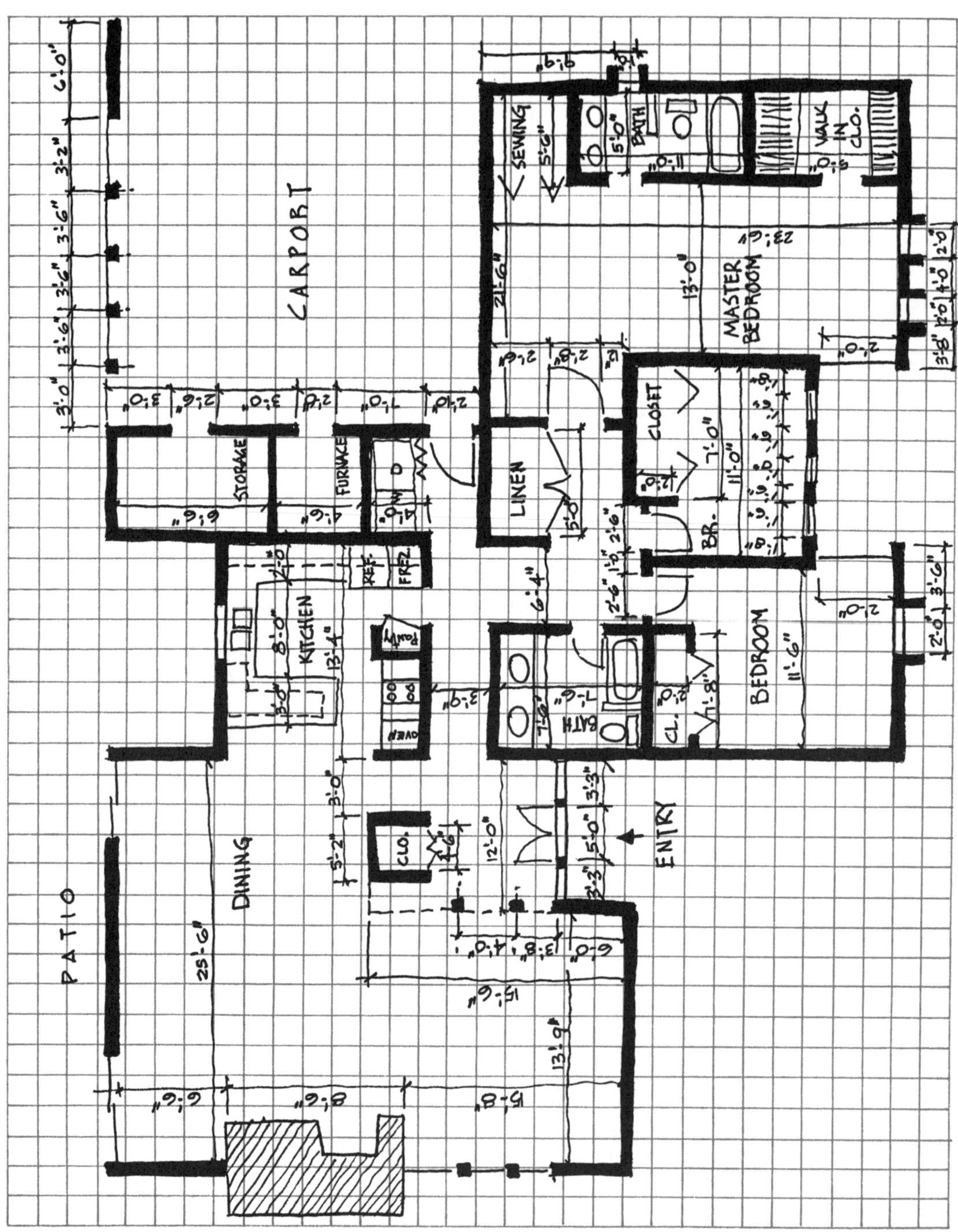

Take measurements and put the dimensions of each space on the floor plan.

accurate scale. Using the ¼ inch graph paper, start with a scale of ¼ inch equals 2 feet. For instance, if a room measures 12 feet by 12 feet, you will draw it on your graph paper using 6 squares in each direction.

First, walk through the house observing the rooms with the drawing in mind. Then, sketch the rooms on the graph paper, estimating the dimensions. After that measure each room with a measuring tape and put the dimensions on your rough drawing. Be sure to include all closets, storage areas, offsets, built-in cabinets, major plumbing fixtures, fireplaces, etc. After you complete the dimensions, redraw the plan accurately on a new sheet of graph paper. Use a double line for typical wall thickness. In a short time you will have a permanent record for your use.

I recommend two people working together, one measuring and one recording dimensions and sketching. It will go faster and be more enjoyable. The whole family will be involved eventually, so start early. If you have unidentified empty spaces on your drawing, walk through again. When the basic plan layout is done, add all large permanent items of furniture. Measure the location of all doors, windows, outside closets, etc., and include them on the plan.

Using the Floor Plan

Some people find it difficult to actually visualize in three dimension. Don't worry. When the "as built" floor plan is in your possession, take a few minutes for the following exercise. As you look at the plan, imagine yourself in different locations within the rooms. For example, you may be sitting on the sofa looking at a fireplace. (You can draw in furniture to scale the same way you draw the plan.) Visualize the walls or objects on each side of the fireplace. Then imagine (still looking at the plan) getting up and walking to the kitchen. Think about your path of travel — what you do and see in getting there. Follow similar procedures until you feel familiar with the space. Go on to other areas and rooms in a similar manner.

This procedure will be useful as you discuss the check lists in the following chapters. With the plan in hand, ideas will develop that otherwise never would have occurred to you. Also, you are better able to work with a consultant, should you decide to.

Doing it Yourself

The cost of labor often is over half of the cost of remodeling. So, if the job isn't too complicated, you may be thinking of doing it yourself.

Do-it-yourself projects require some skill, a little patience, and a whole lot of *perseverance*! Books and articles have been written and illustrated, showing how to build everything from a storage closet to an entire house. It looks easy, and in fact, most construction *is* logical, straightforward, and goes smoothly . . . if you know what you're doing! Doing it yourself can be a very satisfying experience, especially when completed. Just remember . . . be patient and persevere.

Chapter 14, GETTING IT DONE, will explore doing-it-yourself in some detail with helpful guidelines.

Your Remodeling Budget

You may have an approximate budget figure in mind. That's fine. Keep it in mind, but, in the beginning, don't let a budget figure inhibit your ability to develop the *design program*.

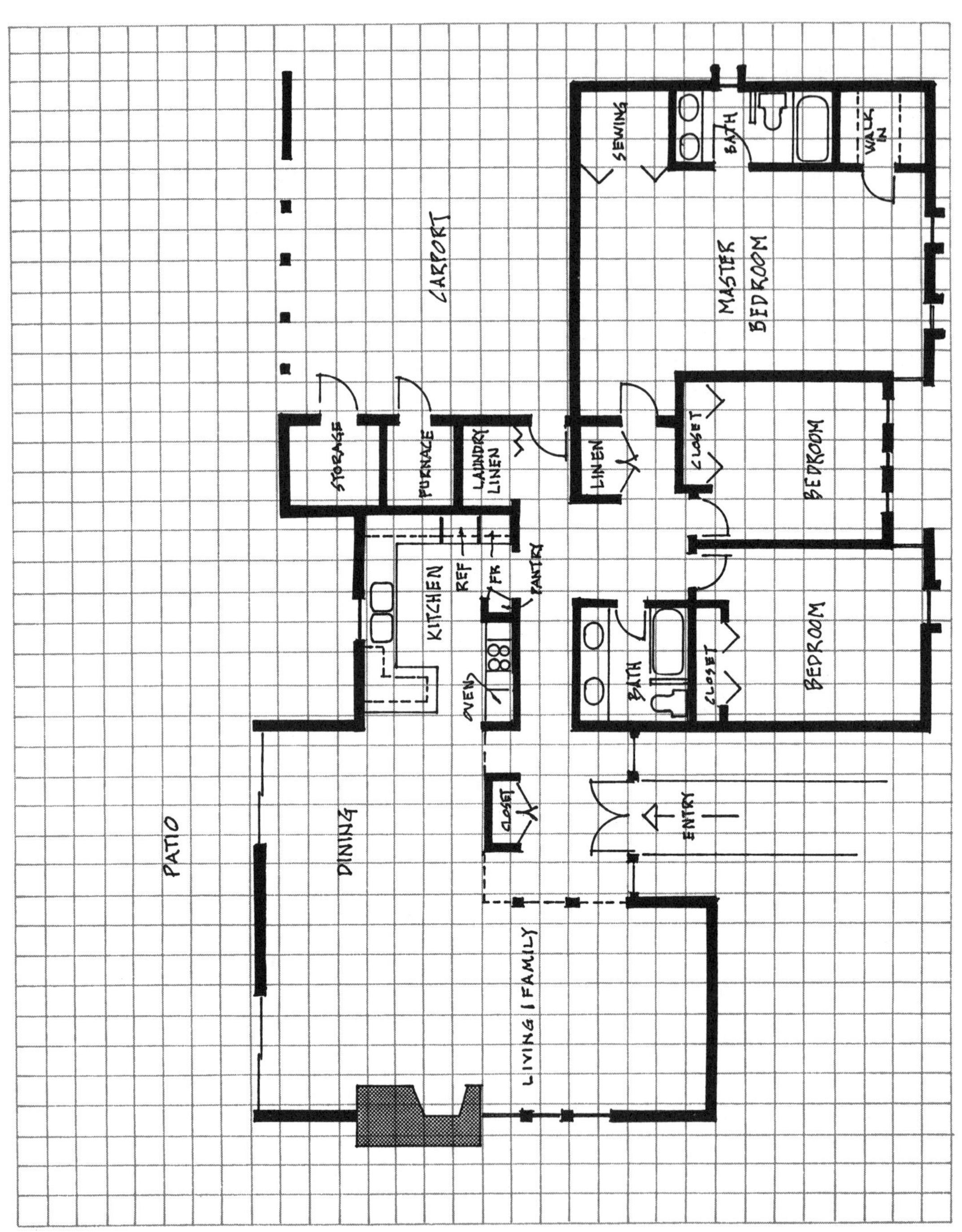

Redraw the floor plan to accurate scale.

The important thing is that you *spend the money in the right places*. To do this, first determine the order of importance of your objectives. Compromise, if it comes later, can then be handled properly.

PHASING THE WORK

If remodeling desires exceed bank deposits, you might decide to do the work in phases, a common practice. Phasing construction is discussed in Chapter 14.

Improve Your Environment

The purpose of this book is a practical one . . . to help you successfully remodel your home. To that end, I express architectural opinion stressing the value of good design and the need for a constant awareness of aesthetic considerations in your home environment. There is good reason for this.

When making home improvements, there is usually more than one way to accomplish a desired end. Why not select the method giving you the greatest *overall benefit*? Look beyond the one isolated task or the one space worked on. Enhance the general atmosphere whenever possible. Following are a few simple examples:

CREATING AN ENTRANCE

You may be adding a new walkway to your front door or increasing the roof overhang in this area for more protection. This is a good opportunity to develop that area a little further. Why not create an entrance court with added landscaping? The exterior approach to your house is an early statement about the atmosphere of your home. Start there creating a pleasant environment.

IMPROVING FUNCTION

Some homes were not planned well. There may be simple annoyances, such as poor access from one area to another. Traffic flow may be through a busy area. Problems of this nature often can be solved inexpensively, as a minor alteration, along with major improvements. Look for these opportunities as you go through the chapter check lists.

A NEW VIEW

You may be adding a fireplace on an outside wall. Since you already are removing a portion of the existing wall, consider adding glass adjacent to the fireplace masonry or nearby. Would the light make that room more interesting, or provide a nice view you had never noticed?

A good example of a beautiful, but unnoticed view occurred a few years ago during construction of a new home. My client's building site was the only lot left in a subdivision of expensive builder "spec"-type homes. We took advantage of the various minor views, but the most dramatic view was that of a beautiful rock-faced mountain. One day the next-door neighbor stopped in to introduce herself to my client. As the neighbor entered a main living space and looked through a glass wall, she exclaimed, "Oh, what a wonderful view you have!" The neighbor, of course, had the same view available, but due to poor design, was unable to take advantage of it.

Finish Building Materials

Variety of finish materials is vast. Almost any color, texture, thickness, or density is available, for any surface. Select materials for compatibility with the overall scheme.

Other chapters mention finish materials for various parts of the house. Here are a few things to keep in mind:

FLOOR

Beyond aesthetic values, function and maintenance most affect floor material choices. For instance, what areas get the most traffic, or will collect dirt or moisture from the outside? Will you need comfort for periods of standing? Are stain resistance and easy maintenance required? And so on.

WALLS AND CEILINGS

The choices are many — from rough-sawn wood, to mirrors. Selections should have meaning to the overall space, mood, and function.

COLOR

Choosing colors is a vital part of design work. Colors can make a space cheerful or dreary, warm or cold, even larger or smaller. Psychologists tell us that colors affect our subconscious state of mind. Probably so, since color is so important to the overall atmosphere.

In color selection, many people need help. If you are unsure of yourself in choosing colors for your remodeled space, seek help from a consultant.

LIGHTING

Correct lighting is important to the atmosphere and function of any space. So important, indeed, that I have included a chapter on natural and artificial lighting in this book.

Furnishings

Nothing in your home more visibly reflects your taste than your furnishings. You can furnish the same room for a few hundred dollars or ten thousand dollars. With *either* budget, it may look ordinary or it can look great. Chapter 11 discusses furnishings and accessories in more depth.

A Family Affair

Remodeling your home can be exciting for the entire family. Consult and consider everyone. Some members need special things and special spaces. Requirements range from group activity to private, quiet corners. Throughout day and night, the family lifestyle and living habits of each member involves one big interaction. Encourage all to vocalize their opinions.

Your Check List Sheets

I have included check list sheets in each of the following chapters. They are the backbone in helping you establish the design program.

In this chapter, the check lists pertain to the *general* areas of your home. Separate areas of your home are discussed in detail in the following chapters.

The check lists in this chapter provide a summary for your *final* thoughts and decisions. When you have finished other chapters, refer back here and complete these check lists by compiling the results of the other chapters' lists. If your concern is isolated to just one area, such as kitchen renovation, then probably you will concentrate on that chapter. I recommend, however, that you do the check lists at the end of each chapter. They are easy to do and provide a good reference for all aspects of your home. A sample is given in each chapter for guidance.

As you review each check list, add any thing that applies to your home which I have not included. For instance, you may want an underground vault, five bedrooms, sound studio, fitness center, etc.

It might help to make copies or cut out the check lists before reading each chapter. Having them handy while you read will let you record your thoughts as they come to you.

FILLING IN THE CHECK LIST SHEETS

Make notations for each space under all

column headings. For instance, under "Quality/Quantity of Space", think about the space quality. Is it too dark, too sunny, too cold, etc. Think about the space quantity. Is it just right, too large, too narrow, etc.

Under the column "Importance to Total Project," you should grade the tentative improvement on a scale of say one to five. Or select your own rating method.

The "Priority Rating" column is the place for the narrowing down and selection process. At this time, the influence of the budget comes into play. (Notice the Sample Check Lists.)

With the guidelines in Chapter 14, GETTING IT DONE, we will take the check list results and decide what to do and how to get it done.

The Planning Adventure

The planning experience is a creative adventure. The goal is to produce something tailored to your own desires and requirements. Until the last nail is driven and finish surface painted, you will be making decisions. Be good to yourself. Take your time, especially in developing the design program. Extra quality time spent in planning is necessary to get the most value for money spent.

If, at any time, you ever feel you have taken a wrong direction . . . *back off!* Rethink the situation. Review your options. Get professional help if you need it. Never go ahead with an unnecessary compromise, or force yourself to live with a decision that can make your remodeling less than totally successful.

Check List
— Interior Space/General Areas —

Interior Space	Existing Yes/No	Quality and Size of Space	New Features, Alterations and Additions Desired	Importance of Change to this Space	Priority Rating for Total Project	Remarks
Entry	Yes	Too small	Increase size	2	4	Increase inside area or add entrance court
Family Room	Yes	OK - dark at fireplace end	Add natural light	3	4	Skylights probably best
Den/Study	No	—	Add study built-in shelving	2	2	
Living Room	No	—	None	—	—	Re-do spare bedroom? Add entr. court/glass door
Dining Room/ Area	Yes	Too dark	Improve with better fixtures	2	3	
Kitchen	Yes	Too small poor layout	More counter & cabs; new layout/lighting	1	1	Change ceiling fixture add wall brackets?
Breakfast	No	—	Add snack bar at kitchen if possible	3	3	Re-design. Extend size new sink & dishwasher
Storage/Pantry	Yes	Too small, bad location	New pantry	1	1	O.K. to use dining area for most eating
Bathroom (Common)	No	—	Add powder room	1	1	Locate closer to sink/ /preparation area
Bedroom No. 1	Yes	O.K.	None	—		
Bedroom No. 2	Yes	O.K.				

Example of How to Use the Check List

Sample

Note: You may wish to remove or copy the check list sheets for more convenient use.

Check List

— Interior Space/General Areas —

Interior Space	Existing Yes/No	Quality and Size of Space	New Features, Alterations and Additions Desired	Importance of Change to this Space	Priority Rating for Total Project	Remarks
Entry						
Family Room						
Den/Study						
Living Room						
Dining Room/ Area						
Kitchen						
Breakfast						
Storage/Pantry						
Bathroom (Common)						
Bedroom No. 1						
Bedroom No. 2						
Master Bedroom						
Master Bath/ Dressing						
General Storage						
Laundry/Work Space						
Recreation Room						
Basement						
Attic						
Special Purpose Room						
Other						
Other						
Other						

Check List
— Exterior Space/General Areas —

Exterior Space	Existing Yes/No	Quality and Size of Space	New Features, Alterations and Additions Desired	Importance of Change to this Space	Priority Rating for Total Project	Remarks
Drive	Yes	Drive too narrow	Widen drive to two car width	3	4	
Garage/Carport	Yes	O.K	—	—	—	
Storage	Yes	Not enough storage	Redesign storage for efficiency. Add space	1	1	
Work Shop	No	—	Would like small shop area-w.6″ work counter	3	3	
Entry Area	No	—	Walled entrance court in front of house	2	4	
Patio/Courts	No	—	Add court/patio noted below	2	4	
Front	No	—	Add entry court with brick wall and patio	2	4	
Side	No	—	Add redwood deck off family room	1	3	
Side	No	—	—			
Rear	No					

Example of How to Use the Check List

Sample

Note: You may wish to remove or copy the check list sheets for more convenient use.

Check List
— Exterior Space/General Areas —

Exterior Space	Existing Yes/No	Quality and Size of Space	New Features, Alterations and Additions Desired	Importance of Change to this Space	Priority Rating for Total Project	Remarks
Drive						
Garage/Carport						
Storage						
Work Shop						
Entry Area						
Patio/Courts						
Front						
Side						
Side						
Rear						
Yards						
Front						
Side						
Side						
Rear						
Landscaping						
Storage						
Decks						
BBQ						
Swimming Pool						
Storage						
Other						

2

Kitchen and Dining

Kitchen remodeling is high on the list of all home improvements. Why do so many kitchens need to be changed? Are that many bad ones built, or must we have every latest gimmick and convenience? The answer is a little of both. There are other more positive and practical reasons, however.

Most houses are built for an average market, but, alas, we're not all average. Also, the layout and design one family considers ideal, may not work at all for the habits of another.

In addition, while most rooms can be adapted to by rearranging furniture, the kitchen is essentially a "built in" space. Therefore, to change the way a kitchen functions usually requires actual reconstruction.

Let's make the kitchen a pleasant space to be in. This chapter includes guidelines to help meet the requirements of cook and family. The check list at the end of this chapter will help to consolidate thoughts, and set priorities.

Multiple Benefits

Redoing the kitchen may provide more benefits, in one space, than is possible with any other room. It's a natural gathering place and often a focal point of the home. Any improvement to the kitchen is enjoyed by the whole family.

Good Value

Well-done kitchen improvements can increase the value and marketability of your home.

Some believe you should not personalize a kitchen because it then might not be saleable to someone else. That ignores basic priorities.

You spend much time in your kitchen. The layout should suit *you*. Have counters where convenient for *you*, storage where *you* need it most, lighting to suit *your* work habits, colors to suit *your* taste, and so forth.

OVERIMPROVEMENT

Kitchen overimprovement is possible, of course. However, fear of overimprovement should be tempered by the value of the improvement to your lifestyle. Is the cost offset by the increased enjoyment of your home?

A common guideline is to balance the spending for kitchen renovation with the general quality of the overall home.

Beyond that, it's safe to assume a great kitchen is a plus for the resale of any home.

Pretty Pictures

Enjoy, but don't be mislead, by kitchens pictured in magazine ads. What you see is often an elaborate mock-up or model kitchen not related to space in a real home. The space required for the model is often out of proportion for an average home. Ads are useful, though, to illustrate ideas, moods, materials, lighting, and color schemes.

KITCHEN STYLE

The style and decor of the kitchen should compliment the house. You may want a colonial kitchen, but if you live in a contemporary home compliment *that* style. With any style, the kitchen still can have a warm and cheerful feeling.

Construction Cost

On a cost-per-square-foot basis, the kitchen is usually the most expensive room to build or rebuild. Because of the high cost of plumbing, wiring, cabinets, and appliances, a renovated kitchen, if planned without proper consideration for cost, can exceed your budget. This chapter includes ideas to help you keep the cost in balance.

APPLIANCES

A large percentage of kitchen cost is in appliances. Careful appliance shopping is a must. I am not aware of any hard and fast rules, but here are a few suggestions:

Manufacturers often offer four or five models of the same appliance. Dishwashers, for example, go from bare bones wash-and-dry, to the top of the line, which appears to do everything except prepare the next meal. Look carefully at the model second from the bottom. Normally it does what you need done and with a much lower purchase price.

Go through this process with each appliance. Cumulative dollar savings can be considerable.

Kitchen Cosmetics

Sometimes new cabinets and appliances are installed simply because the user is tired of the old ones. Old, but still good, appliances often work as well as new ones. New cabinets, counters, and appliances can absorb a lot of the remodeling budget. Unless you redesign the *basic* layout, they don't improve the *efficiency* of the kitchen.

Also, it's relatively inexpensive to have old appliances sprayed another color to match a new decor.

THE KITCHEN CHECK LIST

If you plan to redo your kitchen, go through the check list at the end of this chapter. Give thought to the *efficiency* of your current layout. Consider the plus and minus factors of your kitchen, and define changes required.

To summarize, remodeling efforts should make your kitchen a more efficient, comfortable, and cheerful place. This requires good planning and design, not expensive cosmetics.

Your Kitchen Work Area

The most important space in your kitchen is the work area. Sink, range or cook top, and refrigerator are located here. In or near the same space are counters for mixing and chopping, as well as the major cabinets.

Planning the work area is the most important part of kitchen remodeling. Design it carefully. Other functions are important, but they only supplement the work area.

Years ago, studies showed that women on a daily basis made over 200 separate trips between sink, appliances and work counter.

Since that time, we have seen versatile small appliances and prepared foods of every nature. All save time and steps, but the work area is still key to the basic kitchen layout.

THE WORK TRIANGLE

Many layouts function well. In each one, the main work centers — sink, cook top, and refrigerator — should form a triangle. The three sides of an efficient triangle generally total between 14 to 20 feet.

The exception to the work triangle occurs in a one-counter kitchen, with all functions lined up along one wall. In this case, it's usually best to locate the sink between cook top and refrigerator.

"L" Plan.

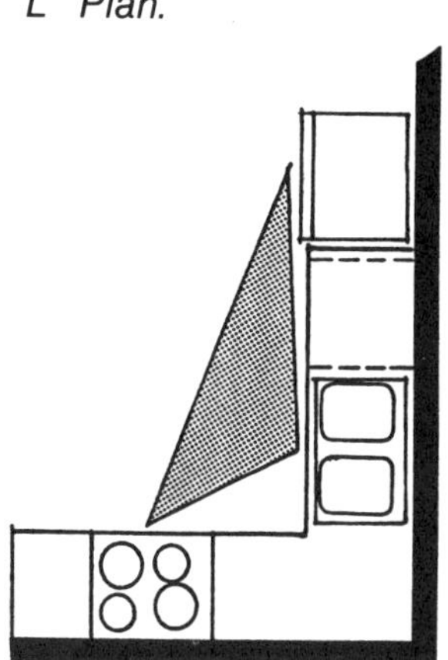

Corridor Plan 2 sides.

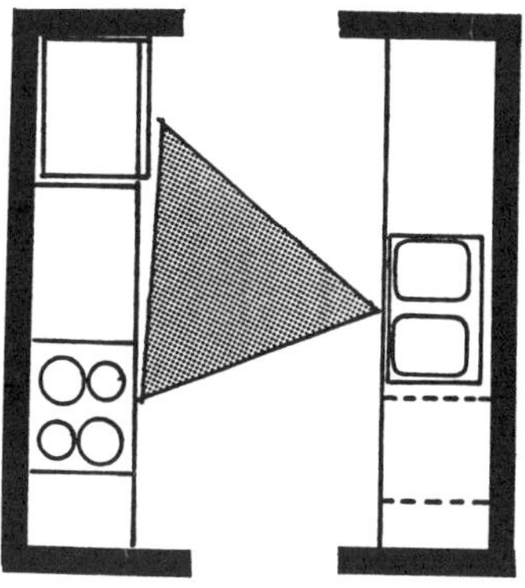

Corridor Plan 1 side.

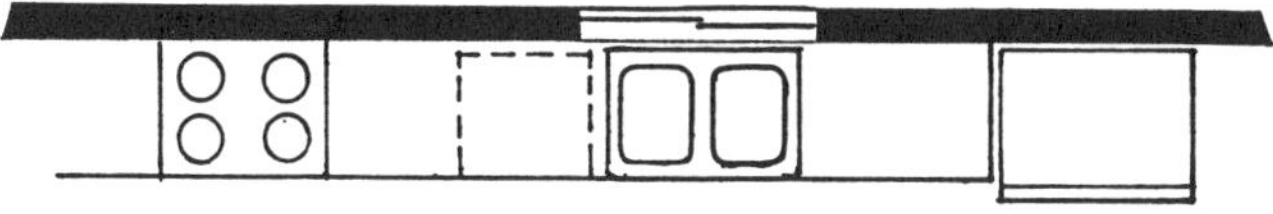

"U Plan with Peninsula.

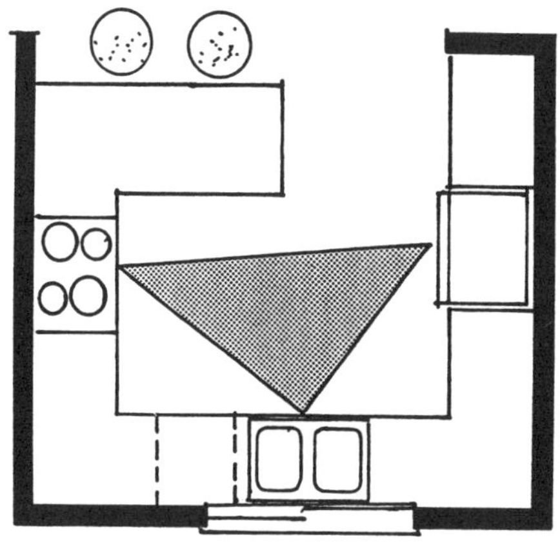

"U" Plan.

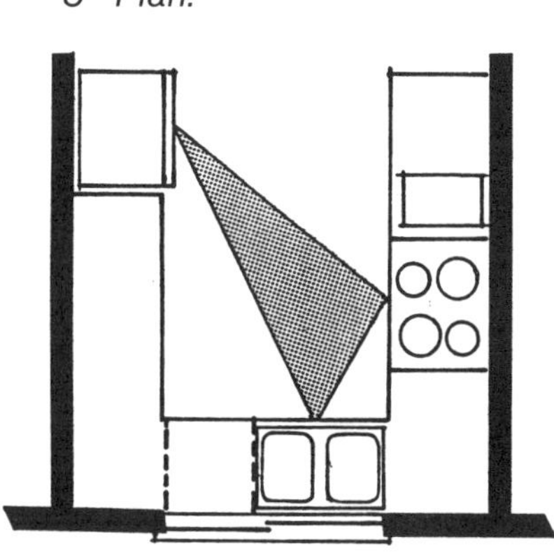

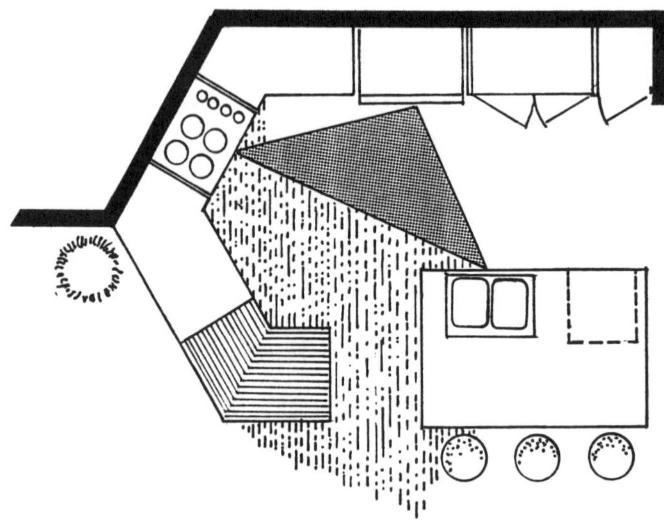

Variation No. 1.

Variation No. 2.

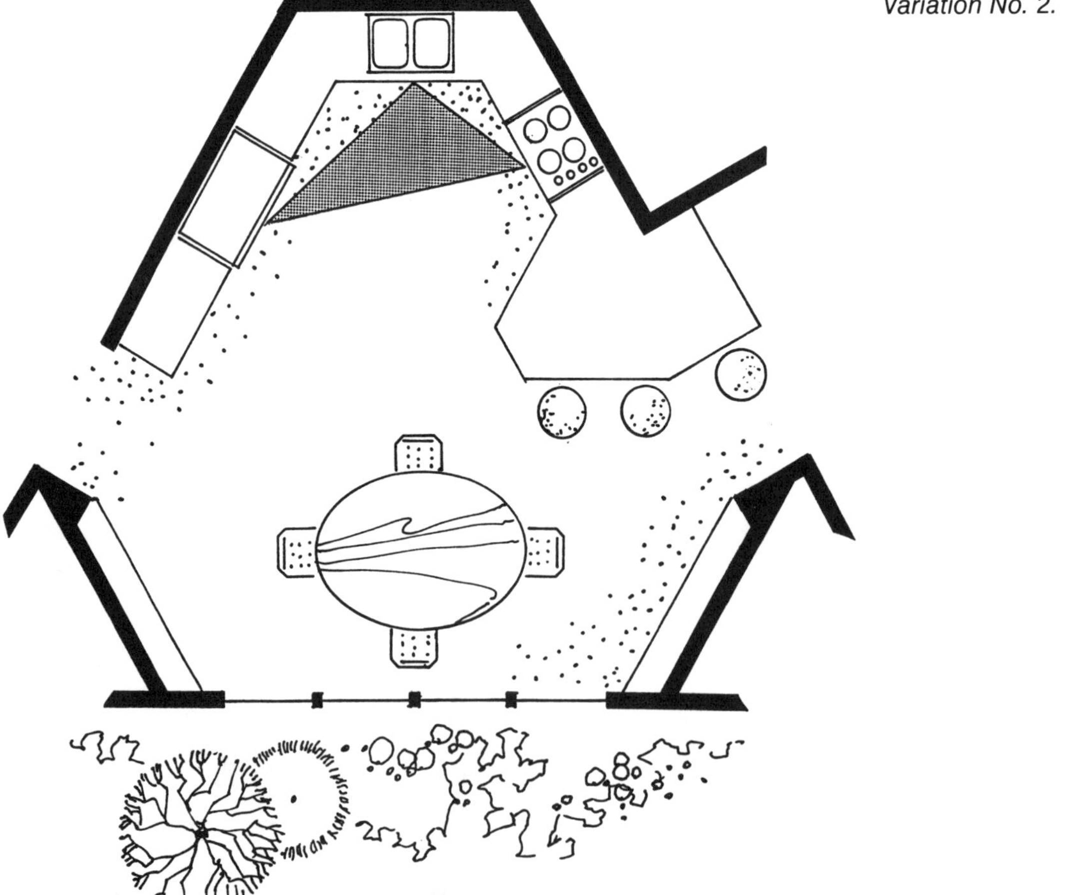

Basic Kitchen Plans

Your floor plan arrangement can form a "U", an "L", a corridor with two counters, one counter, or include an island. It also can be angular or free form. The key is simply a good basic work area.

BREAKING THE RULES

The layouts discussed here — the basic work area and the work triangle — apply to typical kitchen work patterns and are good guidelines. However, as in most design, rules can be broken if the total arrangement doesn't make sense for *your* habits and lifestyle. If you deviate from the typical kitchen layout, do so for good reason, and try to think ahead about any problems which could result.

CAREFUL PLANNING ON PAPER

Work out your kitchen on paper. Make a plan. Imagine yourself working in the space. Go through the check list with the new plan, resolving situations on paper. Changes during or after construction are expensive.

NOTE: It can be useful to have the check list (shown at end of chapter) handy as you proceed through the rest of this chapter.

Planning kitchen storage, like the basic layout, is mostly common sense. Nevertheless, it's easy to overlook storage for some items — such as portable appliances, electrical devices, utensils, trays, etc. Remember those special things that help you function best, in your own unique way, and find space for them.

WRITE IT DOWN

Write down your thoughts about storage needs. File them with kitchen/dining notes, and use them with the check list.

CREATE NEW SPACE WITHIN THE OLD

Conceive the most effective use of all enclosed spaces. Look for wasted space and put it to use. Here are a few ideas to direct your thinking:

1. Organize cabinet space for optimum storage. Adjustable-type shelving is one way. Cabinet organizers are available. Install shelving on backs of doors. Provide rolling extension slides on hard-to-use lower shelves. Ideas generate browsing through merchandise in home do-it-yourself stores.
2. Provide doors on opposite sides of dead corner cabinet space.
3. Create full floor-to-ceiling cabinet storage, two feet deep, in areas where you can give up some counter space. This is effective use of space and works well at the end of a counter. Use roll out shelves.
4. Use stud wall cavity space for narrow pantry type shelving. I first started putting pantry storage within stud walls years ago in apartment kitchens, where any extra storage was a boon.

PANTRY STORAGE

Pantry storage deserves more attention than it gets. Often, pantries are a poorly designed use of left-over space. Give thought to location, size, arrangement, and depth of shelving to best suit your storage. It may be best to have more than one pantry closet. Remember that shallow closets are an efficient use of space for pantries.

SPECIAL STORAGE SPACES

Consider the following:

1. What storage to be near sink?
2. What storage to be near cook top or oven?
3. What storage to be near the serving or eating areas?
4. How will you store pots and pans?
5. Consider storage for special shapes, such as large trays and bowls, tall glassware, portable appliances, and so forth.
6. Will you need a place for storing bottled water and dispenser?

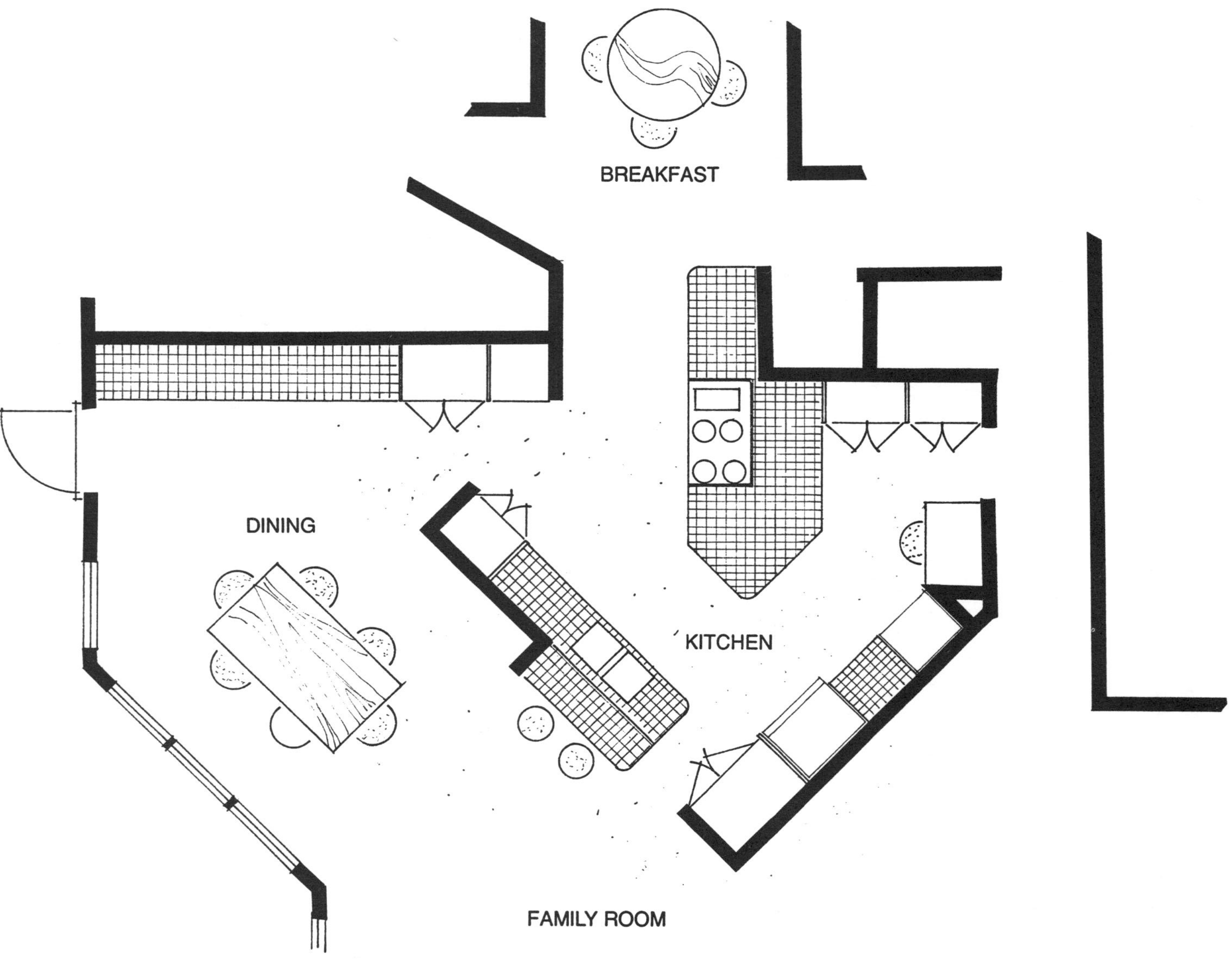

An example of a deviation from a typical layout that works well for this family.

Full height, counter depth storage cabinet.

Using stud wall cavity space for a narrow pantry.

Roll out drawers for easy access to back of shelf.

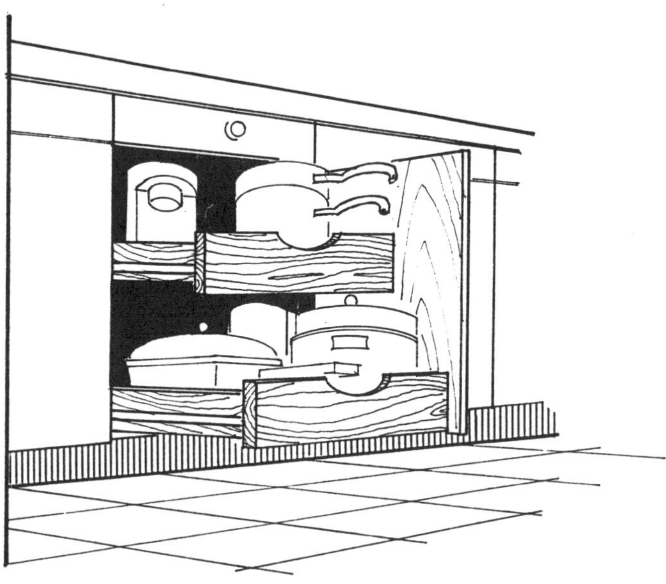

Planning

In new construction, kitchen planning is relatively easy. In remodeling design, the kitchen usually is planned within restrictions of *existing* conditions. That includes plumbing in place, electrical wiring, doors, and windows.

YOU CAN MAKE CHANGES

Economy and good sense dictate that you work within existing conditions. However, don't become mentally locked into keeping all existing openings and utility locations. You might miss out on a new design that would require only minor changes. The expense of such work may be small, with large benefits from a new layout.

I am not suggesting that you throw caution to the wind regarding cost. Just avoid mental blocks and keep all options open.

Making use of a dead corner.

Examples of Variations in Layout

SINK LOCATION

About 40% of kitchen work time is spent at the sink. The advantage of having the sink at a window is obvious. However, in some homes, other locations might be better. For instance, you might rather face an activity area, or look through the windows of an adjacent eating space.

DISHWASHER LOCATION

Moving the dishwasher from one side of the sink to the other usually involves a minor plumbing expense. Cabinet work is also involved and may or may not be minor. However, if it will improve the work center, get an estimate of cost to make the change.

Plan ahead to custom install items such as bottled water coolers.

Storage above deep counter for small appliances and food prep items.

OVEN LOCATION

The oven, in concept, is one of the oldest methods known for food preparation. Its importance is taken for granted. However, review its frequency of use in *your* kitchen. You may choose to move it and create needed space in the work triangle area. For most people, the oven is not used frequently enough to justify putting it in the work triangle.

MICROWAVE OVEN LOCATION

The microwave may prove an exception to the rule regarding oven location. With shorter cooking time, the microwave is a relatively low energy user. And because of its versatility, it might belong in your basic work area.

Looking across breakfast area for an outside view.

Dining

Kitchen and dining spaces are so interrelated that any planning discussion should involve both spaces.

The typical American house has been built to provide two eating spaces — a breakfast area and separate dining room. Whatever your spaces are, now is the time to consider their effectiveness — and the need for both.

THE RESALE THEORY

Realtors have said we need the separate dining room for resale. This might apply to the majority of homes. However, it seems less true as time goes by and space becomes more costly.

DINING SPACE OPTIONS

If you feel the need for a separate formal dining room, then keep it, of course. However, if you think the eating area can be included

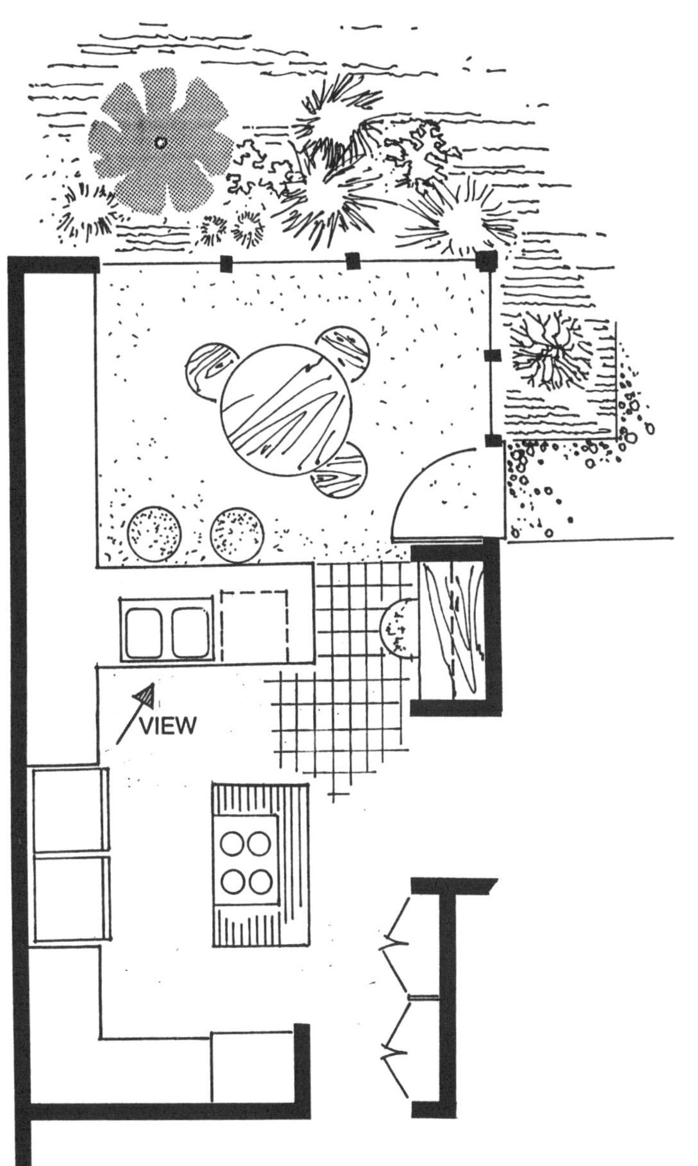

View through another space to the outside.

in another space, some or all of the existing dining room may be used for another function.

If space is at a premium, another option is to retain the dining room as the *only* eating area.

The typical dining room, especially in older homes, is a separate room, and quite inflexible. In that case, consider taking out a non-load bearing wall. Expand the room and create a more cheerful, accessible, and inviting space.

Think about opening up your dining visually to the outside. For privacy, try landscaping or high walls creating an outside court area. In addition, add a door to the area and create an outdoor eating space.

OUTDOOR EATING

An outdoor eating area is a plus to any home. Decide what is needed to make it successful, such as: What time of day will it most often be used? What are the normal weather conditions? What protection do you need? Do you want morning sun at breakfast? Do you want to take advantage of a nice view? And so on.

A Closed Dining Room.

Opening the Dining Room to the outside and part of the kitchen.

Surface Materials

Every surface in the kitchen has its own special criteria for selection. Products for kitchen use are made for appearance, durability, and easy maintenance. Quality control varies, however. Try to check with someone who has used the product. Advantages and disadvantages should be known before making a selection.

In Chapter 14, GETTING IT DONE, I discuss floor and counter top materials. You will find information to help make a final selection.

Cabinets

Cabinets represent a large part of the cost of any kitchen improvement. Take your time in selection. Look at samples available in your area. Get comparative prices.

The three typical materials are wood, laminated plastic and metal. Prefabricated cabinets are less expensive than custom-built. Custom-built cabinets, however, offer total flexibility and design variation.

A spacious Dining Room but separated from other areas.

Walls and Ceilings

Material selection relates to the total kitchen design, and the atmosphere desired. When choosing wall and ceiling treatment, consider cleaning, light reflection, material cost, and color. Wall covering is often used, but, generally, painted surfaces do nicely.

Lighting

Good lighting provides a warm, cheerful atmosphere. Some people prefer well-distributed light throughout the kitchen. Others prefer high intensity lighting in the work center areas only. The key work center areas, such as sink, food preparation, and mixing center, do require the best lighting. Chapter 7, LIGHTING, contains other lighting information.

Plans and Detailed Drawings

In due time, you will draw or acquire the "as built" house plan described in Chapter 1. If you don't retain professional help for redesign, here is a tip: Isolate and make separate drawings of the kitchen space. The drawings should be to an accurate scale. Include the floor plan and an elevation (vertical front view) of each wall showing the cabinets, windows, and doors.

Dining Room becomes dining area — part of a large spacious area.

Final Detailed Plans

When the kitchen redesign is complete, you then need detailed plans of exactly what you want. The need is two-fold.

First, there is a lot going on in one space and, to insure that everything is remembered and fits where it belongs, complete drawings are a must. Also required is a written description of the materials and the finish for each surface.

The second reason is to obtain accurate costs from your builder prior to starting the remodeling.

Detailed Cabinet Drawings

When your builder is selected, spend time discussing the kitchen plans. You both should understand what is expected.

Prior to fabrication of the cabinets, insist on drawings from the cabinet maker showing how he plans to make the cabinets. This is not an unusual service. It should not be an extra cost. Look over these drawings to be certain you are getting everything you want. Insist that the builder or cabinet maker take his own measurements of the space prior to beginning the cabinet work. Ask to see samples of the cabinets you will receive.

Planning Considerations

Following is a list of items to help you complete the check list for this chapter. Consider these items as they relate to *you and your new kitchen*:

1. How many people work in food preparation? (Relates to size and arrangement of work triangle.)

Provide 24 inches minimum on one side of cook top. Provide 36 inches minimum on one side of sink.

Provide 24 inches minimum next to refrigerator.

2. Discuss cooking habits and preferences.
    a. Be honest. Do you like to cook or is it a required chore? (Relates to things such as pantry and freezer size, microwave and oven location, appliances, and *relative importance of total kitchen remodeling.*
    b. Do you like a place for everything and everything in its place? (Relates to needed cabinets and storage.)
3. Family eating habits:
    a. Where do you like to eat breakfast? Lunch? Dinner? What space is needed?
    b. Does the family eat all meals together?
    c. Do you want an eating area: (1) out of sight of kitchen; (2) within sight of kitchen; (3) in the kitchen?
4. What kind of cooking do you do? Do you need: (1) extra storage for ingredients; (2) more counter area for mixing and preparation?
5. Does the family gather in the kitchen during the meal preparation? (Relates to having space near the work triangle for the non-workers.)
6. Does traffic route through the kitchen go to other areas? If so, correct that condition.
7. Total counter space needed:
    a. Do you need all existing counter? What is not well-used may be converted to better space.
    b. At the sink, 18″ to 36″ is required on each side. The amount depends upon your work methods. Have at least 36″ on one side.
    c. At cook top, have 24″ minimum on one side.
       Provide a heat-resistant insert nearby for hot pot parking.
    d. At the refrigerator, a counter 18″ to 24″ at the latch side is usually enough for food on its way in or out.
    e. For food preparation (mixing, baking), combine the uses at one counter space or have separate spaces, whatever your preference. Try for 48″ minimum for combined use.
    f. A serving counter is handy. Located between the work triangle and dining area, it can serve double duty as eating or bar counter.
    g. Do you want an eating counter?
    h. Will you have a wet bar elsewhere? (Relates to storage for beer, wine, liquor, soft drinks, ice, etc.)
    i. Note: Overall, you need *adequate* counter space, not excessive counter space.

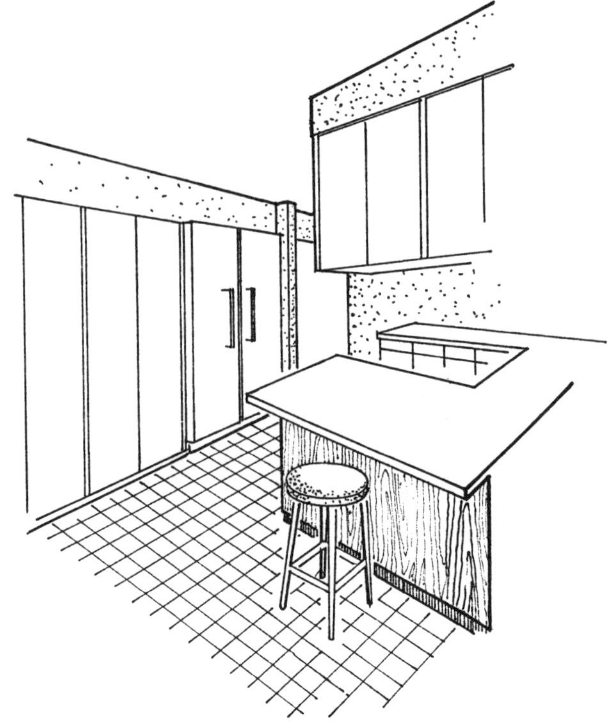

Counter used for refrigerator duty and eating bar.

8. What about counter heights? The standard counter is 36″ high. Dishwashers, trash compactors and full range units are made to fit under or within a 36″ counter. If you like to work at a shorter or taller height for food preparation, change the counter height in that area. If you go shorter, remember that appliances may not fit under in that area.
9. Do you entertain often? Formally or casually? (Relates to serving counter and storage space needed.)
10. Do you need cookbook shelving? Desk space?

For short people, a lower counter in the food prep area. A swing-out seat can be used.

Double duty as a serving counter and eating bar.

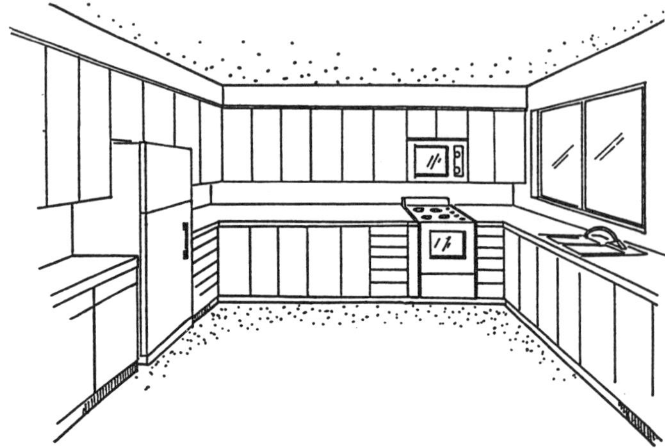

BEFORE *A large kitchen with wasted space.*

AFTER *The same kitchen with peninsula counter added as a food prep area and eating bar.*

11. Do you want a telephone in the kitchen? Where?
12. What is the access between kitchen and dining? Should you improve it?
13. For general storage, think about improvements. For example:
    a. Plan for optimum use of all cabinet space. (Relates to type of drawers, type of shelving and their locations.)
    b. Special spaces for special things, such as knives, trays, large pots, etc.
    c. Check your glassware, silver, portable appliances, etc.
    d. Check needs for linen, paper, plastic wrappings, etc.
    e. Don't forget storage near the cook top for cooking tools, pots, pans, skillets, etc.
14. Define pantry storage requirements. Do you need bulk storage, such as for pet food, as well as for cans, boxes, and bags?
15. What is your oven use? (Relates to location, what kind, and how many?).
16. Are you familiar with microwave or other alternate cooking devices? If not, investigate before planning further. You may decide later that you want it.
17. What kind of lighting do you like?
18. What have you always wanted in your kitchen? Could it be a barbecue grill, a separate freezer, a large chopping block, a rack for hanging pans, etc.?
19. Do you want an island? The island has benefits. It adds efficiency to certain layouts, and the look itself is a feature. However, the kitchen must be larger than average to include it. I feel you should have 4 feet minimum between the island and nearest counter or appliance.

    Some older homes have large square kitchens with wasted space in the center, but not enough to add an island. There are other ways to utilize the space, such as create a peninsula extension on one or two counters, or widen one counter for an eating area.
20. Remember, the most heavily used leg in the work triangle is between the sink and cook top. Locate cook top near sink.

21. The sink is the most used piece of equipment in the kitchen. Its location is key to a good layout.
22. If your work area is efficient, changes may involve only cosmetics, lighting, appliances, or improving amenities *outside* the basic work area.
23. How does the kitchen relate visually and functionally to other spaces? Improvement may be possible. For example, if rooms are small, consider opening up part of the kitchen to the dining area or family activity space.

With total kitchen renovation, it's often wise to seek the help of a consultant involved with remodel work. Further guidelines appear in Chapters 13 and 14.

Check List

— Kitchen and Dining/General Design —

Space or Features	Existing Quality	Desired Change	Remarks: Include materials desired, changes required, etc.
Flooring	Poor	Replace	Change to new material - wood or ceramic tile
Walls	O.K.	Repaint	Repaint to off-white
Ceiling	O.K.	Change w/lighting	Lower part of ceiling for full lighting at work counter
Cabinets and Storage	Fair	Add cabinets	Add 1 full height cabinet and upper cabinets
Below Counter	Fair	Want more drawers	Add drawers to left of sink and to left of cook top
Above Counter	Fair	Need more	Add 3 or 4 feet of upper cabinets if possible
Full Height Cabinet Storage	Do not have	Would like at least one	Add 1 full height cabinet - 18″ minimum width
Pantry	Yes	Increase storage efficiency	
Desk or Writing Area			

Example of How to Use the Check List

Sample

Note: You may wish to remove or copy the check list sheets for more convenient use.

Check List

— Kitchen and Dining/General Design —

Space or Features	Existing Quality	Desired Change	Remarks: Include materials desired, changes required, etc.
Flooring			
Walls			
Ceiling			
Cabinets and Storage			
Below Counter			
Above Counter			
Full Height Cabinet Storage			
Pantry			
Desk or Writing Area			
Book Shelving			
Lighting			
Traffic Pattern			
Within Kitchen			
Through Kitchen			
The Work Triangle			
Doors and Openings to Other Spaces			
Relationship to Eating Areas			
Relationship to Outside			
Dining Space			
Breakfast Space			
Other			
Other			

Check List

— Kitchen Features —

Appliance and Work Centers	Existing Yes/No	Location	Condition or Quality	Remarks: Discuss colors, locations, efficiency, replacement, etc.
Sink	Yes	Good	Chipped and scratched	Location good, want new stainless steel sink
Disposer	Yes	Good	O.K.	Save
Dishwasher	Yes	Good	Poor	Replace with new dishwasher
Range or Cook Top	Yes	Fair	O.K.	Relocate close to sink and refrigerator
Refrigerator	Yes	O.K.	O.K.	—
Freezer	No*	—	—	Freezer in refrigerator*
Other	—	—	—	—
Other	—	—	—	—
Preparation and Mixing Counter	No	—	—	Add space if possible
Chopping Counter	Yes	Between sink and cook top		
Hot Pot Counter Insert	Yes	Between sink and cook top		
Other				

Example of How to Use the Check List

Sample

Note: You may wish to remove or copy the check list sheets for more convenient use.

Check List

— Kitchen Features —

Appliance and Work Centers	Existing Yes/No	Location	Condition or Quality	Remarks: Discuss colors, locations, efficiency, replacement, etc.
Sink				
Disposer				
Dishwasher				
Range or Cook Top				
Refrigerator				
Freezer				
Other				
Other				
Preparation and Mixing Counter				
Chopping Counter				
Hot Pot Counter Insert				
Other				
Other				
Ovens				
Ovens (Microwave/Convection)				
Trash Compactor				
BBQ Grill				
Island				
Snack Bar				
Other				
Other				
Other				

3

Family Room and Living Space

Family and social functions gravitate to that part of the house which gives the greatest feeling of comfort.

The "family room" has come full circle. Some of you may remember that closed off, little used, space called the "living room"? It had the "good" furniture, never occupied. Well, the so called "open plan", combining Kitchen, Family and Dining spaces, was a natural evolution from formal house plans that didn't work.

When housing costs began to rise, a seldom-used living room occupied space too valuable to waste. So, let's talk about *living spaces* instead of living rooms, and discuss how to get the most use from each space — the "most for the money." The trick is to have all spaces well used. To do that each must fit the needs that are uniquely yours. Each space must be an integral part of a total scheme.

A well-used family room is multipurpose by nature. Without good planning, it can look like a dumping ground of toys, magazines, trophies, TV trays, and knick knacks. Because it's the common area of your home, it becomes a showcase for favorite things. It closely reflects your taste.

What are Your "Living Needs"?

Each family member has unique needs. Discuss how everyone feels about the present living, social, and family spaces. Decide what works, what doesn't, and what's needed.

Busy people, with a lot of interests, need spaces that are specially planned to make it all work. You could say to me, "There's no way to add or create enough space for all the things we want to do." Don't bet on it. Creative thinking does wonders.

PRIVATE PLACES

In planning, separate the activities that need privacy. Privacy needs are audio, visual, and psychological. Examples: Play areas for children or adults can be noisy. Quiet space for reading, study, or conversation are needed. Separate music listening areas are helpful. Rock and Rachmaninov are not compatible. Sound control usually means a closed room, but also can be done with separation by distance. Other needs might be met with nothing more than a seat in a bay window, or simply rearranging the furniture.

Valuable is that niche or quiet corner for your private relaxation and detachment from the clamor and chaos of the world. To have a place where you can take a step back and recharge the batteries in quiet perspective is the pause that pays in an active life.

Versatility as a Goal

Pre-planned versatility is the key to having a space that accommodates all your activities without looking cluttered. From VCR, home movies, game table, and computer; to fireplace, wet bar, library, and conversation, a planned space can let it all happen, with a sense of order and cozy comfort.

BUILT-IN ENJOYMENT

Toys, for either adults or children, are often complex and expensive and need their own built-in space. An activity-family area that is essentially *built-in* is a good idea. As you know, built-in means that you can't move things around, so plan it first on paper. Go through the exercise described in Chapter 1, imagining yourself in the space while looking at the plan. Place other people in the space in your imagination. Move people and objects around and see how it all works.

STORAGE

Often overlooked in family/living areas is the need for storage. Good storage reduces clutter, allows versatility, and keeps a room looking warm and friendly.

As an example, select a room of high use, either existing or planned. List the activities that will happen in this room. Think about the multi-purpose aspects of the room. Will there be toys and games for children and the family as a whole? Will an occasional guest sleep there and need closet space? Items like firewood, games, TV, stereo, writing desk or even a guest bed, might require hidden storage space.

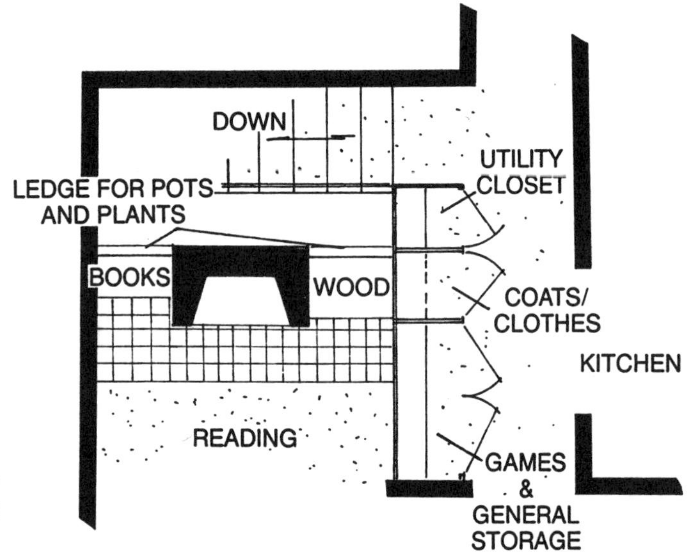

A small preplanned space took care of miscellaneous storage for the general living area of this home.

Multi-function wall storage units allow versatility in family/living space.

WET BAR

There are almost as many ways to handle a wet bar as there are drinkers. Some homes feature an elaborate bar while others put it behind cabinet doors. Success usually is found in between the two extremes — somewhere within the space, but not dominating.

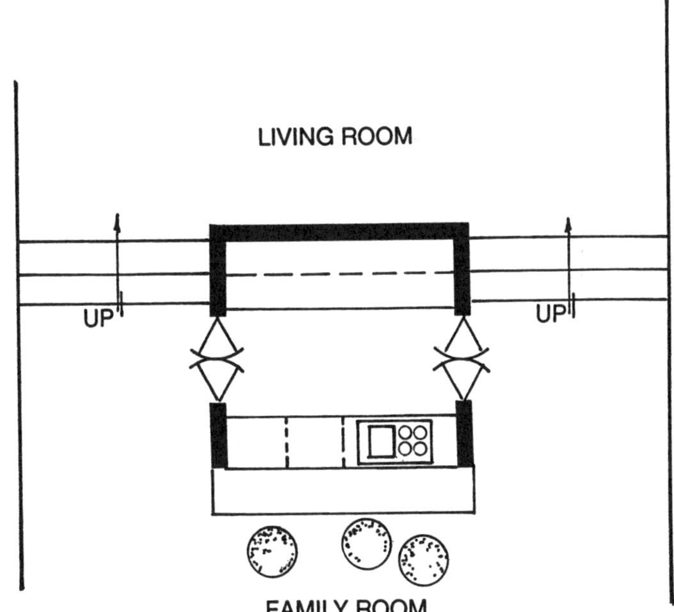

This bar/soda fountain separates the living and family room spaces.

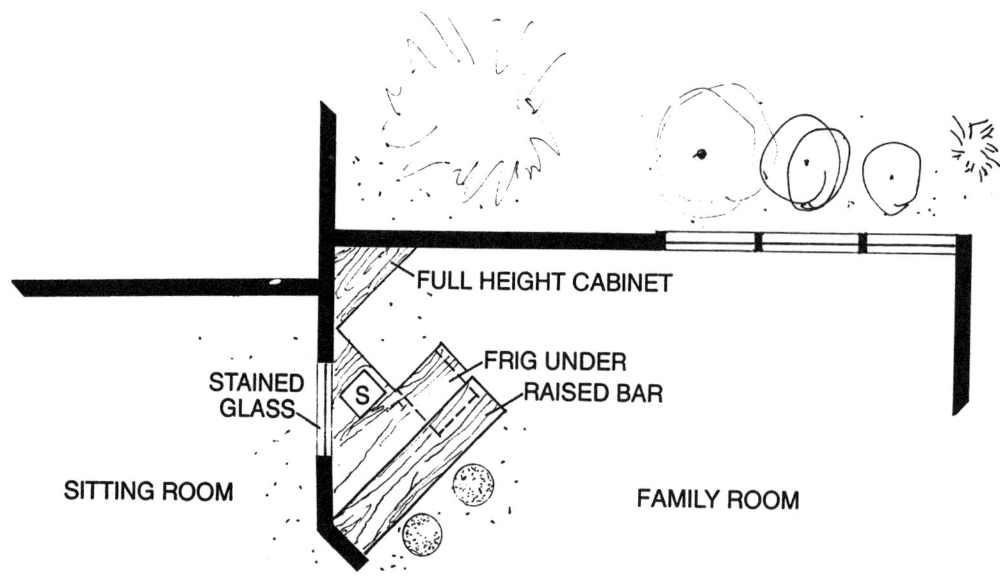

Wet bar tucked in a corner, to serve both sitting and family room.

Entertainment center: One side contains TV, VCR, and storage. Opposite is a bar with sink, refrigerator, bottle wells, and storage.

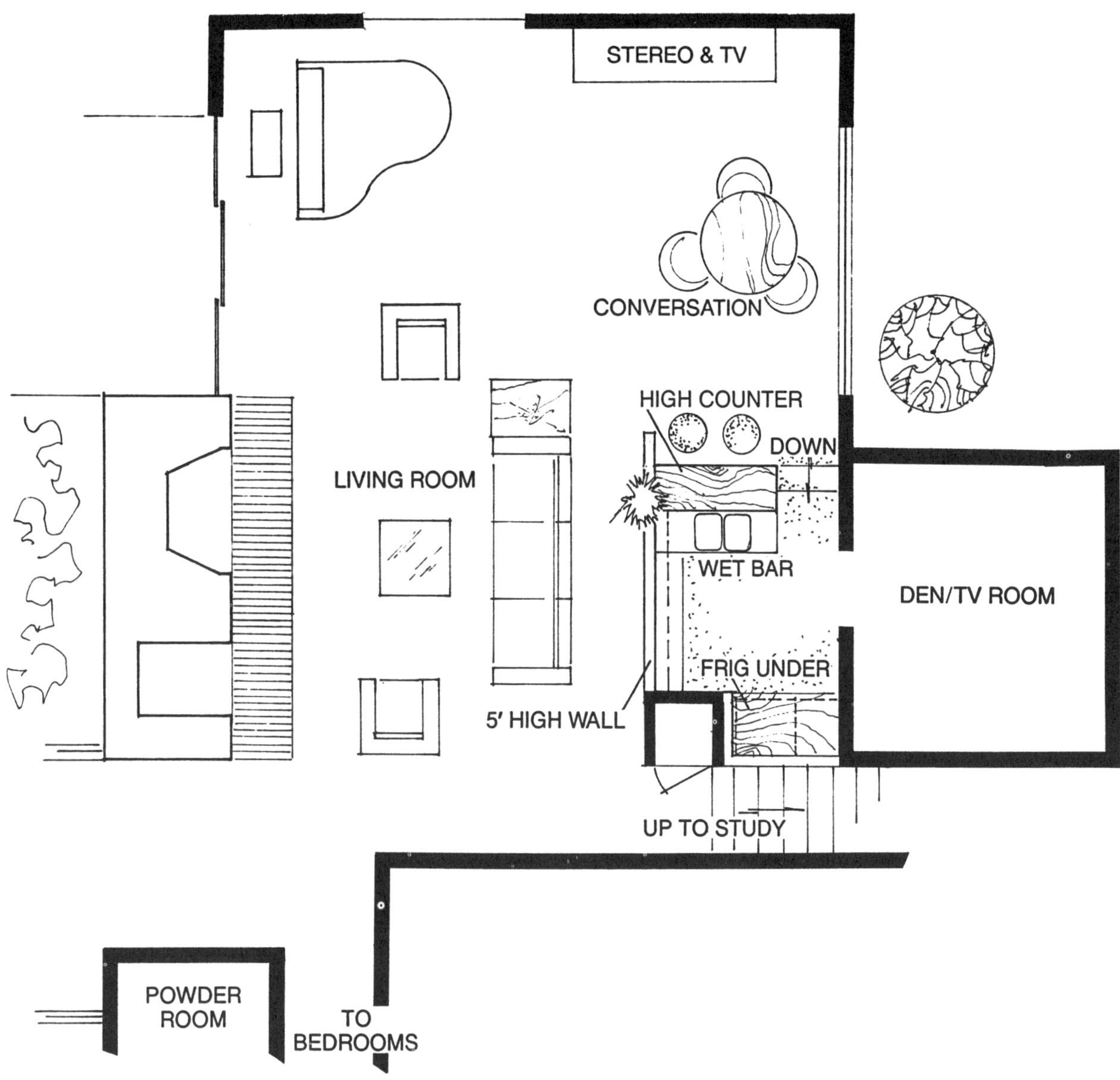

A wet bar that is in he living area without really being in *the area. Physical access with visual separation is the key.*

The Open Plan

Open planning has come to mean opening up the kitchen to dining — to family — to living — etc. Successful degrees of open planning vary with each of us, because each have our own lifestyles and habits.

An open plan might work better for a family with quiet habits rather than noisy. Sometimes open planning works better if spaces are large. Distance and separation provides a degree of privacy, while visual contact and spatial interest is achieved.

On the other hand, many small homes have been renovated to partial open plans, eliminating the feeling of small, cramped spaces. Open planning with remodeling can be more successful than with initial construction. That point assumes that you have lived there awhile and know how the house plan works for you.

TOGETHERNESS ISN'T EVERYTHING

In your planning, remember to think about *all* living habits. Don't lose the ability to have a space for privacy. Togetherness is great, but probably not full time. Leave a niche or two for that quiet time to relax by yourself.

TIME AND PLACE

Opening up a closed plan can be effective for a couple whose children have left the nest. At this time in your life you might be thinking of looking for another home. Consider a few remodeling options first.

An adjacent bedroom can become part of an enlarged living area. Special purpose ideas can be developed and unique areas created. This is also a good time to replace some of that worn furniture and carpeting. Letting space and functions flow together can create a feeling so fresh and interesting that a prior urge to move might disappear.

CHECK THE STRUCTURE

Creating an open plan usually means removing interior partitions, which may be load bearing. Load-bearing partitions can be removed, but the load from above must still be supported. The entire process of removing partitions, walls, or other structural work should be done by a professional. This procedure is discussed in more detail in later chapters.

KEEP IT INTERESTING

Generally a new space that turns out to be fun is the result of a partial rather than total open plan. Good open planning doesn't mean that you should see everything from any one viewpoint. As with views to the outside, it's better to have a surprise or change in atmosphere by turning a corner to another portion of a space. Interest is sustained in this way.

An open feeling can result from just borrowing light or ambiance from another area. To this end, partial openings in walls can be used to pick up light from skylights, a view through glass or the glow of a fireplace.

OPEN FROM THE KITCHEN

Not every cook wants to be isolated in creative privacy. If you feel left out of family activities during kitchen duty, it's a good case to remove walls and bring activities in sight of each other.

DISADVANTAGES

Energy savings may suffer with open planning. It's more difficult to control separate heating and cooling zones. Also you may have to heat or cool a large space when you wish to use only a portion of it.

There are ways to balance mechanical systems to partially offset the control problem with an open plan. In addition, passive and

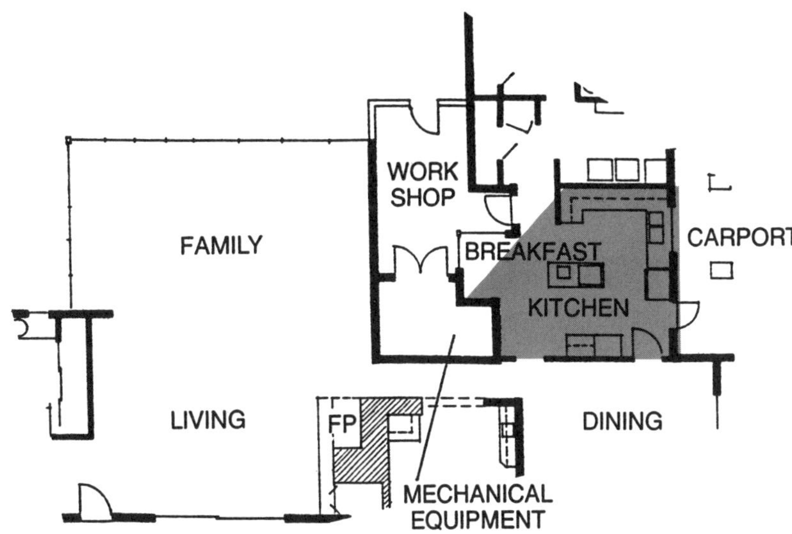

BEFORE *Due to a poorly done previous remodeling, the existing kitchen was isolated from family activity. It overlooked the carport.*

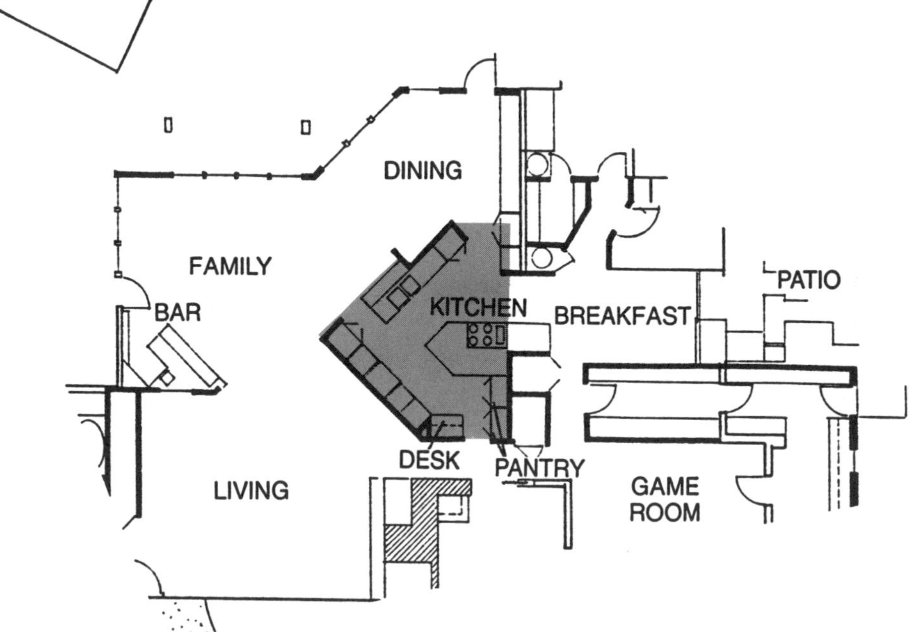

AFTER *A new kitchen was located near family activities with an outside view of the pool area.*

active solar systems can be effective. Ask a local utility company for guidelines.

It's wise to consult with a heating and cooling expert before making changes. Even though making two or three rooms into one large room doesn't increase total area, it probably does affect air distribution. If a duct system is involved, changes are usually required. Brief consultation with an expert might save needless expense.

The Den and Study

Webster describes *den* as a small, cozy room where one can be alone to read, work, etc. A *study* is described as a place set aside

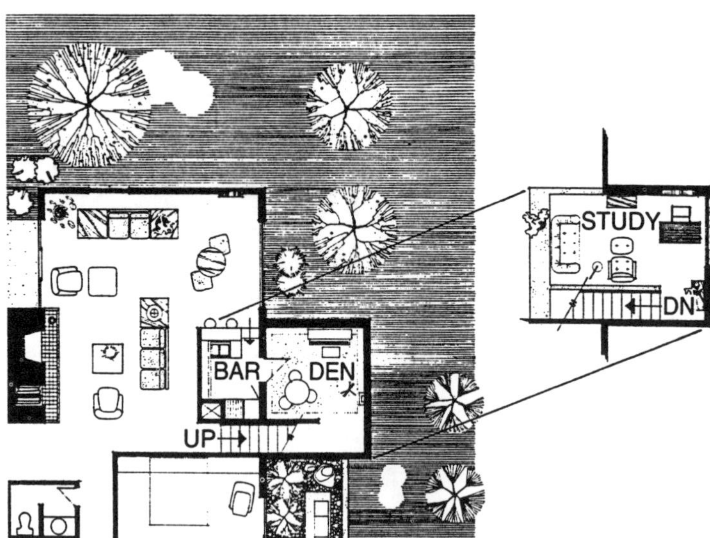

A loft study overlooking a large living area allows privacy without being isolated.

for study and work, usually containing books. They sound much alike to me. Let's say a den is usually smaller and more private than a family room and when it gets very private, becomes a study.

No matter the definition, a den is a handy space. It can be strictly personal and discourage others by that very appearance. Or, it can look so inviting you can't resist the urge to enter.

It contains those "most comfortable in the house" reading chairs. It may double as a small, informal library, or contain a TV. It can be a retreat.

A den is usually near the general living/family areas. It contains choice treasures or art work. It's a nice place to show off or use for a social drink or quiet conversation.

LOCATION

Locate your den or study according to the degree of privacy desired. Unless you poke away at a typewriter, noise coming into the den is usually greater than anything going on there. How organized are you? If you work at a desk and like the luxury of leaving papers and books lying out, then a more private location is in order.

A compromise location is one that gives you a feeling of being exclusive and out of traffic without being isolated. That can be a loft or balcony area, an alcove with folding door, or around the corner in the small leg of an "L" shaped space.

SIZE AND PLANNING

A spare small bedroom might be just right for a den or study. Sketch it in the plan first. Then review the function.

How much of a work area do you need? What size desk, file cabinets, storage space, etc.? Plan the wall space needed for book shelving, TV, stereo, storage. Will you have a home computer set up? Plan the seating required for you and others for reading or conversation. Plan room for a good reading lamp and don't forget task lighting at desk workspace.

Once an Attic

If you live in an older house with a real honest-to-goodness attic, remodeling options are greater. Most homes built since the 1930s don't have an attic that you can actually stand up in. It's a bonus if you do.

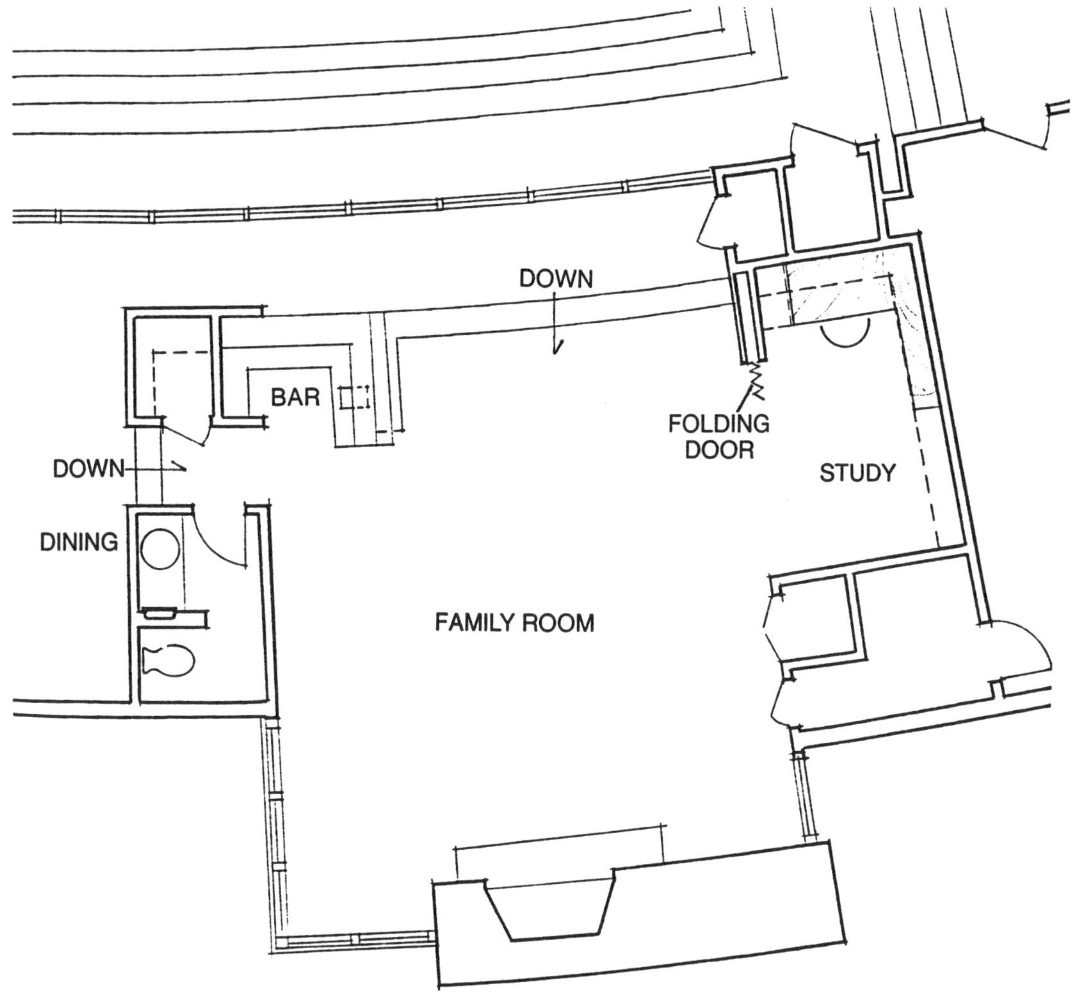

A convenient study off the family room, with folding door for privacy.

HOW TO USE IT

In the planning stage, check possible attic use based on access to the space and functions that might take place. Access to attic space can be improved by creating a new stairway. Consider opening up the space to become an open loft or balcony.

BASIC IMPROVEMENTS

To make attic space livable, it surely will cost something, but only a portion of the cost of adding on comparable space.

Electrical, heating, cooling, and ventilation systems have to be worked out. The structure must be checked. The existing attic floor may be only ceiling joists which will have be to replaced or reinforced. Consult with an expert about the attic floor and the supporting walls below. You will probably want to add to the roof and wall insulation before finishing out the space.

Exit from the space must be adequate for any emergency. Also, this is a good time to add smoke alarms to your house if you haven't already. They are a good feature in any house. They become even more important with two or more levels, where exit to the outside is less flexible and takes more time.

HOW TO USE THE SPACE

Do you need a children's play space? Some parents want the children playing within sight and sound. Others prefer respite from the noise and clutter, with the kids having some privacy, too. In the latter event, a converted attic space might be a winner. A lot of play can happen in a modest area. It needn't be large. Make it colorful and bright. Try out some of those super graphics you have wanted to do.

OTHER OPTIONS

Converting your attic to a study is a popular option. It's a good get-away place to create your own atmosphere. Also, any number of special purpose functions work there, such as an art studio or dark room.

It Used to be a Garage

Garage or carport conversions work well in warm climates where vehicles can be left out or under a new carport. It's a large space, economical to transform for indoor living.

During remodeling, remove that part of the driveway abutting the newly created living space. Replace it with landscaping. This helps erase the remodeled look. Then redesign the drive, if necessary, to make it look planned.

When you do create the new family room, or whatever, it's a good place to add storage closets.

Basement Fun

A well-built basement invites many possibilities. This is cost-effective remodeling. It doesn't have to be a drab place either. You

BEFORE *This family needed a large general activity and recreation space.*

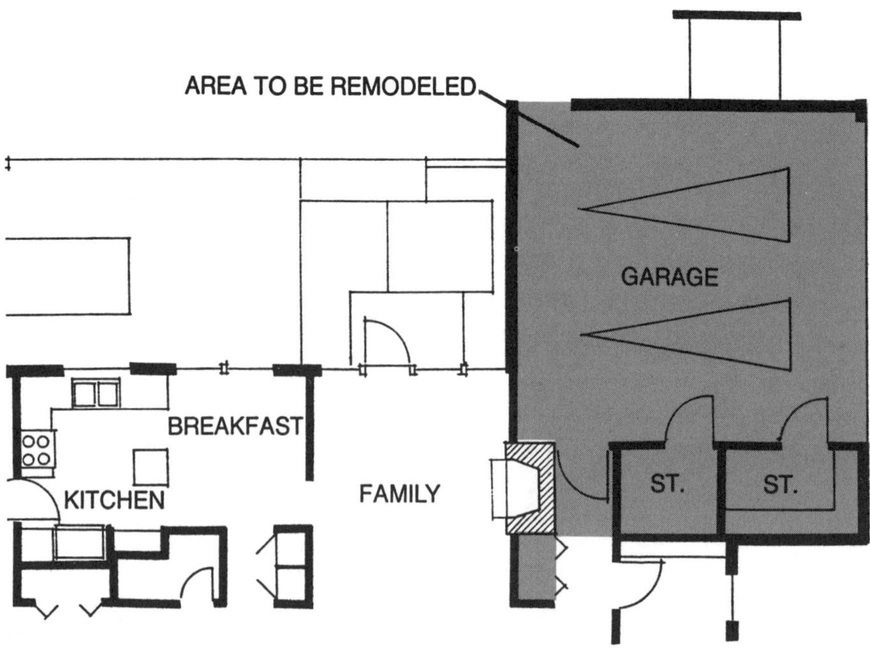

can let in new sunlight, build new stairways, and create color and warmth. Provide good exits, with outside access if possible.

Basement environments are easy to control. For this reason, as well as remoteness, they are a likely place for special purpose, as well as living/family spaces. Craft or hobby, work shop, wine cellar, dark room, music room, home gymnasium, spare sleeping quarters, game room/recreation space, are just some of the popular basement conversions. Adding a bath in the basement, when feasible, makes it more livable for all things.

AFTER *In addition, the kitchen-breakfast-family areas were opened to each other for a more spacious feeling.*

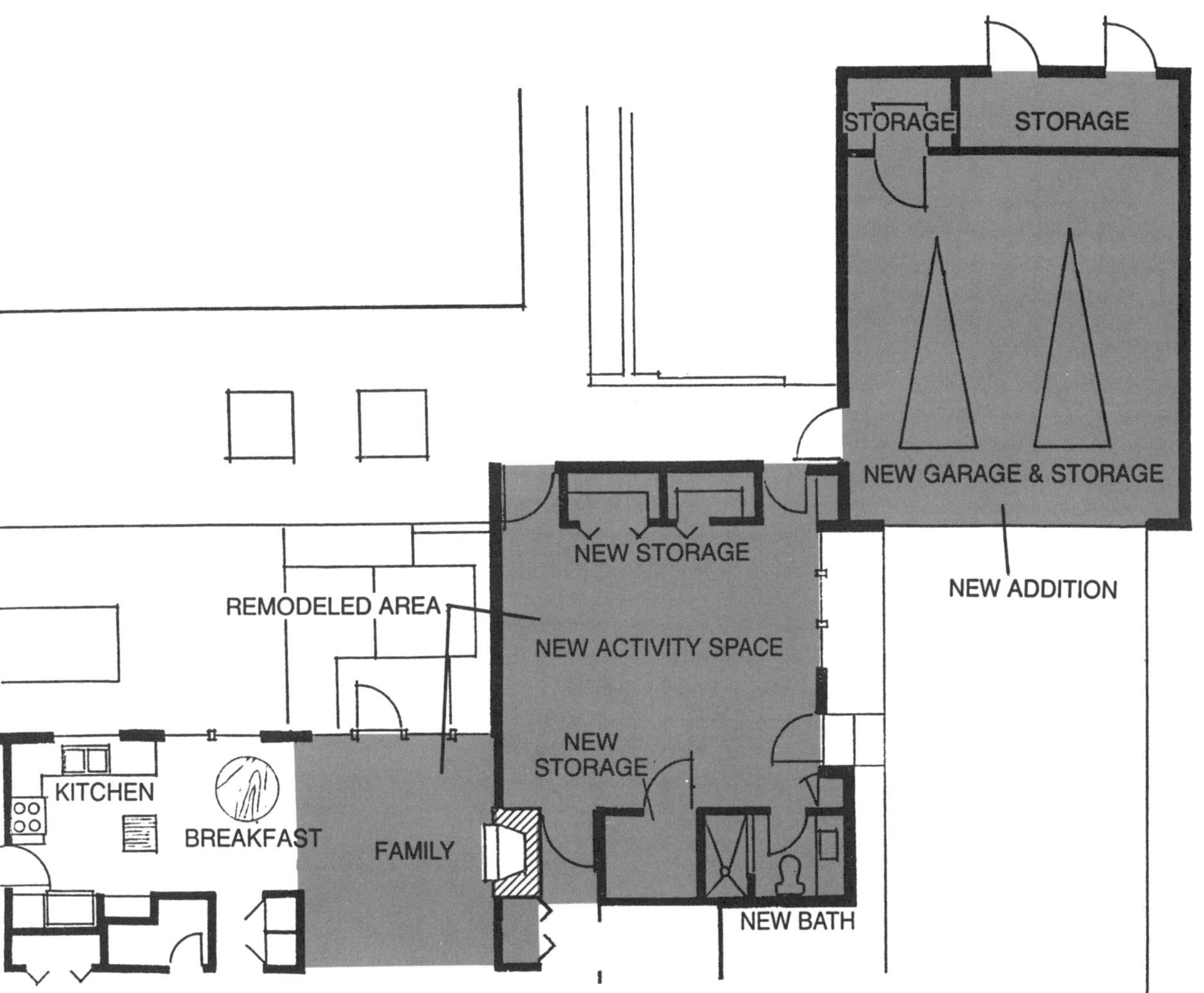

A Place for Books

A space set aside as a library, with good lighting, reading chairs, and maybe a small desk is one obvious solution. Spreading books around is another way. In a family where everyone is a reader, several mini libraries work well. Each member has favorite reading places.

Creating built-in shelf areas is easy and won't break the budget. Book shelf areas also can be part of a total design of built-ins including TV, music system, computer, desk, and art objects.

MAGAZINES

Eliminating magazine clutter is easy. As part of the book shelf area, one or two shelves can be set aside for magazine display. For easy reference, slightly tilt up the back of the shelf and provide a lip on the front edge.

Adding a Fireplace

Adding a fireplace makes a big difference in any space. The anticipation of enjoying the warm glow on a cold night makes this part of your planning special. A common mistake is to assume there is no good or economical way to add one in your existing plan. There usually is, with a little resourceful thinking.

FIREPLACE DESIGN

Several designs are shown on these pages. There are hundreds more.

A fireplace can be modest or can dominate a room. Either way, if the fireplace

Book shelves combined with a major design element.

A manufactured metal fireplace built into frame construction with raised hearth and storage units.

A manufactured metal fireplace built into an existing outside wall. Outside enclosure is required for fireplace and flue.

is built as part of a wall, the entire wall should be planned and designed as a visual unit. With a new furniture arrangement that area will become a focal-point.

Interesting things can be done with a fireplace wall. If planned for an existing room, think beyond the fireplace alone. Now is the time to add new: glass to the outside, mirrors, book shelves and built-in cabinetry, flooring materials, skylights or lighting fixtures, and color schemes.

LOCATION

Decide where the fireplace would be most enjoyed. Then consider what kind of fireplace would go best in that space. Some considerations are size, materials, height/size of room, hearth height, and wood storage. Think about furniture arrangement, traffic patterns, and generally how the whole room will be used.

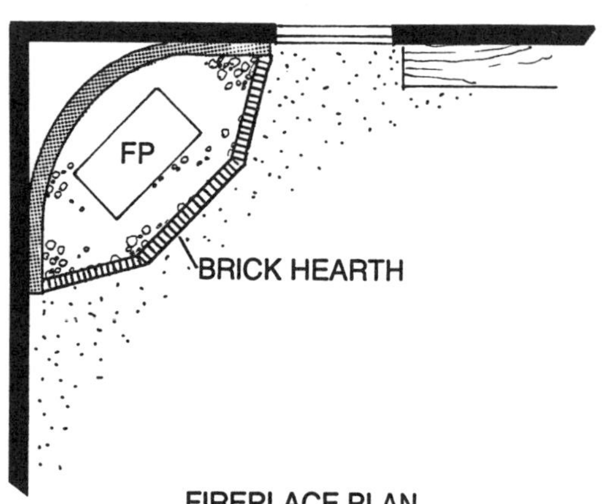

FIREPLACE PLAN

Adding this corner fireplace was an economical way to create a warm glow on a cold night.

Room for All

Living spaces that are large enough and planned for versatility can work for the whole family. You can be together, but stay out of each other's way with good zone planning.

Some methods used to make it work are: changes in floor level, furniture arrangement, lighting arrangement, and using built-ins. *Lots of storage space* in this area makes everything easier.

When it seems necessary to build a separate space or room for children, also plan for the future. If possible, make it useful for purposes after the children leave home. Customizing also can include flexibility. Include storage closets with versatile shelving and drawers.

A space-dividing fireplace serving two areas.

The fireplace becomes a focal point within the space.

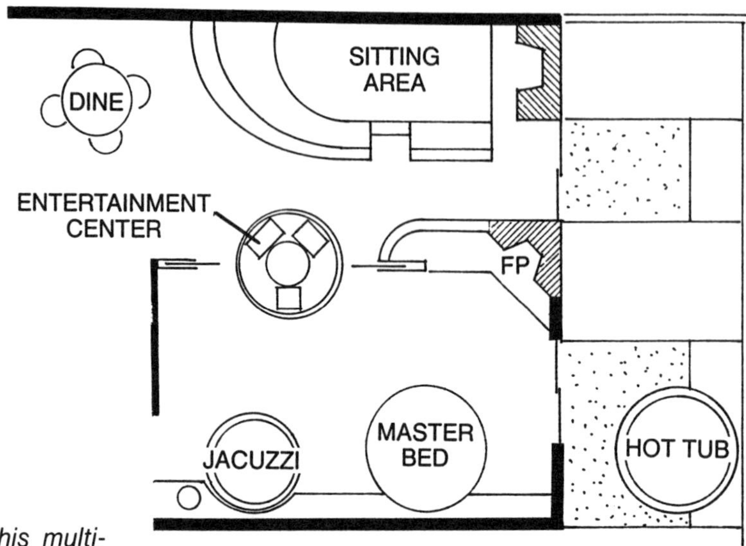

Preplanned versatility is the key to this multi-purpose, space saving design.

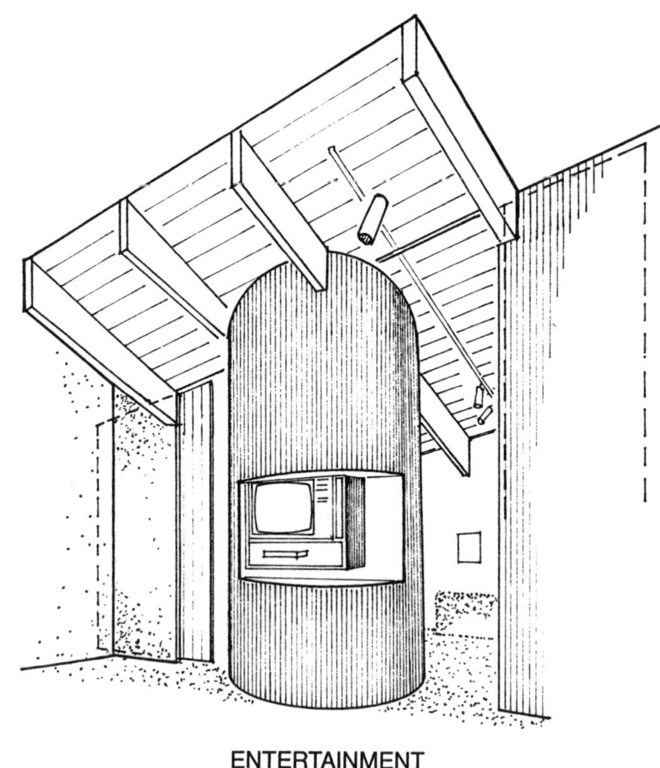

ENTERTAINMENT
CENTER

New Space Within the Old

Much remodeling involves the desire to change the feeling and function, of spaces without changing the actual shape or size of the home. All of the work is within.

Often it seems impossible. Rooms, as well as outside walls, seem restrictive. Please believe, usually it can be done. Casting off old habits and setting priorities from your "want list" help to loosen up your thinking and get the inventive juices flowing. Before long a solution will be found where you thought none existed.

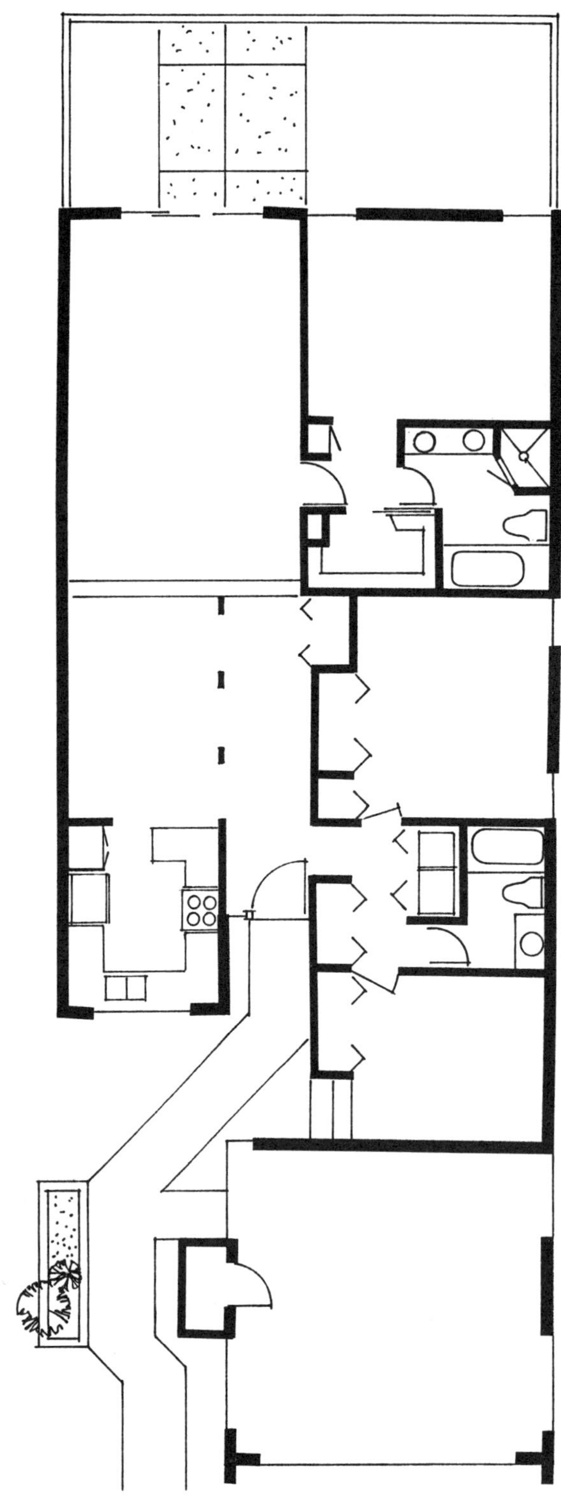

Major surgery was performed here. This couple thought their condo was very ordinary, had a cramped feeling and was not conducive to a relaxed life style. A small expansion at one end absorbed the old carport, and the interior living and master bedroom space was re-done.

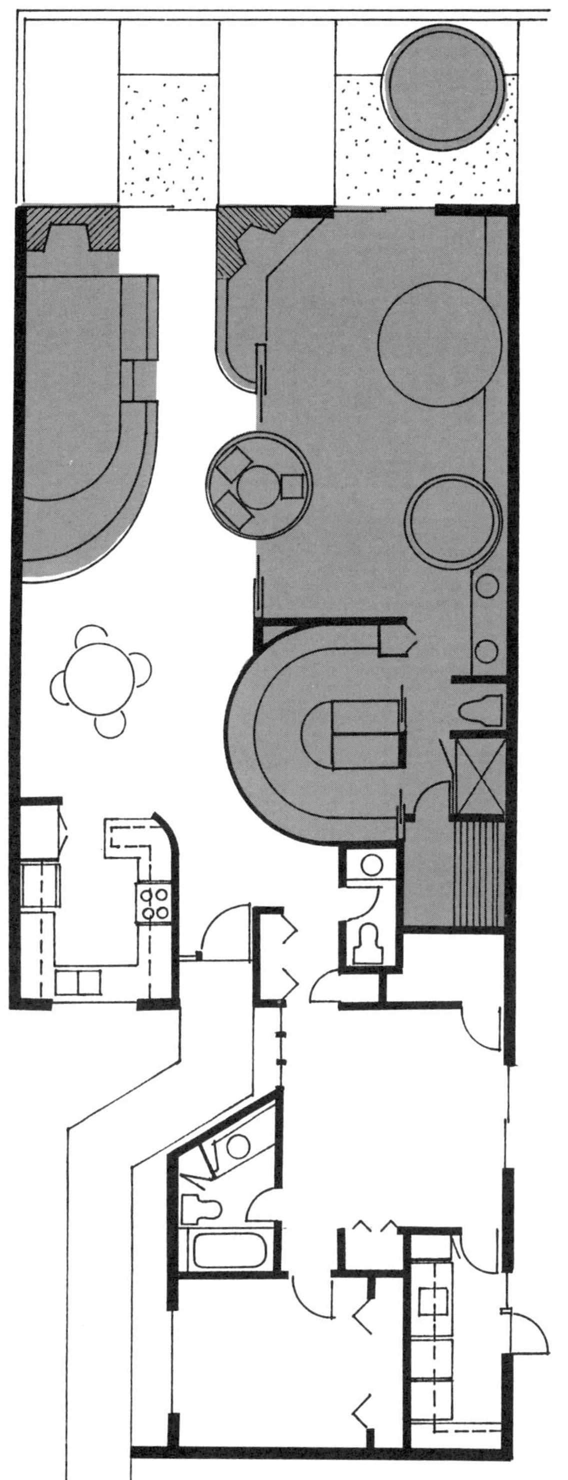

Revolving entertainment center for living and bedroom areas contains TV, stereo, VCR, bar, sink, microwave, refrigerator, and storage. Floor to ceiling pocket doors, each side, complete the flexibility.

Check List

— Family Room/Living Spaces —

Space or Room	Existing Yes/No	Quality and Size of Space	Changes Desired	Remarks
FOR THE FAMILY UNIT:	Yes	Fair - Average size	Add to storage and recreation area	Transfer some use of Fam. Rm. to Liv. Rm.
Family Room	Yes	Fair - Not used Average size	Convert to adult social and library	Increase use of this space
Living Room	No	—	—	
Game/Activity Room	No			
Library				

Example of How to Use the Check List

Sample

Note: You may wish to remove or copy the check list sheets for more convenient use.

ADULTS:	No	—	—	Use new redone Living Room
Den/Study	Yes	Limited	New space in redone Liv. Rm.	Set aside
Reading	Yes	Fair		
Social				

...EN.	Yes	Fair - Fam. Rm. and Bedroom	Create better reading area	Redone Liv. Rm. to include reading area
Reading/Study	Yes	Fair	Improve an area for child. social	Fam. Rm. redone to improve child. social
Play/Social	Yes	Fair to Poor Bedroom only		
Private Space				
Other				

Check List
— Family Room/Living Spaces —

Space or Room	Existing Yes/No	Quality and Size of Space	Changes Desired	Remarks
FOR THE FAMILY UNIT:				
Family Room				
Living Room				
Game/Activity Room				
Library				
Social/Conversation				
Multi-Purpose				
Breakfast				
Den				
Other				
FOR ADULTS:				
Den/Study				
Reading				
Social				
Private Space				
Other				
FOR CHILDREN:				
Reading/Study				
Play/Social				
Private Space				
Other				
Other				

4

Hobby and Recreation

For identification, let's call recreation an activity of leisure and enjoyment. Hobby is a special interest or avocation for fun or profit.

Hobby

What comes first, the hobby or the space required for its function? It really doesn't matter. How often have you heard, "I would like to do such and such, if only I had the room for it?" Another common example are the clients who tell me to provide a space for hobbies although they don't currently have a hobby.

Space for a hobby is a delightful luxury and one of the cheapest spaces to provide. It normally doesn't have to be large, complex, or expensively appointed. If you provide for it in your planning, there is a good chance it will be well used. In fact, the demand might be strong enough to warrant the space becoming multipurpose.

Multipurpose Space

The number of uses to which a space can be put are endless. Combinations include: hobby with recreation, hobby with hobby, hobby with utility, recreation with social, hobby with social, etc., etc. Let's assume you want to create a two-person hobby space. The following discussion might typify a planning scenario.

OBJECTIVES

In this hypothetical example, wife and husband want to share a designated space for different hobbies — not always an easy thing to do.

Defining objectives is very important here. Will both use the space at the same time? Are the hobbies of equal importance to each person? Is one hobby quiet and one noisy? Is one clean and one messy? Does one require a lot of equipment and another less? Is strong lighting needed for one or both? Continue this line of questions until you've covered the subject. Be realistic. The space won't *work well* unless *planned well.* Conflicts are not difficult to imagine.

An easy example of conflict is a four letter word — *mess*! Some hobbies are messy, i.e., pottery, painting, woodworking, etc. The unique thing about a messy hobby is that the person making the mess doesn't mind it at all. And, leaving the space messy can be a time-saver, so they say. (I know I've said that!) But, for anyone else, the mess can be intolerable.

So, if you want to share hobby space, get the ground rules established. Plan

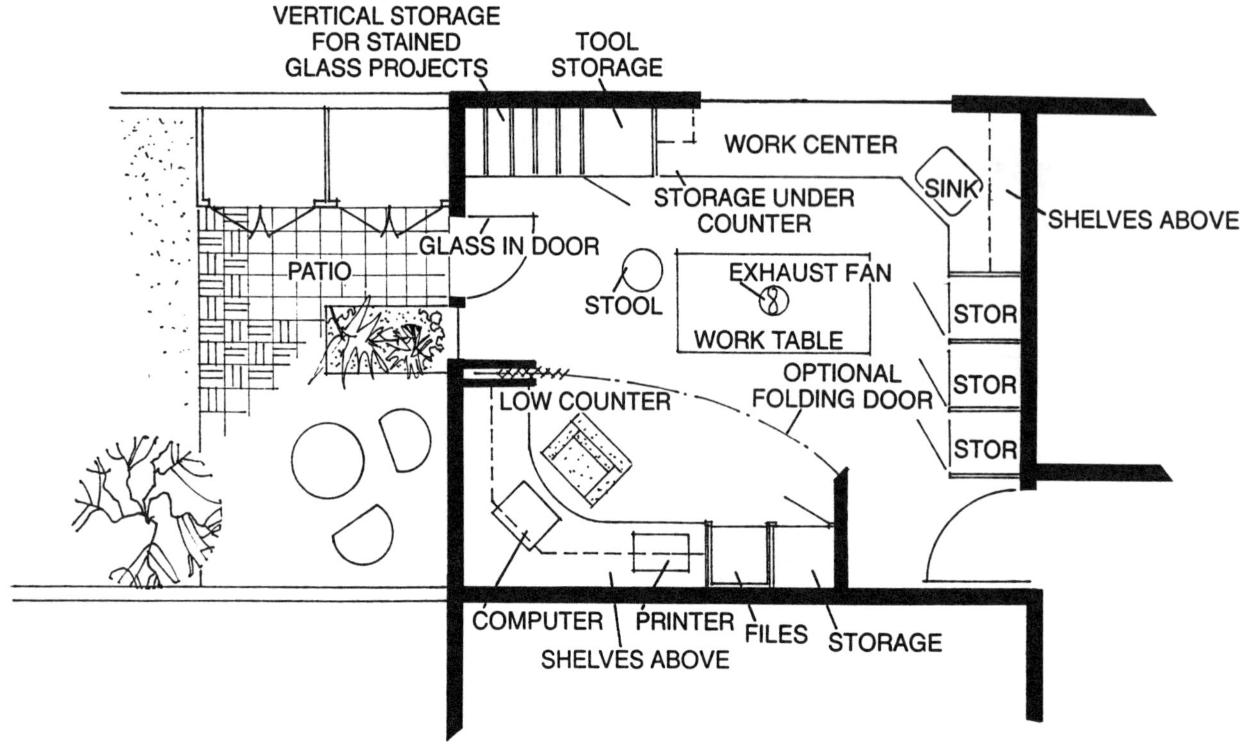

A multipurpose hobby space: With children grown and moved from home, the family room is converted for dual hobbies — computer center and stained glass shop.

carefully what work space is needed for each hobby. Storage space is vital. Keeping the area tidy is possible only if there is ample and convenient storage for all tools, materials, and partially-finished projects.

COSTS AND EQUIPMENT

Costs for tools and materials to perform your hobby are on-going and not part of construction. But, consider what custom equipment is needed to be built-in. Do you need special electrical, such as a separate circuit for computer equipment or 220 volts to operate a machine? Do you need special heating, venting, or cooling? (Film development, for instance, requires a good exhaust system, as well as custom lighting.)

A work surface may need to be impervious to cutting or burning. Should it be dark or light, smooth or textured? Will it work for both users?

If you are considering a multi-purpose hobby space for use by two or more people, assess the compatibility. If you feel that compatibility is probable, then develop the space. If it appears that conflict will result, consider a separate space for each person.

STORAGE

It's hard to imagine a hobby that does not require lots of storage space, usually more than you have. Hobby storage doesn't have to be closets built into the house. Many hobbies, in fact, are better served by storage in cabinets, bins, adjustable shelving, or specialty devices. Portable storage containers can be especially useful in making multi-purpose spaces work.

Indoor Recreation

A cost-effective recreation space usually

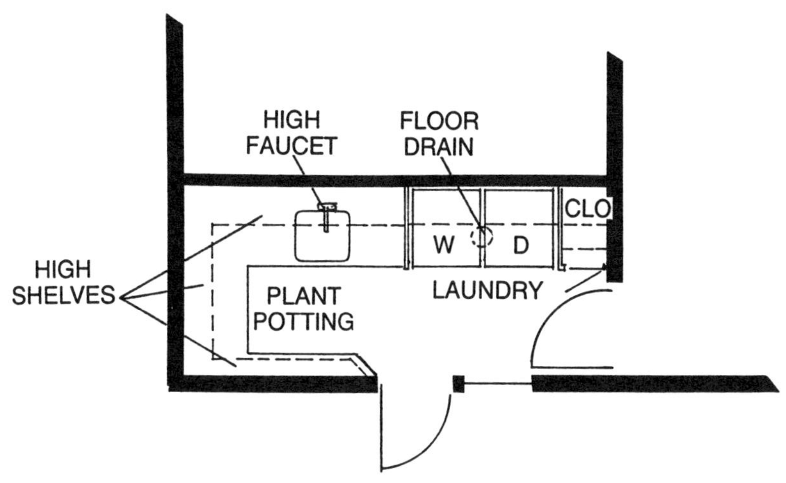

Potting space and laundry in a small room.

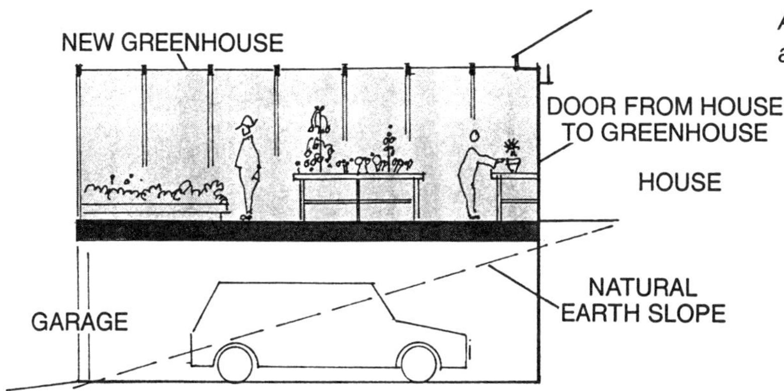

After reinforcing the roof of a flat roofed garage, a greenhouse was added.

is one that serves several functions. The most cost-effective method, and probably most common, is to use existing spaces (family, living, dining, etc.) and alter each space as needed for various activities.

USING EXISTING SPACE

After defining objectives for indoor recreation, lay out your existing floor plan and with tracing paper overlay, work on the spaces. A better expression might be to re-work the spaces.

THE ROOM ARRANGEMENT

Draw the furniture to scale (sometimes using cut-outs for furniture is the best way). Arrange it to best suit the primary use of the room and still leave space for games, music, or whatever the recreation will be.

Many homes are over furnished. Review your habits with each room, especially family and living rooms. Decide what furniture is seldom used or doesn't really benefit the room. Still using the tracing paper overlay, discard that furniture and rearrange the rest. New space for fun activities may be found.

FINDING STORAGE SPACE

Check walls and corners for new places to add storage for games or recreation equipment. Check cabinets, under tables, etc. With rare exception, you can easily add new

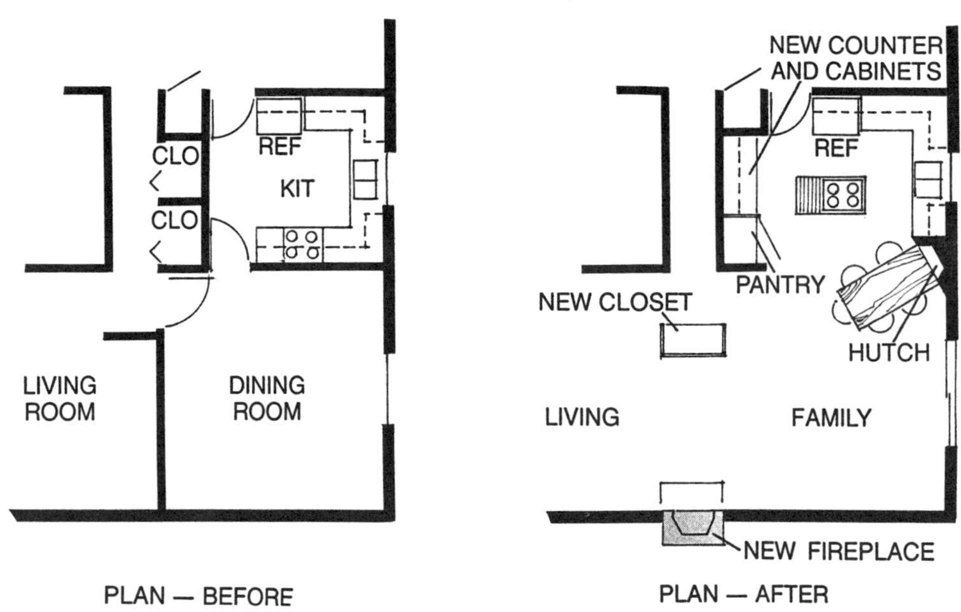

A relaxed, informal family lived with a plan of closed rooms and too many doors. They chose to trade the dining room for a kitchen opening to family activity. The result was a spacious, cheerful atmosphere.

storage to any existing room. By so doing, you make the room more adaptable for multi-purpose use.

CONVERTING SPACES

If you have an unused basement or attic, suitable for habitation, you are lucky indeed. Be sure the space is dry, insulated, safe for use and has proper exits for emergencies. Then, let your imagination take over and create new places for fun and games.

Other convertible spaces include that spare bedroom, part of a garage or carport, an enclosed patio or porch.

WHEN NEW SPACE IS NEEDED

Certain leisure activities interfere so severely with normal household functions that they demand separate space. Some of those are: (1) pool or billiard tables, (2) video theatres, (3) customized audio with special acoustics, (4) active games such as ping pong, darts, etc., and (5) a good case can be made for having separate space for children's indoor play.

New space is found in various ways. One way is described above under "Converting Spaces". Another is to plan and construct an addition. And yet another method might present itself as you proceed through the "design program" and complete the check lists. It's always possible that existing functions can be consolidated and new spaces made available when renovation occurs. An example of this would be to eliminate a separate dining room with the redesign of kitchen and eating area. Or, you could decide that a game room would get more use in the space now called the Living Room.

CHILDREN

It is said that the most used, and creatively useful, object for young children's outdoor play is the sandbox. I believe that. Those activities imbued with the least gimmicks and devices, most often inspire creative thinking in children. However, little children, mimicking "role models," eventually discard industrious simplicity and become technology captives.

(That's not to say that manufactured products inhibit thinking.) Some beautiful toys are carefully devised to provide both aesthetic pleasure and mental stimulation. And, certain toys (for children *and* adults) with electronic and computer parts require creative thinking for good results.)

If your renovation is occurring at the time you've started a family, consider the needs of children at play. If you decide that children need space in which to be inventive and messy, plan the space.

When looking for new indoor space for children, remember the example of the sandbox. Children don't seem to demand large spaces in which to create their world. The space can be small as long as *it belongs to them.*

Outdoor Recreation

THE TRANSITION SPACE

Screened-in porches and protected patios are great places to extend indoor activities to the outside environment. Most climates allow their use for at least, part of the year. They're also a place to be when outdoor activity gets rained on. Of course, it depends on your social and recreation habits, but these transitional spaces usually are well used, enjoyed, and can add good value to any home.

BEYOND THE SANDBOX

Clients have often said, "Someday I'd like to have a place for ______ ______." The blanks could be filled in with a number of items including: horseshoes, boccie ball, badminton, volleyball, a tennis court, swimming, croquet, or a putting green.

Some of these items (tennis court and swimming pool) require a permanent installation. Required also is a greater commitment and expense. Planning decisions, therefore, involve more than desire to have it and the place to put it. It's back to priorities.

Few of us have unlimited outdoor space. Therefore, the idea of setting priorities for ways to use it is just common sense. Of course, multipurpose use of certain areas happens all the time. Many different lawn games and social functions use the same space. On the other hand, several activities dear to our hearts limit the space they occupy to one use. A swimming pool, concrete shuffleboard, children's climbing bars and swing sets, for example, are all one use items.

PLAN FIRST

Planning a yard for recreation is a routine matter, done without complication. It only gets involved when you want a lot to happen in a relatively small space. That's when it pays to plan first on paper. When you do, use a site plan drawn to an accurate scale for planning the space. Chapter 9 outlines a method to create such a plan, but your own situation might allow a simpler procedure.

Priorities confirmed with the enclosed check list should be combined with those of Chapter 9, ADDITIONS, and Chapter 10, EXTERIOR IMPROVEMENTS AND LANDSCAPING. Settle on the most important ways to use the space and plan it for maximum pleasure.

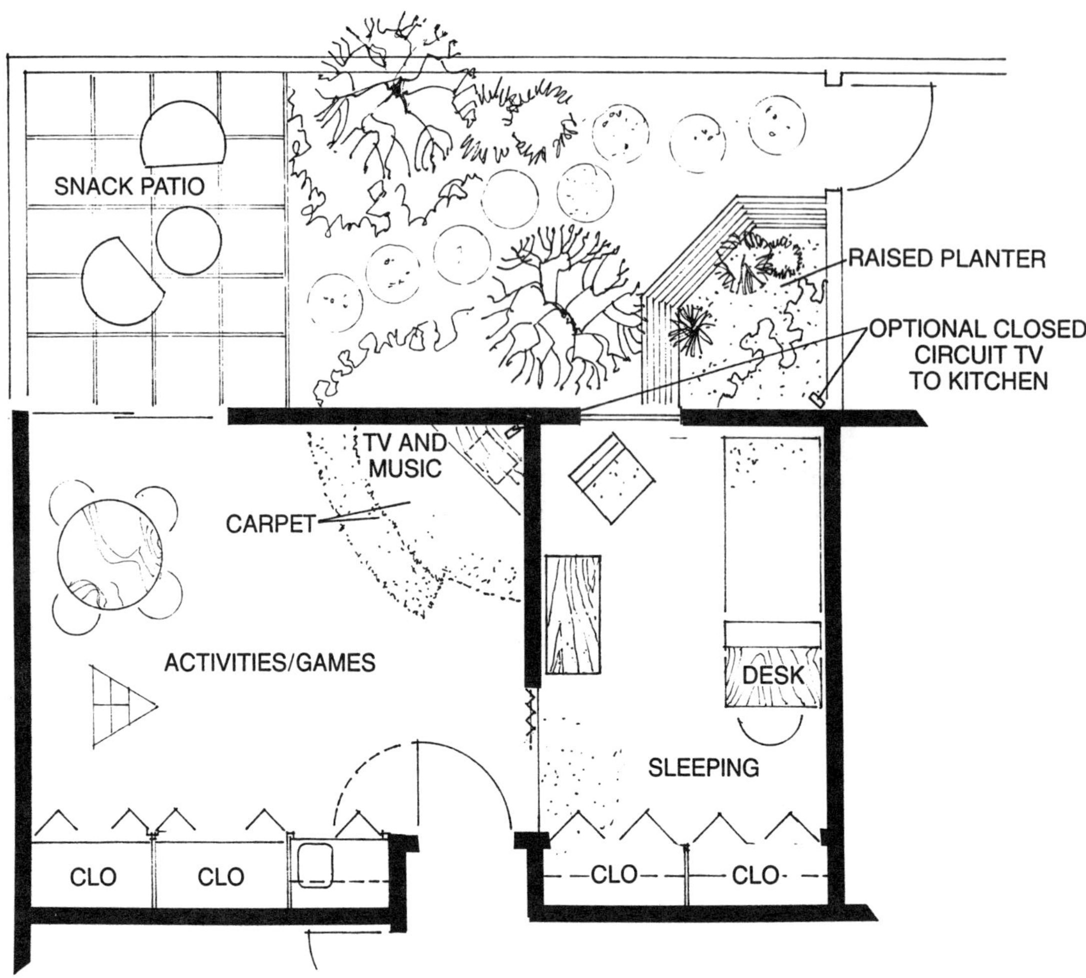

A child's private area set up for easy future conversion.

The first change will convert the play area to a bunk room for 2 or 3 children. Smaller room becomes a play room.

With the future conversion, the large room becomes an adult den-hideaway and the small room used for hobbies.

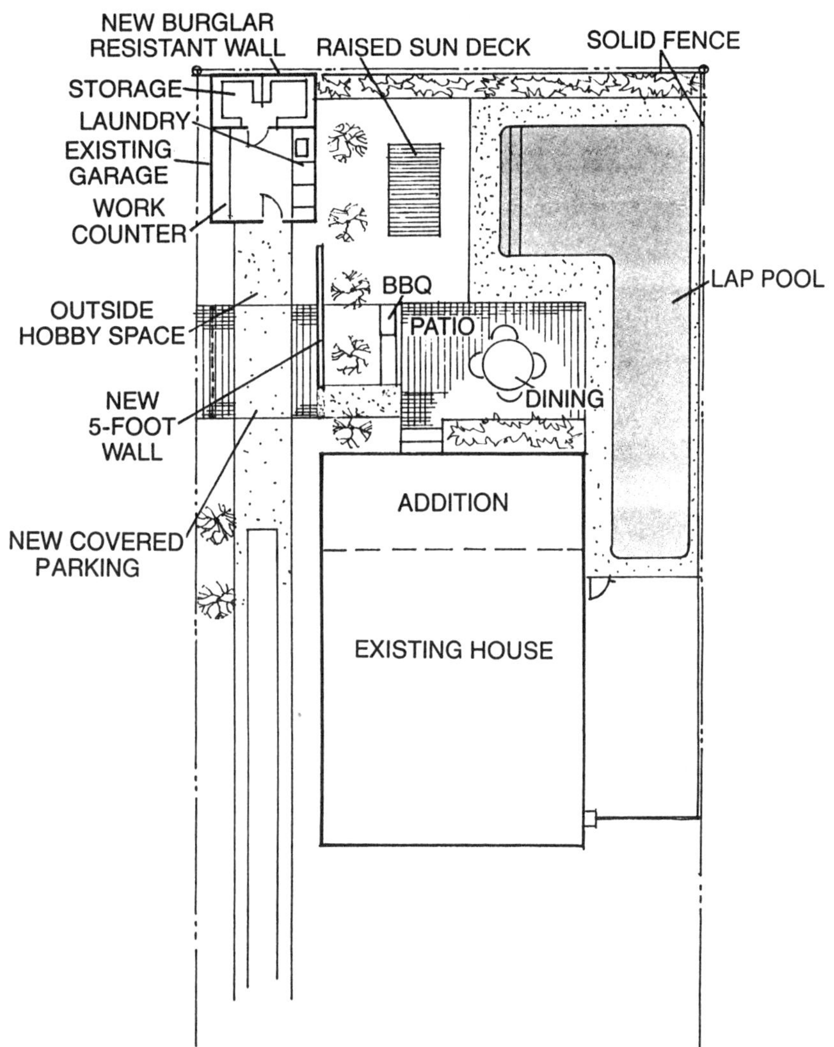

This house, on a narrow lot, was purchased by a young couple. In addition to interior improvements, their lifestyle needs required careful planning for the rear yard and unused garage. Both serious swimmers, they wanted a lap pool which, with a small "L" at the end, added to the atmosphere.

Check List
— Interior — Recreation/Hobby —

Interior Rooms and Spaces	Existing Yes/No	Present Use of Space	Remarks
Recreation Room	No	—	Don't need
Family Room	Yes	Conversation, TV, reading	Add cabinets and shelving. Rearange furnishings and add game table with 4 chairs
Spare Bedroom	Yes	Sewing, storage and misc. Not organized	Convert to Multi-purpose space for computer and sewing
Hobby Room	No	—	Sewing center designed into Spare Bedroom - opposite computer station
Sewing Room	Yes	Small projects on one counter and storage	Move storage to new area. Add counter and shelving.
Work Shop	No		

Example of How to Use the Check List

Sample

Note: You may wish to remove or copy the check list sheets for more convenient use.

Check List

— Interior — Recreation/Hobby —

Interior Rooms and Spaces	Existing Yes/No	Present Use of Space	Remarks
Recreation Room			
Family Room			
Spare Bedroom			
Hobby Room			
Sewing Room			
Work Shop			
Enclosed Patio or Porch			
Attic			
Basement			
Storage			
Other			
Other			

Check List
— Exterior — Recreation/Hobby —

Exterior Spaces	Present Use of Space	Remarks
Patio (Covered)	Occasional sitting area	Add partial wood shade screen. Install new brick surface on existing concrete
Yards: Rear	Storage building and dog run	O.K.
Side	Pool and decks	Add pool equipment storage space
Front	Yard and entrance	Adding entry court
Pool	Swim/lounge	Condition of pool O.K. for now.
BBQ Area		

Example of How to Use the Check List

Sample

Note: You may wish to remove or copy the check list sheets for more convenient use.

Check List
— Exterior — Recreation/Hobby —

Exterior Spaces	Present Use of Space	Remarks
Patio (Covered)		
Yards: Rear		
Side		
Front		
Pool		
BBQ Area		
Storage		
Child's Play		
Garden		
Other		
Other		
Other		

5

Bedroom and Bath

Beginning and ending the day in a warm, cheerful atmosphere is the least we should expect in our daily living. Therefore, those elements of design which create a good space and a feeling of well being are important to the bedroom area. Selection of the right furniture, colors, and accessories rounds out the picture.

Bedroom Locations

A good and workable relationship of bedrooms, to each other and to other spaces within the home, is important for family harmony. As families change, so do room arrangement needs. Let's look at optional locations for bedroom areas:

MASTER BEDROOM

Some parents want all bedrooms in a cluster for ready access to the children's rooms. Others prefer the master bedroom separated for more privacy and less noise.

UP OR DOWN

When you bought your home, upstairs or downstairs location was determined for you. However, in remodeling, you can be choosy.

Review your habits and ask yourself some questions. For example: (1) How often, during the day, do you want access to the master bedroom? (2) Is there a physical problem with using a stairway? (A stairway lift is expensive but may cost less than constructing a new master suite downstairs.) (3) If the bedroom is upstairs, should you add a small refrigerator, coffee maker, blender, etc., . . . ? (4) Do you want an at-home office or reading area near by? (5) Would you like access to an outside deck, court, or pool area?

GUEST BEDROOM

A *true* guest room, set aside exclusively for the comfort and convenience of a guest, is a luxury seldom seen today. For cost effective planning, today's guest room is more likely a multi-purpose space. The *dominant* use among the multi-purpose functions probably will dictate the room location within your home.

If guest room location is based upon *convenience* for *guests and family*, then consider the following:

1. Locate the guest room so that guests can come and go without interfering with family functions.
2. The room is best located away from other sleeping areas.

3. The guest room requires ready access to a full bathroom, preferably one for that space only. However, a compartmentalized bath can also serve as a powder room.
4. The importance of the previous three items varies with the frequency of guests in the home.

Built in furnishings and storage can work to maximize the efficiency of a guest room.

A cheerful atmosphere, combined with high utility, makes this a successful master bedroom-bath suite.

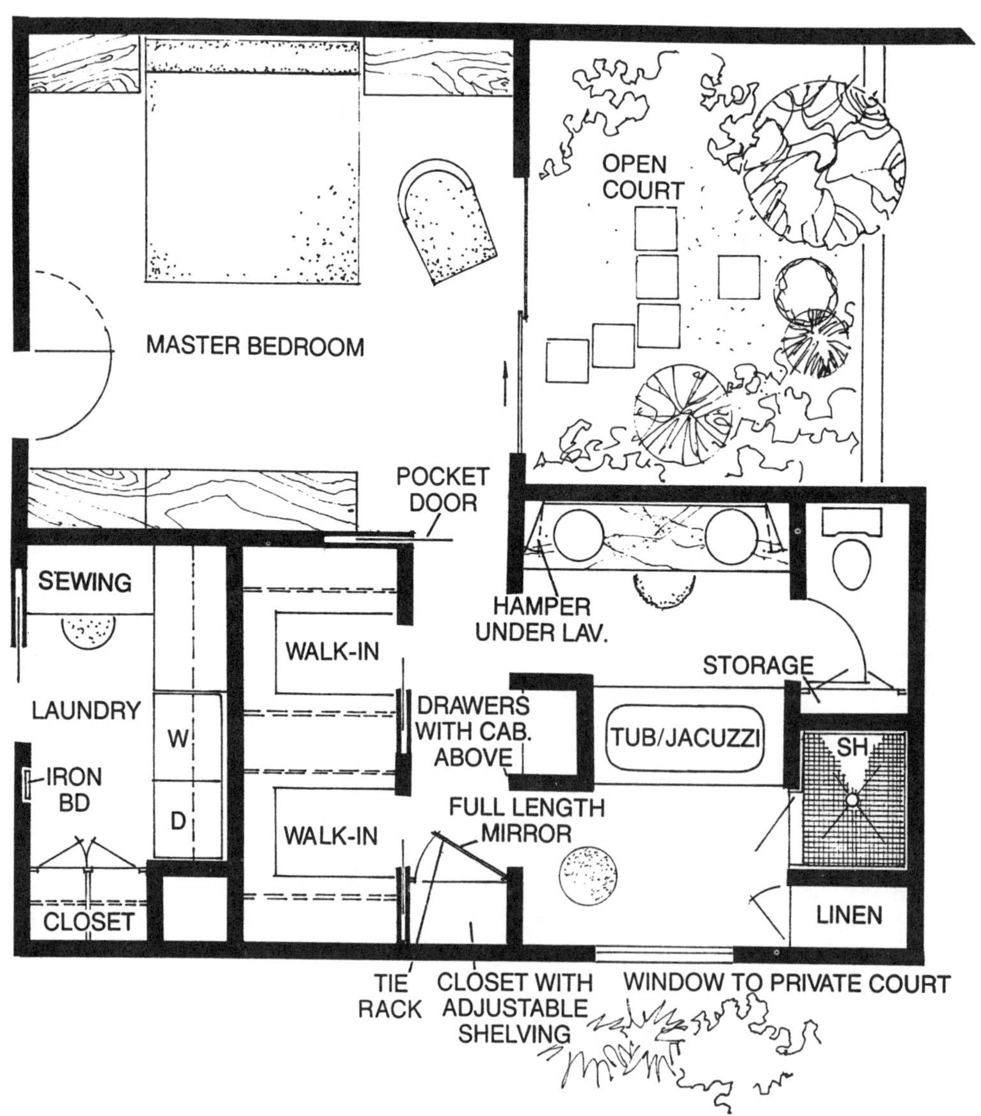

Under furnishing the room is another good idea for several reasons: (1) A room cluttered with your personal trappings is not always comfortable for a guest. (2) A modestly but tastefully furnished room appears larger and more accommodating. (3) A slightly, under-furnished room allows space for guests' belongings.

You can achieve an uncluttered look and still include features such as:

a. Cheerful accessories or art work.
b. Place for magazines or books.
c. Good lighting and a reading chair, if space permits.
d. Full-length mirror.
e. Closet space for the guest wardrobe.

Cut-away view of bath-dressing area.

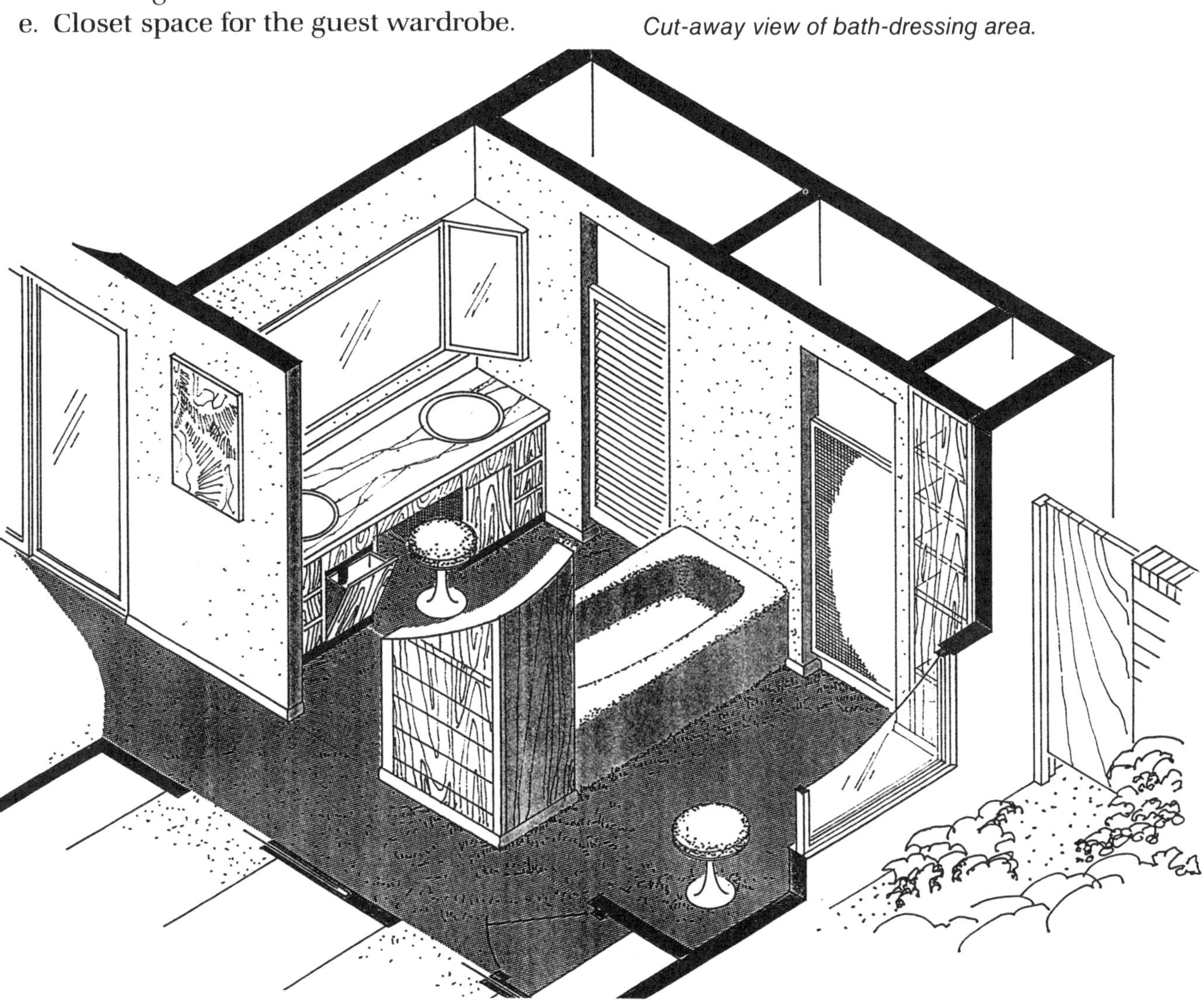

A walled courtyard off the master bedroom is enclosed to become a new reading/sun room. Skylights, stained glass, and extra closets were added.

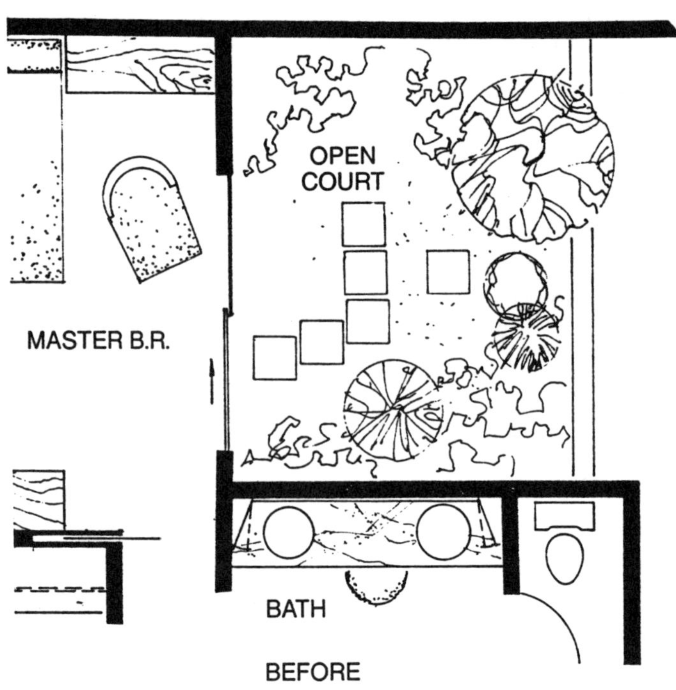

BEFORE

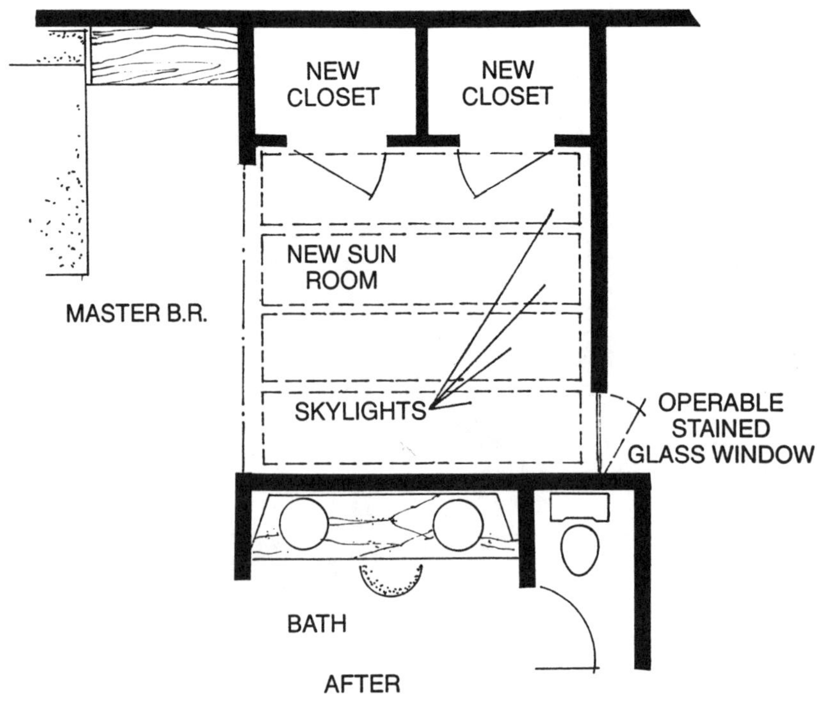

AFTER

I have known people who limit guest closet/storage space in proportion to the length of time they want guests to stay. I'm not sure if that works or not.

CHILDREN'S BEDROOMS

Locations are as varied as your requirements. For instance, assume that you need *additional* children's sleeping space. If a new master suite is created, consider converting the old one to handle two or more children. Several methods may be used, from dividing the space to installing dormitory-type furniture.

OTHER OPTIONS: (1) A flexible room, serving as play area and sleeping space, is

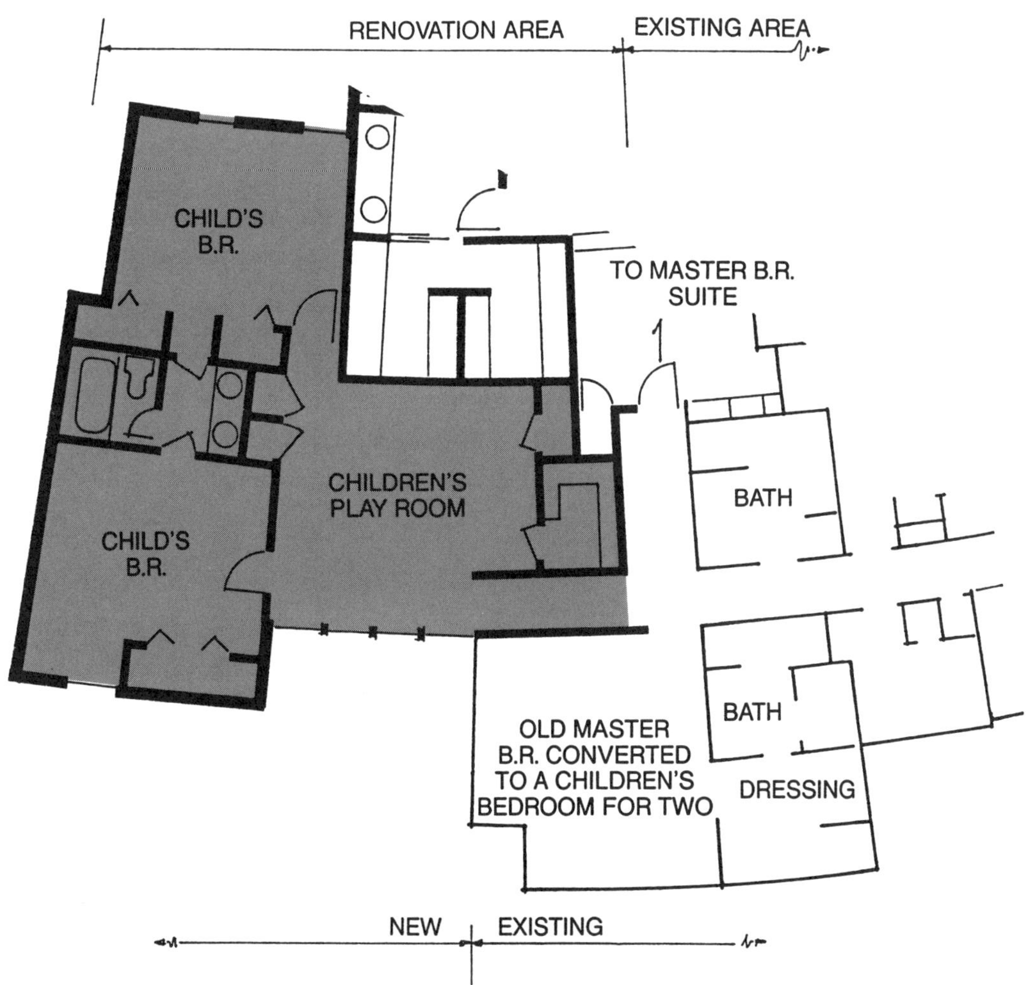

A house, originally designed for a bachelor, became home to a family of seven. A three bedroom addition was created. The children's play room became a well used hub of activity for the bedroom wing.

workable if extra storage is provided. (2) If children's rooms are grouped together, consider a common play room. A room set aside specifically as a common play area doesn't work with all families. If it does work, and if space permits, it's a luxury. As an added bonus, privacy is increased in the children's bedrooms.

Furnishings and Accessories

The bed, because it's a large piece of furniture, is usually the starting point for the layout of a bedroom.

LOCATION

In a room of modest size, bed location normally is limited to one or two choices. A larger space provides the opportunity to be more creative. Considerations are:

a. View — both the view of the bed as you enter the room and the view from the bed.
b. Location in relation to light source for natural ventilation.
c. Location of auxiliary functions, such as bath, dressing area and closets.
d. Location of TV, small stereo, fireplace, or reading areas are items affecting overall layout.

Bed *location* and bed *design* should be considered together. Relative items: How will the bed be made up? Must you have access to three sides? How will the traffic in the room work? How to get to closets, bath, etc.?

BED DESIGN

A wide choice of ready-made beds can be found. Available designs seem to cover all possibilities. Sometimes, however, a custom designed bed is the answer for certain rooms.

For example, bed and accessory design might include:

a. Storage under, using all available space.
b. Headboard shapes to utilize corners or a niche.
c. Habit requirements such as special lighting, reading material, stereo, master

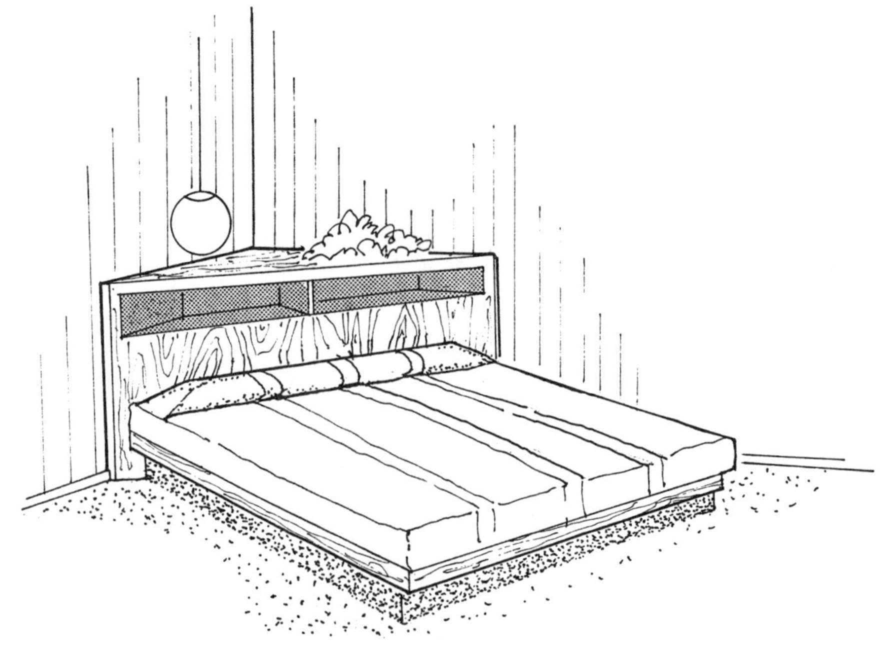

Variation with furniture arrangement, and a new look, is achieved with corner bed unit.

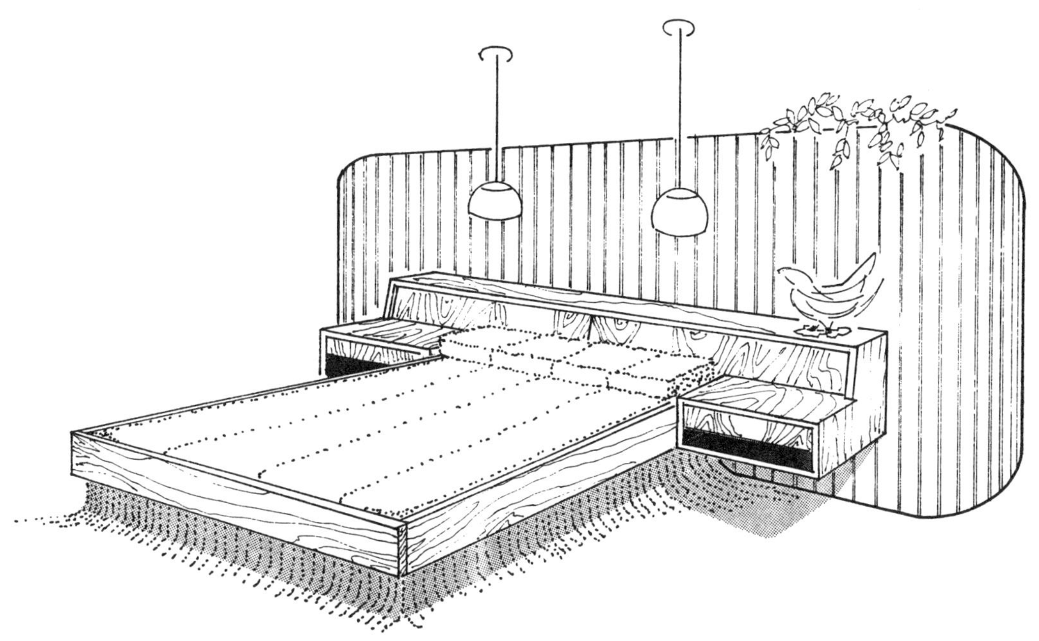

A built-in unit with drawers and accessory storage in headboard, behind sliding panels. Built-in storage under the bed is an option with this design.

Two single beds.

This corner arrangement allows daytime seating with easy roll-out for bed conversion.

switching, wine coolers, etc., can be built in.

An off-standard bed dimension sometimes will better fit in a tight room. Custom-made mattresses are available at a modest extra charge. If the dimensions vary greatly, custom linen is another expense. Being handy with a sewing machine is helpful.

THE PLATFORM BED

The platform bed, although it appears to be a grand idea, is usually a mistake. It consumes extra space which normally can be used in more interesting ways, such as other furnishings, a fireplace, plants, extra storage, etc. The step-up (and step-down) platform also can be a hazard in the dark.

Sketching the Layout

Chapter 1 tells how to draw the plan of your existing home. With it you can isolate areas for special attention — in this case, a bedroom/bath area.

As described under "Using the Floor Plan" in Chapter 1, visualize yourself in the bedroom space and think about living habits. How do you like the bed located in relation to bathroom, dressing area and closets? How about reading, TV, views? Think about air movement from windows, air conditioning or heating. How would you like the room lighted and where should the switches be?

Draw furniture to scale on the plan, or use cut-outs of furniture drawn to the same scale as the plan. (Cut-outs might be the best method for you.)

If you want built-in cabinets, drawers, and shelves, draw elevations (the vertical wall and cabinet surfaces) to scale. Then lay tracing paper over those drawings to develop your ideas. Make over-lay sketches in this manner until you're satisfied. Paper is still cheap.

Bedroom Storage

Chapter 6 specifically relates to storage throughout the house and will supplement the information in this chapter.

FOR CHILDREN

Space needed for children's clothing is typically less than adults. More space is needed, though, for toys, games, sporting

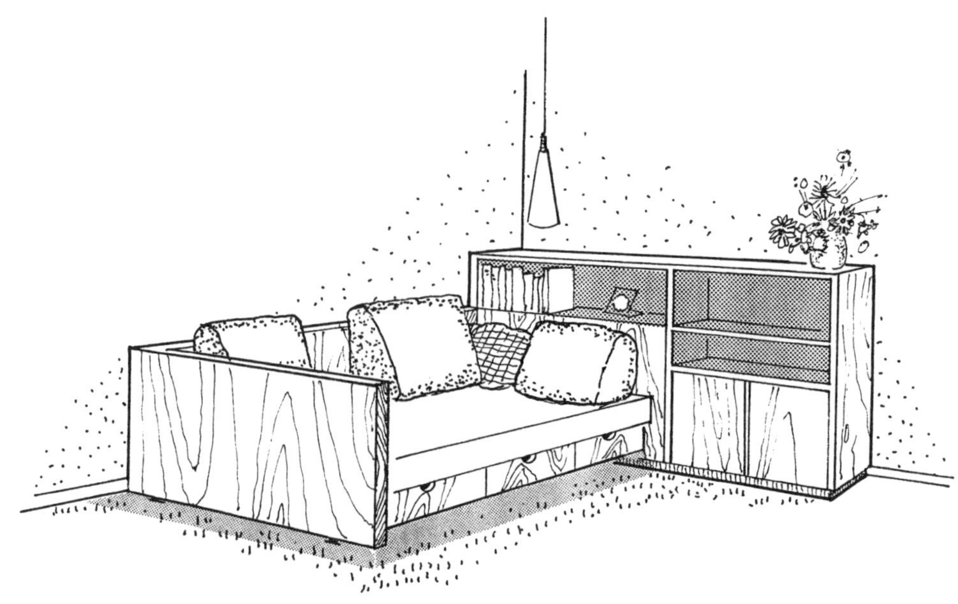

A custom corner design for storage, seating, and sleeping.

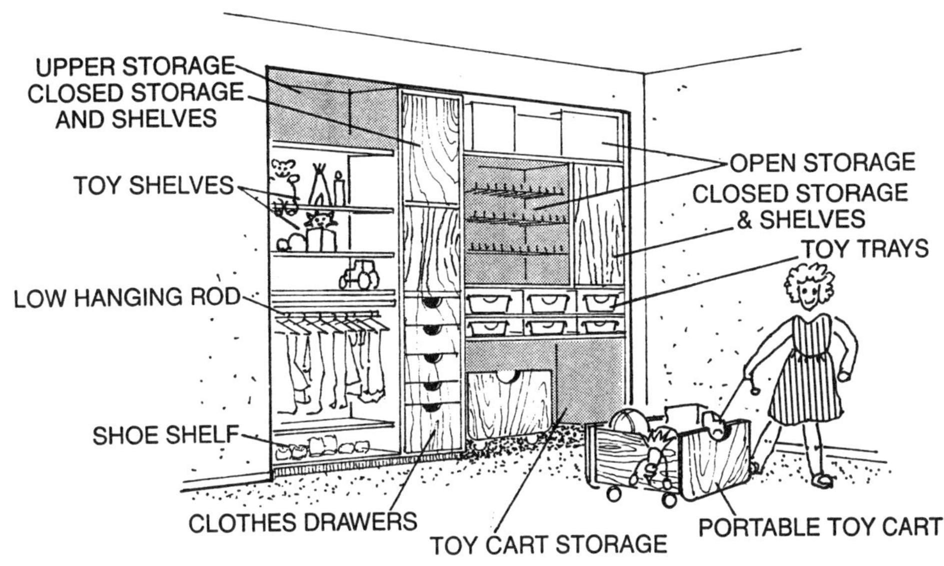

Children's Storage Area.

One of many variations. It can be re-arranged as needs change.

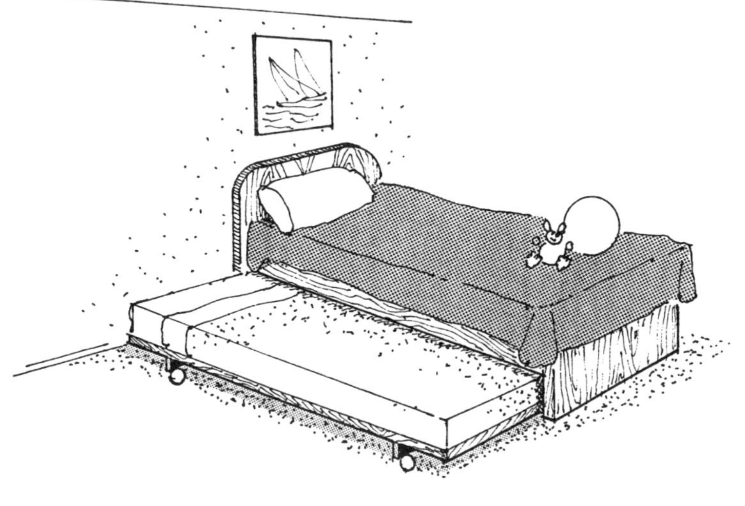

The roll-under trundle bed works well for occasional use.

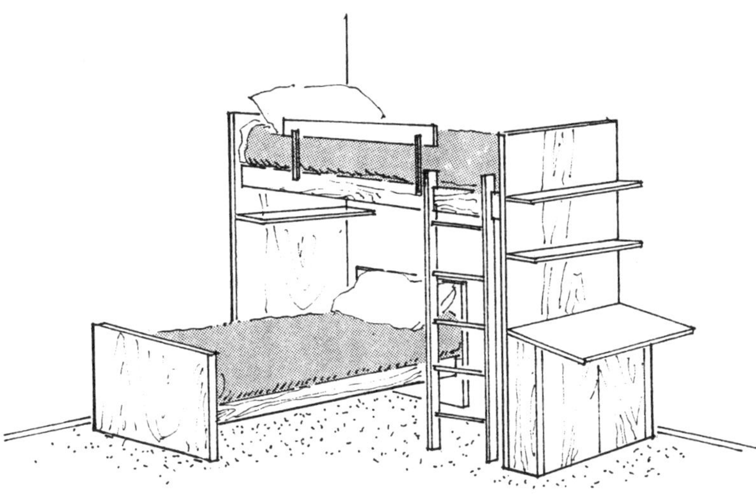

Youth Bunk Beds.

A right angled arrangement for variation.

equipment, junk, and wonderful treasures. It's a sure bet that whatever shelving, cabinets, built-in under bed storage, etc., is provided, it will be used. High and low hang rods for clothes is a good idea.

To create more *usable* bedroom area, try bunk beds or trundle beds. They save floor space and will accommodate stay-over friends.

ADULTS

Is there ever enough closet space? We do accumulate! Renovating bedrooms and redesigning closets is a good time to inventory the wardrobe and even discard a few items.

If all household storage is being improved, try to find or create a closet elsewhere for off-season clothes.

Closets and Storage

Usually, without great cost, you can provide either more or better closet space. That doesn't mean that your wardrobe won't expand to fill it, but that's another matter. Chapter 6 will help you find new space and improve the old.

Surface storage on the inside face of swing-type doors is common. (An extra hinge on the door might be needed.) The outside face is better used for a full length mirror. I advocate an air supply duct to each closet. That feature, omitted in many homes, is very helpful — not for heating and cooling, but simply to circulate the stale air.

Dressing Area

Economically efficient "dressing" space normally is available in the general area. No separate, designated space is needed, but you shouldn't have to sit on the edge of the tub to tie your shoes.

Whether dressing for work, play or the evening, give yourself enough room, enough mirrors (one full length), and accessories to support image enhancement. This applies to men as well as women. And, if a woman's makeup space is desired, put it in. The space required is minimal.

Customized storage, in a modular arrangement, for efficiency and organization.

MIRRORS

It's difficult to imagine a bedroom area that won't accommodate a full-length mirror someplace. For grooming, side view and rear view is easily accomplished with swing doors on side-mounted medicine cabinets or hinged mirrors.

LIGHTING

When planning the space, remember to provide lighting so the light is on the *person* when looking at the mirror. Sounds simple, but again, it's one of those things often overlooked. In addition, it's no fun to select subtle shades of clothing in semi-darkness, so good general lighting is needed. If precise color fidelity (for makeup, etc.) is important, consult a lighting expert for bulb selection.

ACCESSORIES

Storage and maintenance of clothes, shoes, etc., should be made as easy as possible. Don't forget requirements for shoe shining, a clothes hamper, tie rack or purse storage.

Three-way viewing is achieved with beveled and mirrored medicine cabinets on each side.

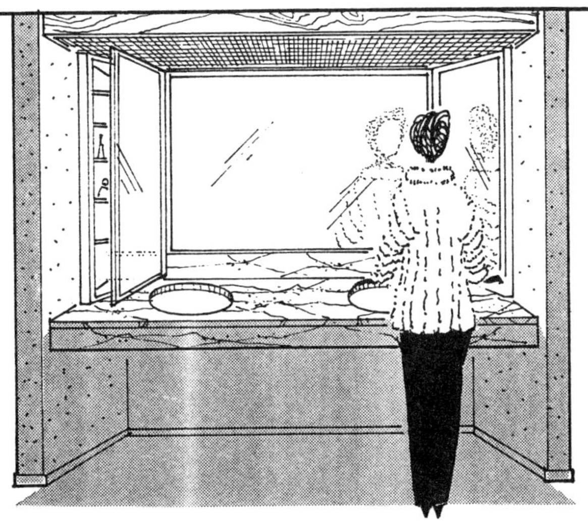

Checking Out the Bathrooms

The most lasting impression, after house shopping, is probably the kitchen and next the bathrooms. The bathroom has evolved, from a space hardly mentioned, to become an important sanctuary in many homes. It's where we begin the day. Consciously or not, a sparkling, cheerful, color coordinated, and well planned bathroom is a positive space. It's another part of the overall home environment which contributes to your life style and sense of well being.

The Bath

As the automobile becomes a personal cocoon in the outside world, the bath is, for some, a personal retreat within the home. In the room itself, the tub is the place of refuge and relief from stress.

Relaxing time for yourself may be only 15 minutes. That's an important 15 minutes and it's brevity only accents the need for comfortable surroundings. Colors, textures, controlled lighting, and the type of tub itself should be selected with care.

THE SPA

Of the billions of dollars spent yearly on bathrooms, oversized tubs, soaking tubs, or water action tubs account for a lot of the money. Luxuriating in your private spa with hot water pulsating against tired bones may or may not be of any real physical value. But, the psychological value is there, without question.

Subdividing Bathrooms

A private bath is always desired, but shared baths can easily serve more than one bedroom.

With two or more children using one bath, traffic jams occur. However, if your final priorities and budget restraints tell you that adding a new bath is impossible — don't despair. There are several ways to improve the situation with changes to the existing bath.

As shown in these illustrations, separating functions with walls and doors is one of the easier methods. Adding fixtures is another.

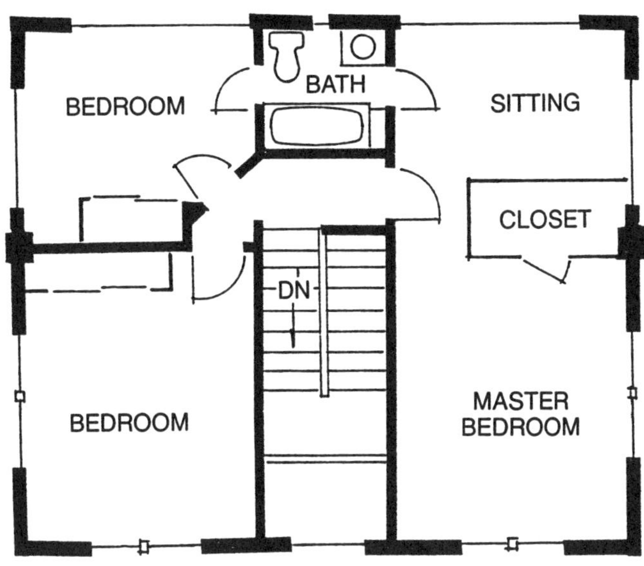

BEFORE *Master bedroom shared a bath with two other bedrooms. Closet space was not adequate.*

AFTER *A 12 foot addition allowed room to create a spacious master bath, reading area, balcony, and two walk-in closets. A new closet was added in the second bedroom.*

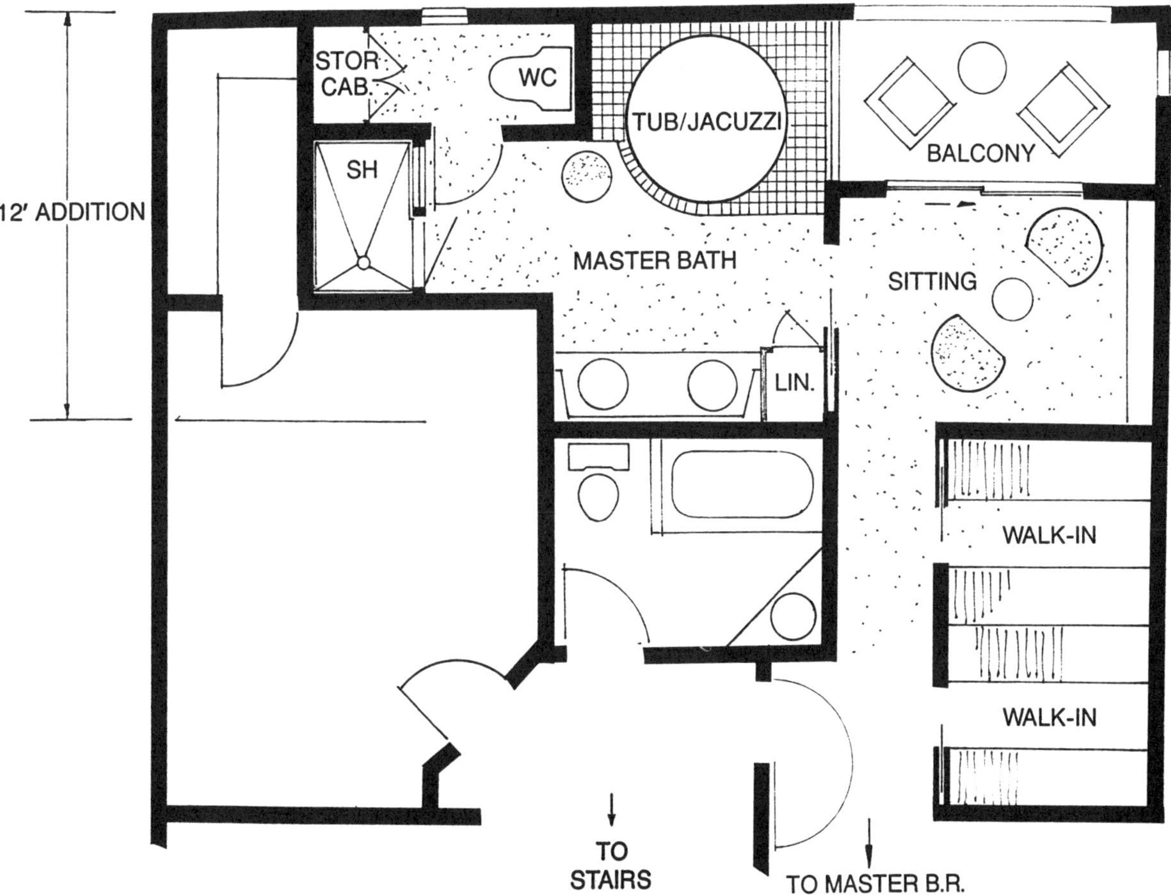

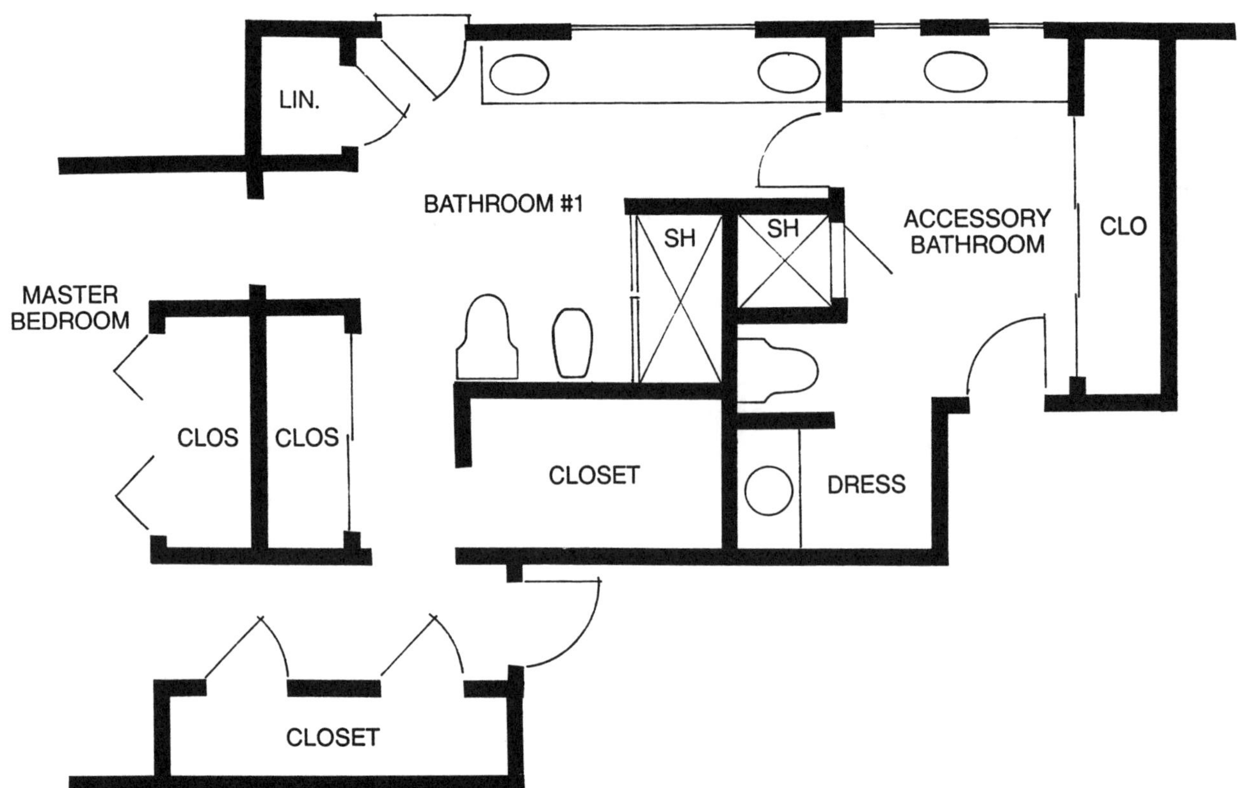

BEFORE *This master bath and dressing area had poor use of space for all functions, with no tub. The adjacent bath, needed only as a powder room, had much wasted space.*

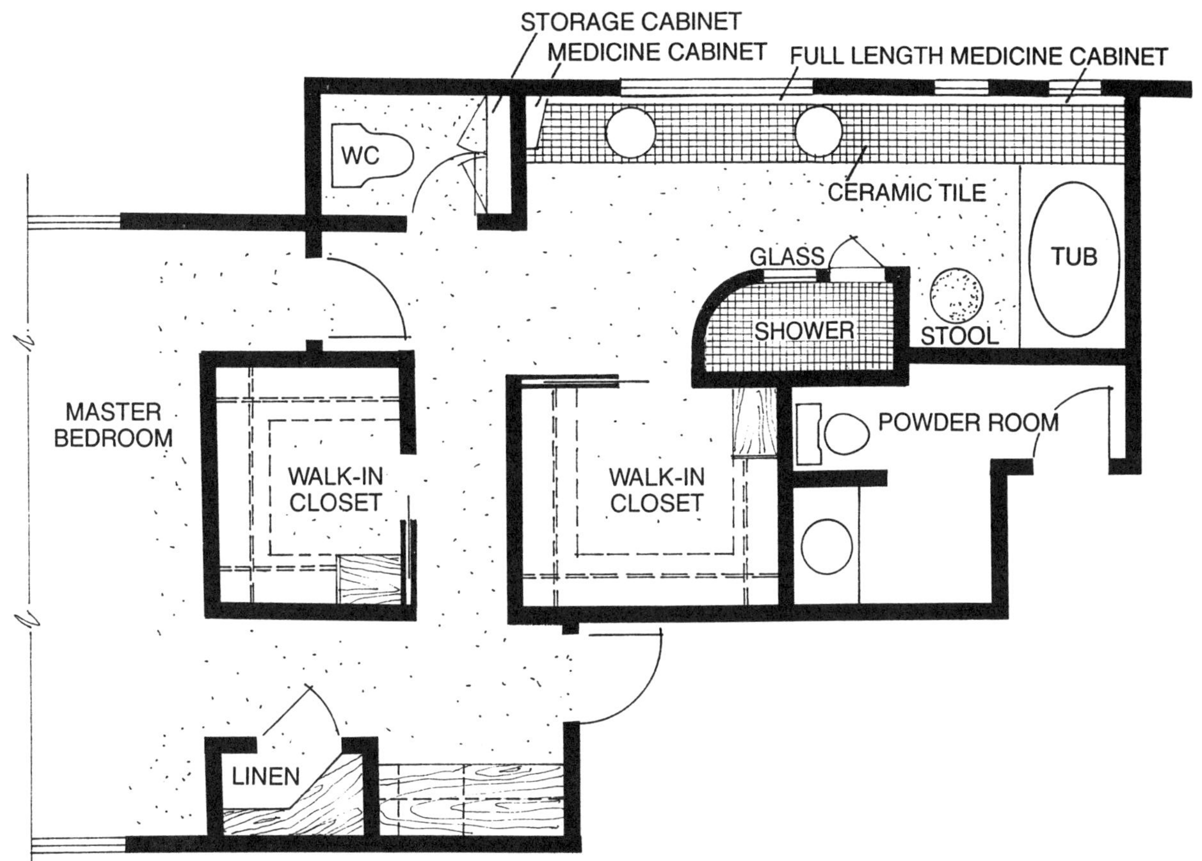

AFTER *The new plan shows a better closet arrangement with more hanging space. Bath layout adds a tub and private toilet compartment. Revision shows general improvement in atmosphere and use of space.*

Check List
— Bedroom and Bath —

Existing Spaces	Size	Remarks	Needed Space or Amenity
Master Bedroom	14″x17″	Create bay in south wall for reading area	More natural light with adjacent reading area
Closets	2- 24″ deep by 60″ long	Include space from closet in adjacent room	Add space for 2 walk-ins
Dressing	—	—	None
Bath	O.K.	Add hamper under sink	Skylight - hamper
Jacuzzi/Sauna	—	If possible: change tub to Jacuzzi	Jacuzzi desired - same size as existing tub
Reading Area	—	New bay in south wall adjacent	Room for 2 chairs and small table
Exercise Area	—	—	None
Other	—	Add someplace in general area	Linen Closet
Bedroom No. 2	11′x13′	Replace bed with bunk beds	Sleeping space for 2 people
Closets	24″x72″		
Bath			

Example of How to Use the Check List

Sample

Note: You may wish to remove or copy the check list sheets for more convenient use.

Check List

— Bedroom and Bath —

Existing Spaces	Size	Remarks	Needed Space or Amenity
Master Bedroom			
Closets			
Dressing			
Bath			
Jacuzzi/Sauna			
Reading Area			
Exercise Area			
Other			
Bedroom No. 2			
Closets			
Bath			
Bedroom No. 3			
Closets			
Bath			
Guest Bedroom			
Closets			
Bath			
Sofa Bed			
Closets			
Powder Room			
Other			
Other			

6
Storage and Utility Spaces

This chapter is about very private spaces. Closets, drawers, and out of sight niches are where you stash and stuff everything under the sun that you don't want seen. For most of us, that's a lot of things and therein lies the problem. There's never enough very private space.

Storage space is either found or created. It can be obvious or elusive. But remember, there is *always* a way to create extra storage space in any home. Believe that first and then go looking. With pad and pen in hand, check every room and closet in the house. Note areas with potential for improvement, no matter how slight the potential.

General Storage

Storage spaces come in two basic types: small closets, cabinets, and niches, or large closets; and small rooms. A typical home has small to average closets and cabinets. I advocate including a large storage closet in your renovation, if possible.

A large closet, say six feet by eight feet, if well organized, is convenient and time saving. It's an ideal place to consolidate your possessions. Also, you don't have to remember which little closet contains something you haven't seen in two years.

An understandable resistance to the large closet idea is the difficulty in committing that much space in one area. It's such a large chunk out of a plan, just for storage. However, while a lot of small spaces don't look like as much, they probably take up more space. Also, many small cabinets and closets cost more to build than one large closet with organized shelving.

Keep both types of spaces in mind during your planning. A combination of several small closets and one large is a good compromise and might offer the greatest convenience.

Inside Storage

Earlier chapters contained storage tips for certain areas. A more consolidated approach is presented here.

KITCHEN

In keeping with the national trend, (having less space, but more money to spend filling it) many space-saving gadgets are available. Kitchen accessories have shrunk in size over the years. Some cookware looks good enough to go from cooktop to tabletop. Microwave ovens of less than one cubic foot capacity are plentiful, with smaller dishes to match.

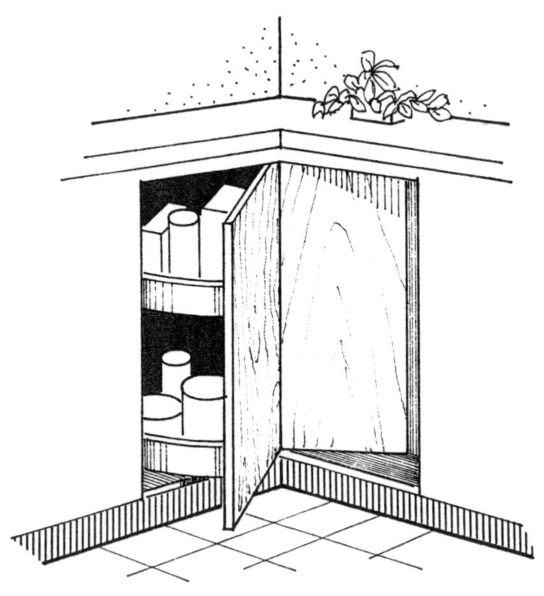

A lazy susan turns a dead corner into effective storage.

INCREASE STORAGE WITHOUT ADDING SPACE

Following are some ideas to help you maximize storage in your existing kitchen/eating areas:

1. Adjustable shelving in cabinets.
2. Roll out lower cabinet shelving for access to rear of shelves.
3. Access from both sides of deep cabinets, if feasible.
4. Add Lazy Susans at inside corners.
5. Add 3½" deep cabinets between wall studs at exposed wall areas.
6. Install tall, skinny pull-out pantry cabinet in left-over vertical space.
7. For access to wasted corners add a door to the outside face of lower cabinet corners.
8. Under sink cabinet, add side shelves adjacent to plumbing, at mid-height.
9. Add a floor to ceiling, full counter depth storage cabinet, 18" to 24" wide. (Do this if you can afford to lose the same width of counter space.)
10. Racks or shallow shelving built onto inside face of closet doors.

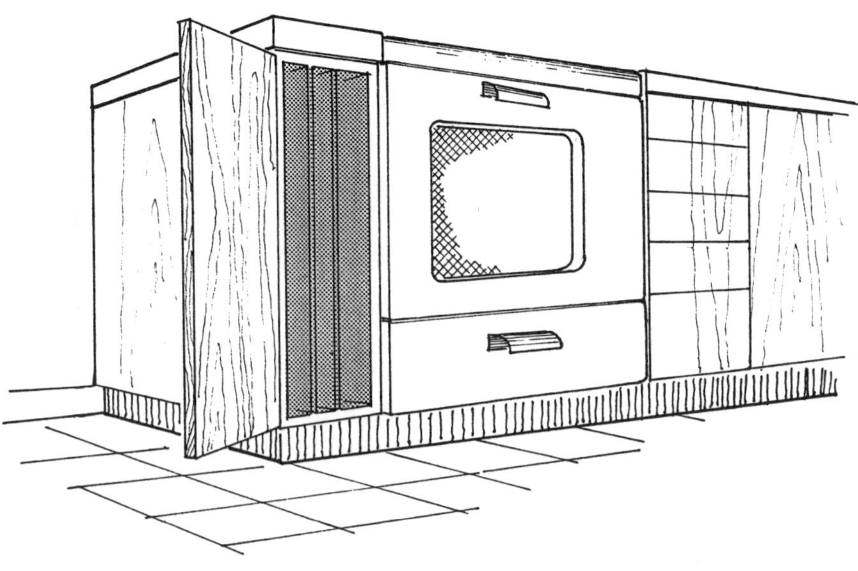

Vertical tray storage created in narrow, left over, lower cabinet space.

Pantry and Utility Closets.

Racks or shallow shelving on the inside face of closet doors hold a lot of storage. Adding an extra hinge is a good idea.

A deep sink cabinet provides storage on the opposite side. Additional storage is gained above.

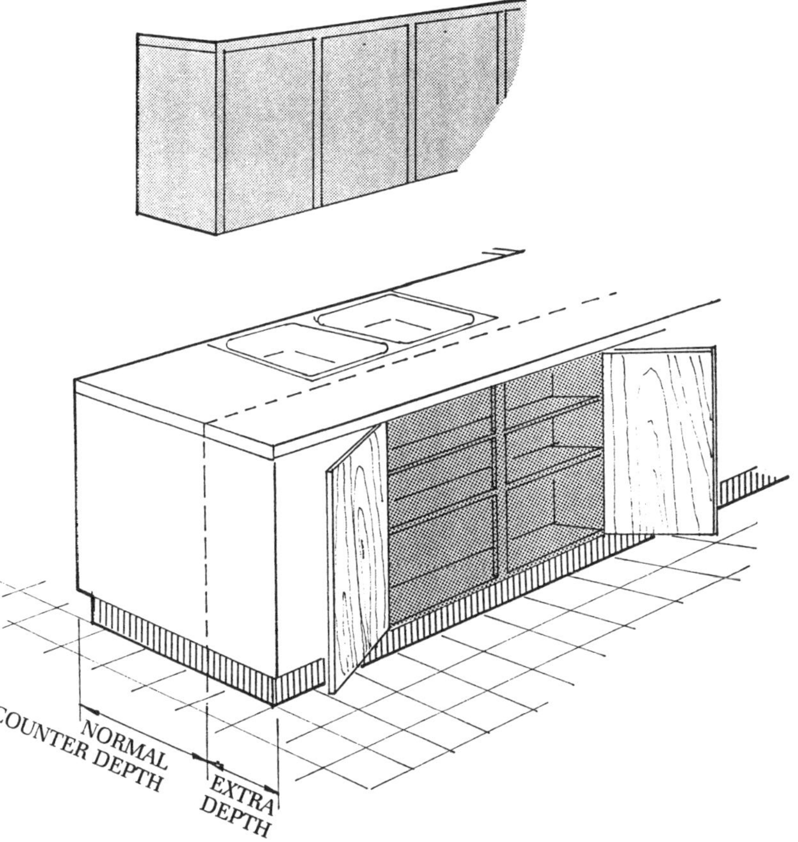

FURNITURE FOR STORAGE

Wooden trunks, used for tables or room accessories, also double for storage. A pine chest is good when a flat table top is needed.

Entertainment center furniture is mass produced. Cabinets combined of doors, drawers, and shelving to accommodate stereo, TV, accessories, cassettes, disks, records, and books are available.

Another choice is to custom make the furniture to fit your particular situation. By so doing, it fits to room scale and decor with finesse.

BEDROOM

How important is bedroom closet storage? Important enough to have launched a new service industry called "closetology." Services in the marketplace will custom design any closet, promising to take advantage of every cubic inch.

A common stumbling block to increasing storage is our own reluctance to *rearrange* closets. If that is your problem, a "closetology" service can take over the job. Or, take up the challenge to create order out of chaos and customize your own closets.

REPLANNING THE CLOSETS

Take inventory of your clothes and accessories. Categorize your possessions according to frequency of use — often, seldom, seasonally or, not in the last three years! Decide what you can do without and never miss! Then decide what should be hung, put on shelves, in cubicles, or given away.

By redesign, you can frequently add enough storage capacity, within existing closets, to handle your needs. A few methods of closet subdivision are: (a) redesign or add to the shelving, (b) create more hanging space with high and low rods, (c) add accessory storage to inside face of doors (d) shop for various devices made especially to contain everything that the body can wear.

For maximum use of the space you may have to remove all existing shelving and rods and re-do the closet from scratch.

Estimate the hanging space needed for each length of garment. The reason: Shirts and blouses are short, so why waste the space underneath? Have two tiers of hanging in the same vertical space, and sometimes three. Build shelving or cubicles sized for your shoes

Add side shelves under sink for extra storage. Leave access to repair the plumbing!

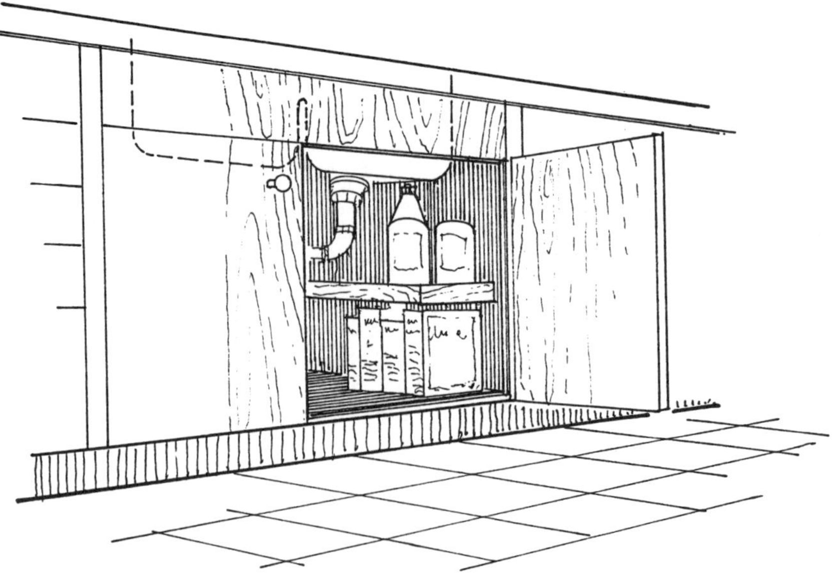

and accessories. Stop planning when you have maximized all the space — floor to ceiling.

In addition to "closetology," another industry flourishes making under-the-bed storage containers, often in see-through plastic for easy viewing. If not already existing, we might soon find stores which specialize only in containers, organizers and devices for household storage.

I once remodeled a home wherein the most demanding storage for the master bedroom suite was the Master's collection of 900 different T-shirts. Storage space was saturated, so we re-designed the bed providing custom sized drawers under each side. Storage under beds is as old as beds. The trick is to customize for maximum use.

BATHROOM

Illustrations best describe methods to increase bathroom storage.

Space under lavatory is put to good use with a hamper. Cut out for plumbing "P" trap.

Exterior Storage

Exterior storage often means little more than things piled up against a wall somewhere. It doesn't have to be that way.

There are ways to find exterior storage space, but not many ways that haven't been tried before.

1. Under roof overhang. Seldom done but it can be effective. The trick is to complement the house exterior when adding the space.
2. Add a large storage room against an outside wall, or as a free standing unit.
3. Other methods such as under porches, outside stairs or raised decks, within a space created by free-standing walls etc., depend upon your particular situation.

Carefully survey the outside area. Chances are you will find a way to get the storage you need.

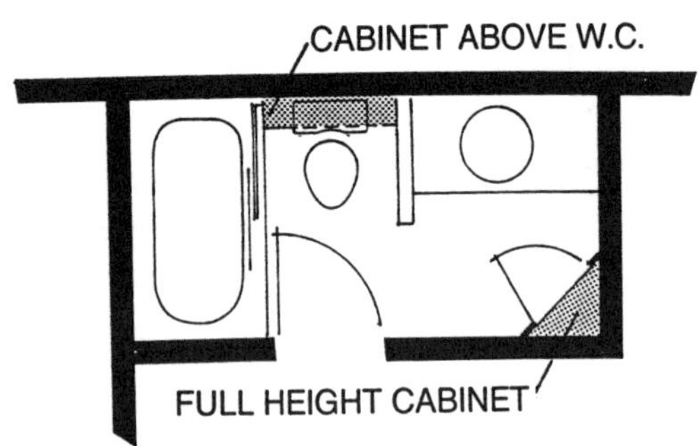

Cabinets above water closet and filling a corner, make good use of unused space.

Shallow cabient above water closet adds a lot of extra storage in a small bathroom.

Garage

Anything that won't fit in the house ends up in the garage. Some garages are so full there is no room for the cars. When that happens, the solution might be to either change your habits or build another garage for the cars.

Another solution is to organize the garage interior for maximum storage with car space included. A garage sale might take care of the remainder — for fun and profit.

Keep in Mind:

1. Literature galore is available on wall shelving for equipment, hooks for ladders, and various hanging and storage devices.
2. Overhead racks should be constructed with care for structural soundness and safety for people below them.
3. Home do-it-yourself stores and magazines are good sources for all sorts of bins, racks, hangers, and storage modules to help you compartmentalize and consolidate.
4. Between the studs works for small tool storage.

Basement

A well constructed, dry basement helps to solve dozens of renovation needs. Storage is certainly one of those and much the same thinking used for garage storage applies here.

Under stairs storage is typical. As with any enclosed space, don't store combustible materials under stairs. Stairs are needed as an exit and it's good practice to surround stairs (including underneath) with fireproof material.

Items that benefit from being stored in a cool place are good candidates for the basement.

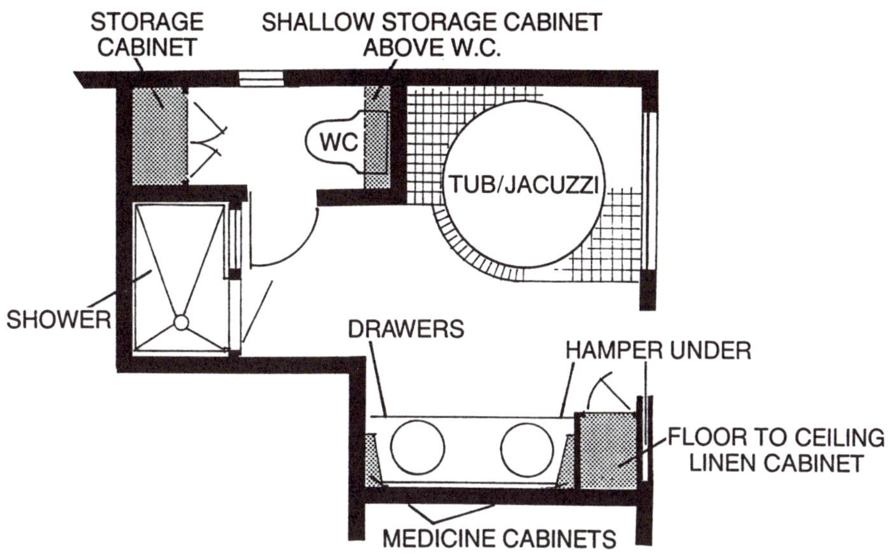

A large bath with enough tucked-away storage for both bath and bedroom use.

Adding storage units to the carport.

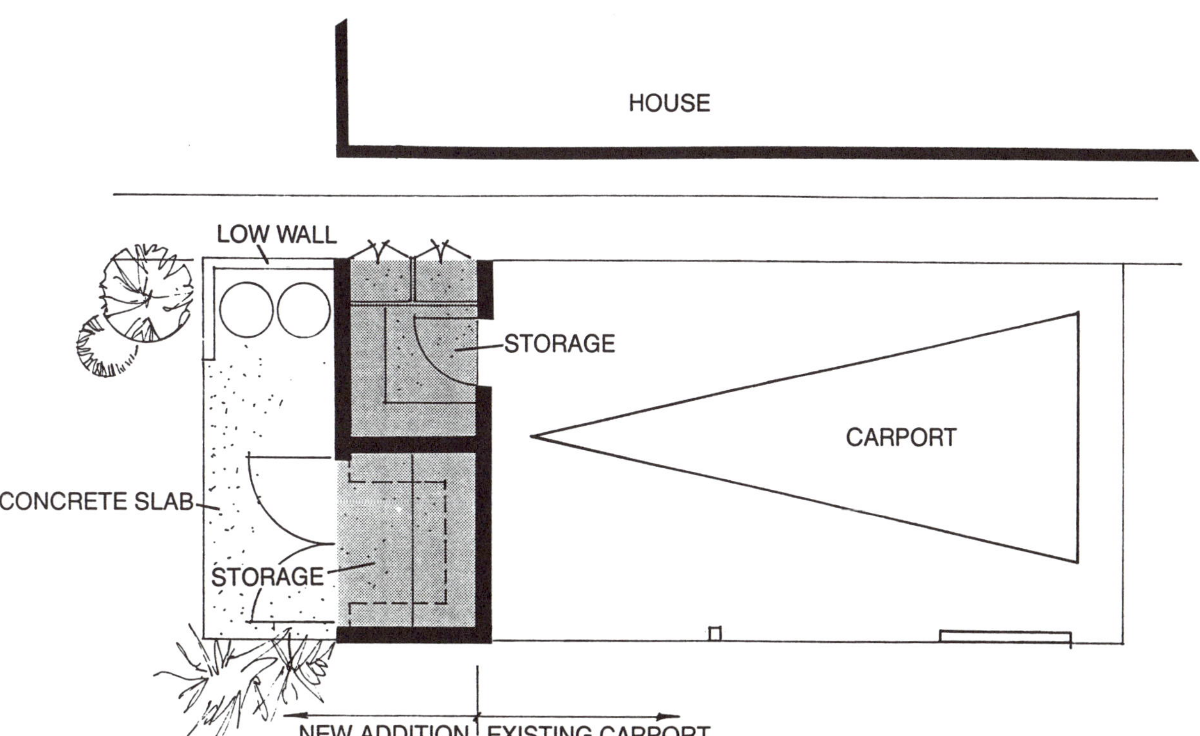

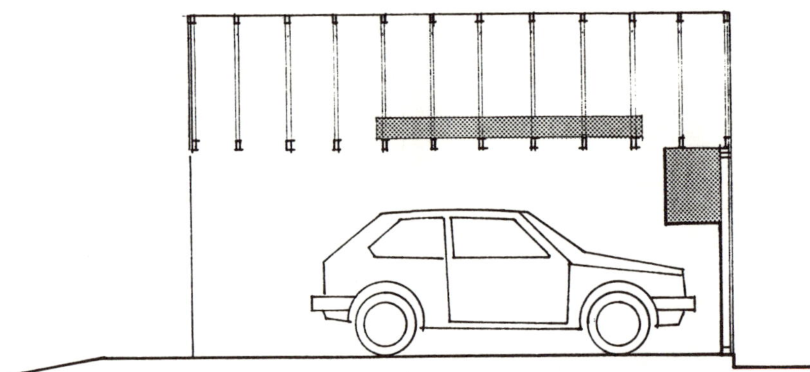

If overhead storage is used, verify the ability of the roof and wall structure to carry the load.

Small tool storage in cabinet between studs.

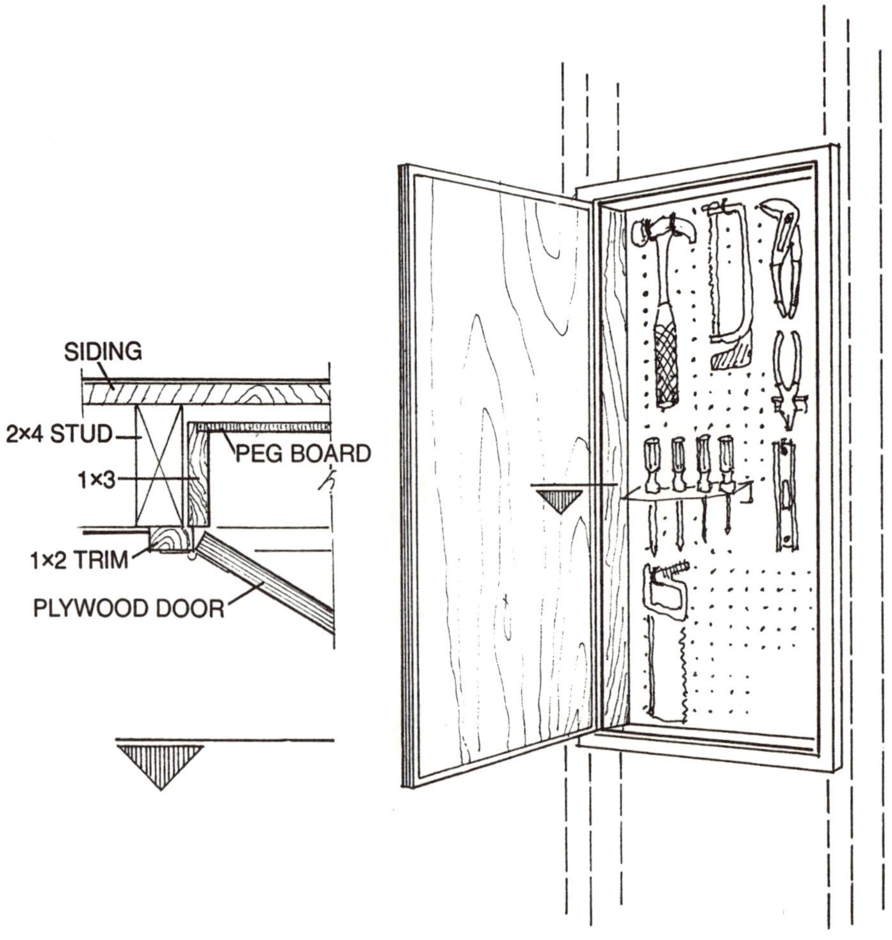

A major interior renovation was performed here. A condominium, under construction, was transformed to accommodate the owner's relaxed life style.

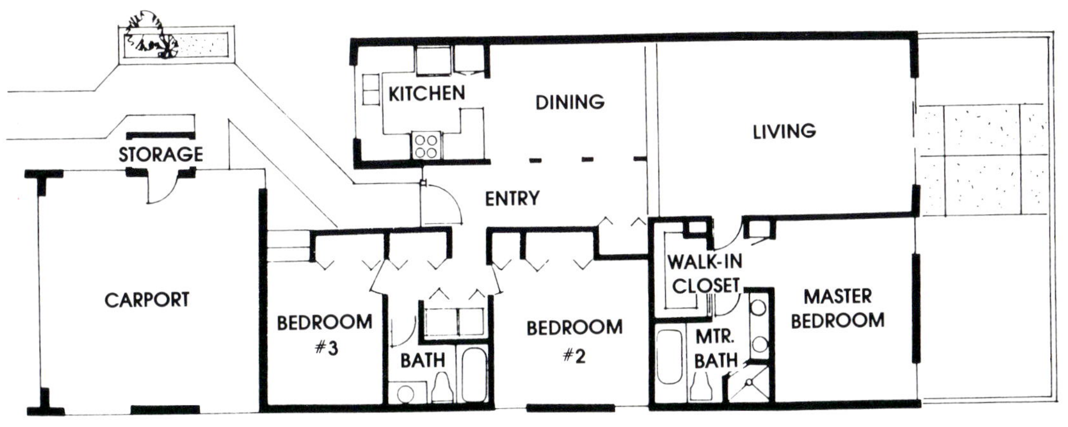

BEFORE

PHOTOGRAPHER MARK BOISCLAIR

PHOTOGRAPHER MARK BOISCLAIR

The revolving entertainment center contains TV, stereo, VCR, bar, sink, microwave, refrigerator and storage. It was originally designed in molded plastic. The owner elected to spend more to have it constructed in oak.

Note the circular bed converting to daytime sofa.

The built-in seating area fronts a fireplace. Flooring is oak through-out.

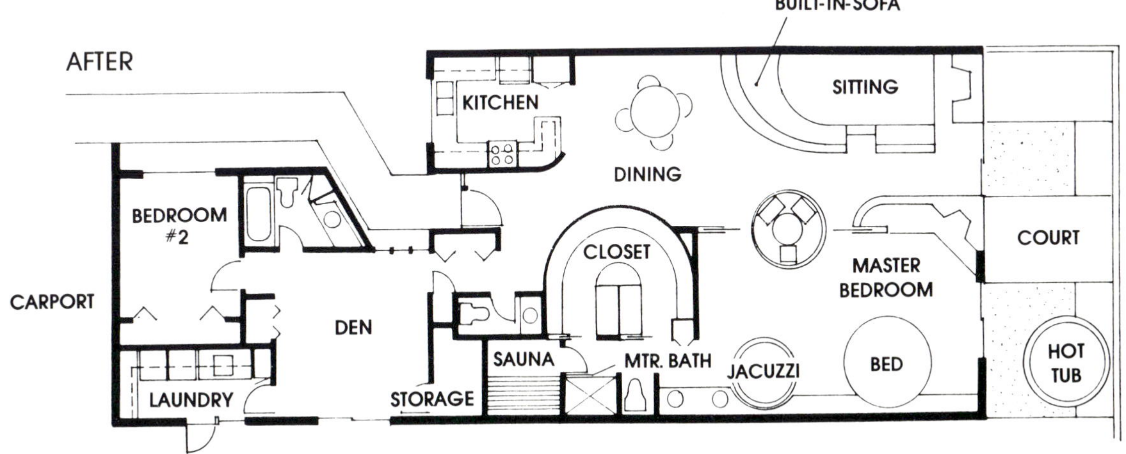

This home contained an unused interior open court space, 8 foot by 8 foot. The space was enclosed providing a gallery for the owner's sports photo collection.

Interest was created by adding furring, sheathing, and cedar shingles to portions of the masonry wall.

BEFORE

AFTER

This couple wanted to add a hobby space with good natural lighting. They created a sun room projecting into the rear yard, using a pre-fabricated structural glazing system. Access is at grade, and with a spiral staircase from above.

Utility Spaces

A bona fide utility room is a combination room for: laundry, ironing, cleaning items (mops, brushes, or just about anything), and a mud room. It has a floor drain, utility tub (laundry sink), electrical and plumbing for washer and dryer, ironing board space, and an assortment of cabinets and shelving for storage.

If you don't have room for all that in one place, look for a smaller space for the messy jobs. Other functions can happen in their own separate spaces.

Laundry

There is no reason for any space in your home to be less than cheerful and uncluttered. In the laundry, uncluttered is accomplished by installing enough shelves and cabinets. Cheerful means good lighting with nice colors and finish materials.

LOCATION

Most homes are built with the everyday entrance starting in the garage, through the laundry, into the kitchen. Aside from creating an entrance not particularly charming, the laundry usually doesn't belong there anyway.

Many people do cook and wash clothes at the same time, and for them it might be a good location. But, if you don't dress in the kitchen or store clothing and linen there, the general bedroom area is a logical laundry location. Available space is often found nearby and it saves carrying laundry back and forth. So, if you want to add a laundry, or create a new one, look to the bedroom wing as an option.

ADDING A LAUNDRY

For economy of installation, examine areas adjacent to existing plumbing and electrical power. For plumbing, you need hot and cold water and a waste line.

Adjacent-to does not necessarily mean in the same room. The space can be on the opposite side of a wall or in the near vicinity. What is needed is *vertical* space within which to create a cavity for the water, waste, vent, and power lines. Remember that walls can, quite economically, be furred out (made thicker) thereby providing a space for new utility lines.

The trick is to locate the laundry so that changes to existing walls and utilities are minimum. And, if the overall remodeling scheme agrees with a particular utility location, it's a bonus. However, don't let that be a requirement that becomes false economy. If the location, chosen because of existing plumbing and power, doesn't work with your overall scheme, look for another. A short run of utilities may be a worthwhile expense to insure remodeling success. That's especially true if, in so doing, you save space and economize elsewhere.

Keeping in mind that adding new storage space can be done without great cost, converting an existing storage closet into a laundry is a strong option. Or, check out the possibility of creating a mini-laundry in an outside closet with access from the inside.

APPLIANCES

Washer and dryer are a good percentage of the laundry expense. Careful shopping helps and finding what you want on sale is always nice. Beyond that, I have one suggestion.

Often, a manufacture will offer four or five models each of washers and dryers. With washers it can go to six models, adding feature upon feature and larger load capability. Look carefully at the model second from the bottom. It might be the best value, doing what you need at the lowest cost.

Mud Room

In theory, little kids (and big ones) will leave all wet things, dirt, and mess in a little place called a mud room. This room acts as the transition between the hazards of mother nature and your tidy home inside. Active families in wet, cold climates make good use of a mud room, at least for part of the year. Keep materials basic, impervious to water, and easy to clean.

Mechanical Systems and Solar Adaptations

Retrofitting solar equipment to existing homes is a thriving industry. The literature available for practically any application is voluminous. In addition to information available from suppliers, the government has stacks of data ready to send you. Listed below are a few sources which have helped me with solar and other natural forms of energy.

U.S. Department of Housing and Urban Development, Washington, DC

U.S. Department of Energy, Washington, DC

Conservation and Renewable Energy Inquiry and Referral Services, P.O. Box 8900, Silver Spring, MD 20907

National Solar Heating and Cooling Information Center, P.O. Box 1607, Rockville, MD 20850

Your local utility company is another source for information.

If you decide to pursue some form of solar energy, use a few simple guidelines: (1) Get firm prices for the system, installed and

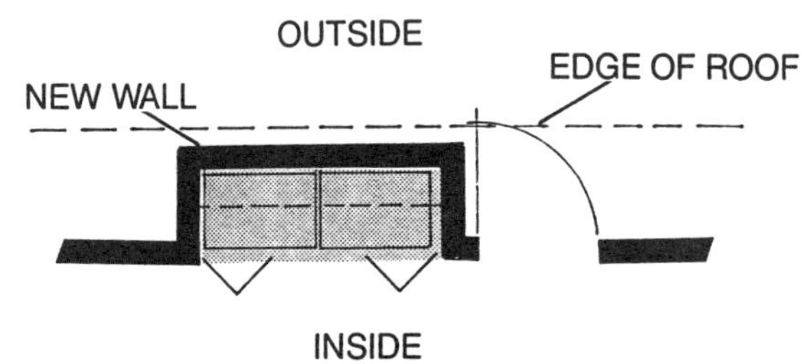

New mini laundry under an existing roof, with inside access.

Outside storage (shown here under roof overhang) should be done with concern for aesthetic appearance.

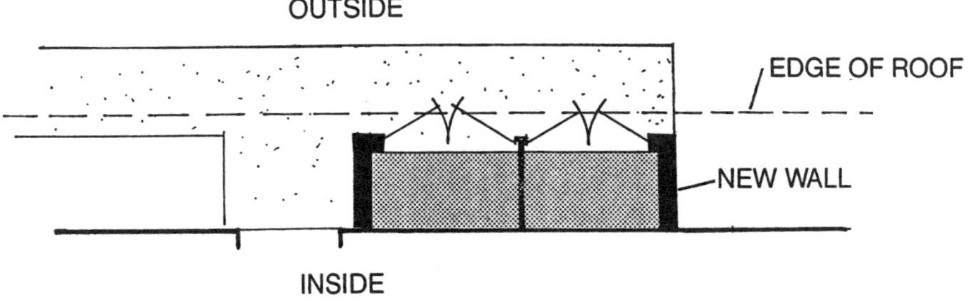

operating. (2) Estimate on-going maintenance expense. There will be some. (3) Calculate the projected savings in energy costs using solar equipment. (4) Estimate the time it will take to recover the cost of the installed equipment. (5) Have the foregoing information at hand before making a final decision.

Check List
— Storage Spaces —

Location	Storage/ Existing	Storage Desired	Remarks
Family Room	None	Books-games-stereo VCR-tapes-albums	Add upper and lower shelving and cabinets at north wall
Den/Study	None	Built-in shelving	Spare bedroom - Converting to study
Living Room	None	—	—
Dining	China cabinet	Cabinet for linens	Built in cabinet if possible
Kitchen	Average	Small appliances Large pots and pans	Not sure where to acquire space
Breakfast	—	—	—
Pantry	Small cabinet	MORE	Add shallow pantry storage at 2 narrow wall spaces
Other	Entry	—	—
Hall #1	Two closets	General household items	Remove hanging rod. Redesign closet for maximum capacity
Hall #2	—	—	—
Bathroom (Common)	Linen closet	Hamper	
Bedroom No. 1			

Example of How to Use the Check List

Sample

Note: You may wish to remove or copy the check list sheets for more convenient use.

Check List

— Storage Spaces —

Location	Storage/ Existing	Storage Desired	Remarks
Family Room			
Den/Study			
Living Room			
Dining			
Kitchen			
Breakfast			
Pantry			
Other			
Hall #1			
Hall #2			
Bathroom (Common)			
Bedroom No. 1			
Bedroom No. 2			
Bathroom			
Master Bedroom			
Master Bath/ Dressing			
Recreation Room			
Basement			
Attic			
Other			
Garage/Carport			
Other			

Check List
— Work/Utility/Storage —

Existing Function	Existing Space	Remarks	Desired Space/Features
Washing	Garage to Kitchen	Too small	Want larger space - location not critical
Drying	Garage to Kitchen	Too small	Need larger space
Laundry Sink	None	Sink not required	—
Counters	None	No room for sorting, folding, etc.	Need minimum 3 feet of counters
Hanging	None	—	Want small hanging
Storage	One upper cabinet	Minimal	
Ironing			

Example of How to Use the Check List

Sample

Note: You may wish to remove or copy the check list sheets for more convenient use.

— Utility Systems —

Equipment	Condition	Desired Changes	Remarks
Hot Water Heater	Fair	Need 60 gallon tank or recirculating pump	Replace tank soon
Gas Furnace	Fair	None	
Central Air Conditioning	Good. New compressor	None	

Check List

— Work/Utility/Storage —

Existing Function	Existing Space	Remarks	Desired Space/Features
Washing			
Drying			
Laundry Sink			
Counters			
Hanging			
Storage			
Ironing			
Sewing			
Mud Room			
Other			
Other			

— Utility Systems —

Equipment	Condition	Desired Changes	Remarks
Hot Water Heater			
Gas Furnace			
Central Air Conditioning			

7

Lighting—Natural and Artificial

Ancient builders left an opening in the roof to light the interior space. Later, clerestory windows were used high in the walls, providing what became a more lasting method for letting daylight in. Later still, in Christian churches, the development of stained glass techniques and artistry elevated a functional requirement into a permanent art form. And so it goes throughout history, each age and society addressing a similar problem in its own way. In this century, glass-sheathed buildings have become a cure-all for many designers.

The above examples introduce an important point about remodeling, to wit: Where lighting interior space is involved, any number of different solutions may be used to accomplish the same thing.

Lighting Effects

In this chapter we discuss the use of both artificial light (incandescent and fluorescent lamps, etc.) and natural light (daylight).

When we visualize the space within a home, it's usually in the context of daylight. Home buyers invariably look at a prospective home only in daylight. That's fine up to a point. When the sun goes down some homes become downright dreary, inside and outside.

Aesthetically pleasing lighting design adds so much to the pleasure of any interior space. Variations and areas of interest can be created through an interplay of light and shadow. Well designed light, both natural and artificial, will introduce benefits to a space similar to the effect of good background music, colors, and fine furnishings.

The psychological effect of natural and artificial light in a room is very real and should not be left to chance. Lighting has an impact on the behavior of people. This effect, subconscious and conscious, begins the moment you enter the space.

Well-planned lighting will enhance colors and textures, bringing surfaces to life.

The sensation of pleasure and mood contentment produced by lighting happens some place in every home. My intention for this chapter is to make it happen more often in yours.

If you doubt the emotional influence of light, consider the natural effect of a gorgeous sunrise or sunset, or the soothing and almost hypnotic effect of firelight! What happens to your mood on a cloudy day? A rainy day?

Soft overhead light for a conversation area. Dimmer controls should be used.

Recessed downlights illuminate the living area with an overall spread of general lighting. Track mounted spots provide accents by highlighting paintings and wall above the fireplace.

PLANNING THE METHOD

Don't hesitate to multiple-switch a series of lights instead of putting them all on one switch. House builders typically put too many lights on a switch. It's less costly but often a mistake for good lighting. More switches provide the flexibility of using only lights needed at the time, whether for effect or function.

Also, it is sometimes preferable to have more than one lighting system in a given space — a low voltage or indirect system as well as a standard, direct-lighting system.

In some spaces, especially those most used for family and social activity, I advocate using more lights and more switches than are commonly used. Let me explain this apparent extravagance.

You will be lighting feature areas such as art work, potted plants, reading areas, conversation areas, wet bar, etc. To accommodate the various situations noted above, *without flooding the general area with light,* requires flexibility. Flexibility is achieved by having an adequate number of lights separately switched. Another way is the use of dimmer switches. Dimmer switches allow you to adjust room atmosphere instantly. They also let you light different room functions with the same fixture. Usually, a combination of extra switching and the use of dimmers, with good fixture selection, will do a fine job.

Focus attention on potted plants with adjustable down lights that vary from narrow to wide beam.

Uplights on interior plants is another way to enhance their appearance and cast interesting patterns on the wall.

Extra cost for lights and switches used in a feature space may be offset by energy saved in reducing the amount of over-all light required.

REVIEW AREAS AND LIGHTING NEEDS

Consider the examples listed below. In a typical family or social activity space, the following areas and their lighting requirements might exist:

USE OF SPACE	REQUIRED LIGHT
a. Traffic circulation	Low to moderate
b. Conversation area	Moderate, diffused
c. Reading area	Higher level, concentrated or generally brighter
d. TV/Video viewing	Low to moderate, indirect
e. Game table	Moderate to high
f. Art work on walls	Moderate, concentrated
g. Potted plants	Low to moderate, concentrated or general
h. Social function	Moderate, diffused
i. Create mood	Low/moderate/ concentrated

Some or all of the above should be found in any average family living space.

Each use area mentioned above may not require its own specific light source. For example, traffic and conversation areas can be served by the lighting needs of an adjacent space. On the other hand, a reading space usually needs its own light source. TV viewing is best when light comes from a source out of direct view.

Quality of light is important in a space used for social functions. At the time the space looks its best, the *people* should also look their best.

Recessed niche in a hallway is lighted for mood and circulation.

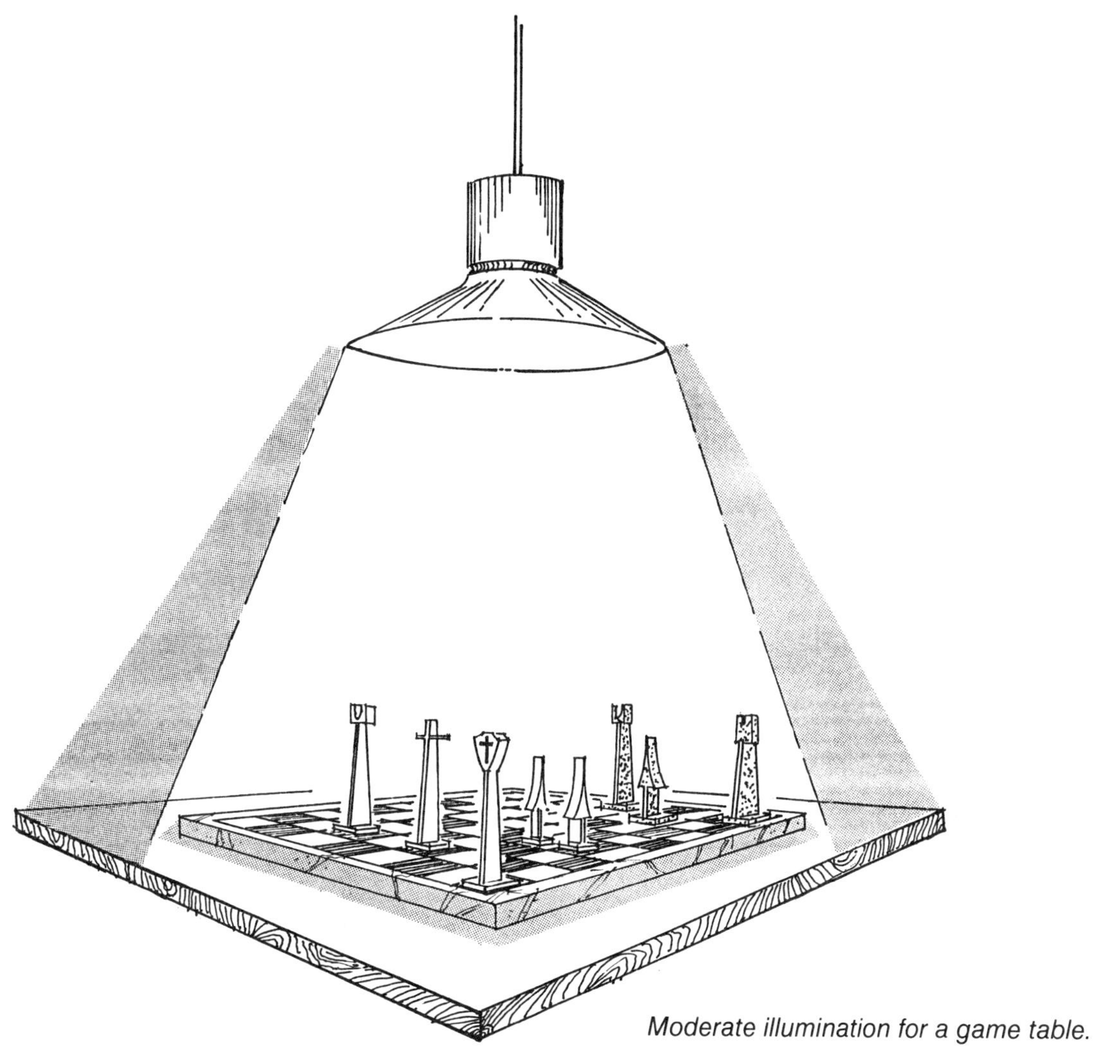

Moderate illumination for a game table.

Remember Aesthetics

Lighting should improve the aesthetics of any space, inside or out. It's not difficult to bring a proper foot candle level of light to a given space. But, lighting for function alone is not enough. Also consider comfort, color, balance, and atmosphere.

DESIGN FLEXIBILITY — FUNCTIONAL AND ARTISTIC

Think about the real *use* of lighting in your home. Why is lighting needed and how much? To create light for traffic, conversation,

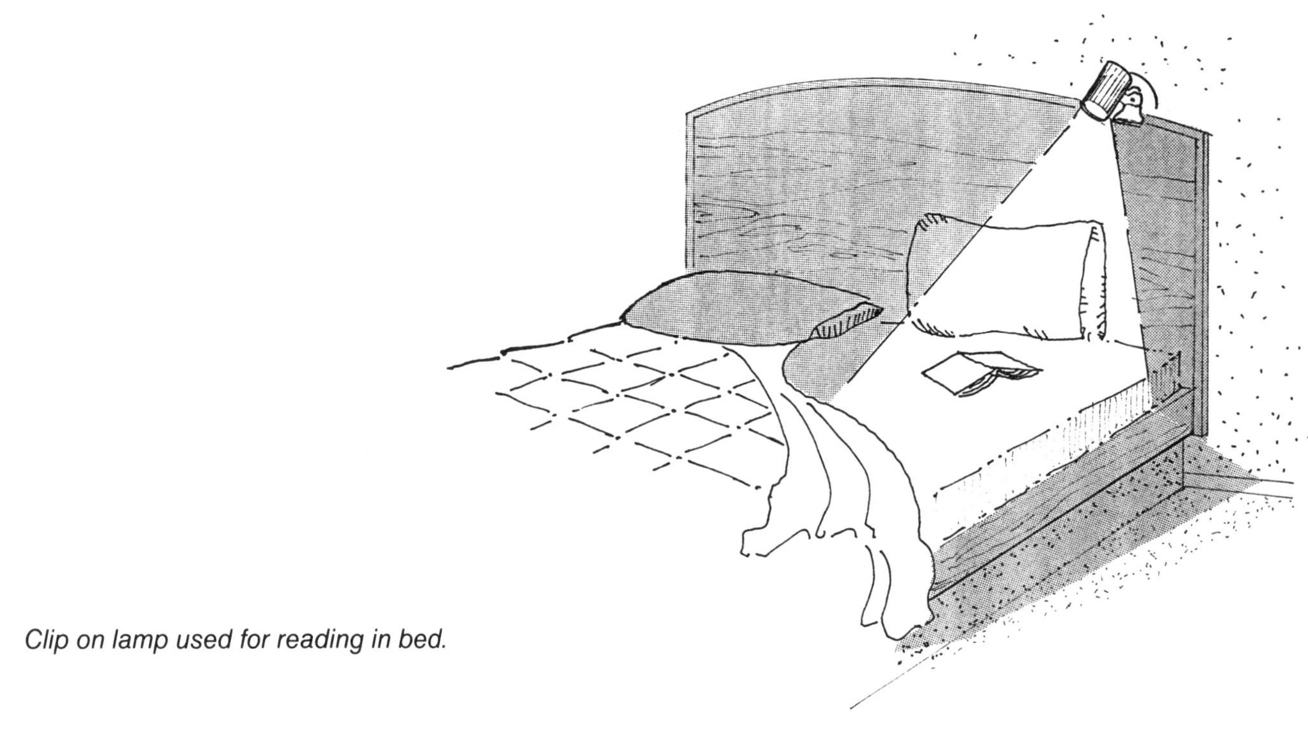

Clip on lamp used for reading in bed.

Track lighting for art work and potted plants. (Low Voltage)

Eye level when seated is approximately 40" above the floor. This is an important consideration when the light source is positioned near the side of the reader.

A large-scale fixture used with a dimmer spreads a warm glow throughout a dining area. Good lighting is flattering to diners and makes food appealing.

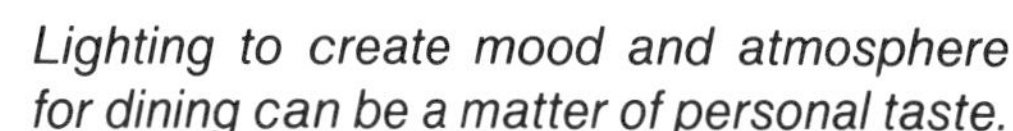

Lighting to create mood and atmosphere for dining can be a matter of personal taste.

TV viewing, reading, etc., you may utilize one of many sources. A partial list, with examples, is shown below:

(a) Indirect area lighting
(b) Decorative chandeliers, lanterns
(c) Lighting used for artwork display
(d) Decorative portable lamps
(e) Lighting used for accent plantings
(f) Pendant fixtures
(g) Wall wash, up-lighting, down-lighting
(h) Track lighting
(i) Low voltage (12 V.DC) or normal house service (120 V.AC)

The wall washer fixtures, which highlight the painting, soften shadows and offset the effect of strong downlighting on the table.

Good lighting can make a blah room delightful, a cold room warm, or a small room appear larger than it really is. Remember, though, it goes both ways! A room which may be exciting by daylight can be dismal at night with bad lighting.

Lighting can direct attention to virtually any part of a room, focusing on a favorite object, painting or plant. Accenting these points of interest can be subtle or dramatic, depending on the type of fixtures used and the intensity of the lamps.

Suspended downlights can cause harsh shadows and should be kept away from people's faces and confined within the table perimeter.

Wall washer fixtures are used where uniform illumination of a wall from an inconspicuous light source is desired.

Versatile track lighting wraps around the corner.

One of the oldest forms of portable lighting for the house is table lamps or floor lamps. There is a floor lamp or table lamp designed to accommodate virtually any need.

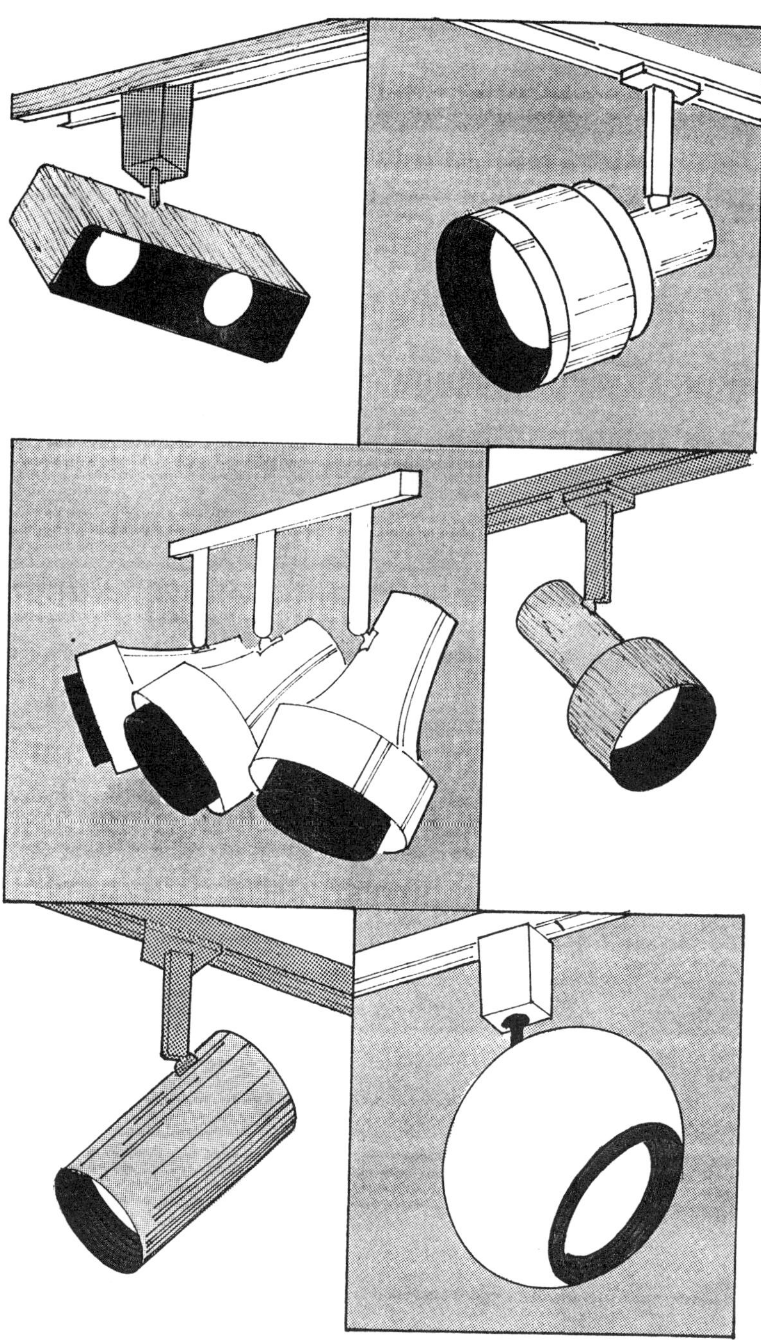

A few of the many light track fixtures available.

Examples of suspended fixtures.

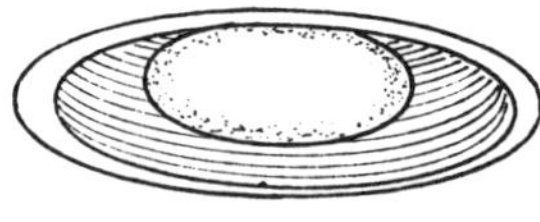

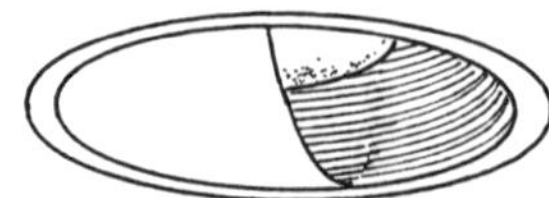

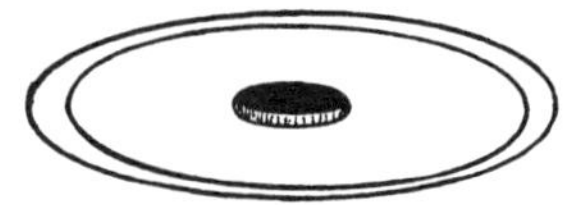

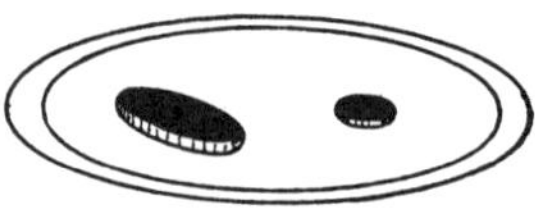

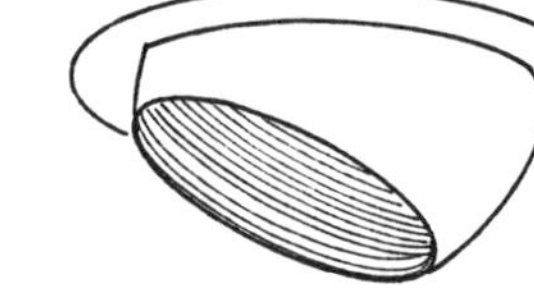

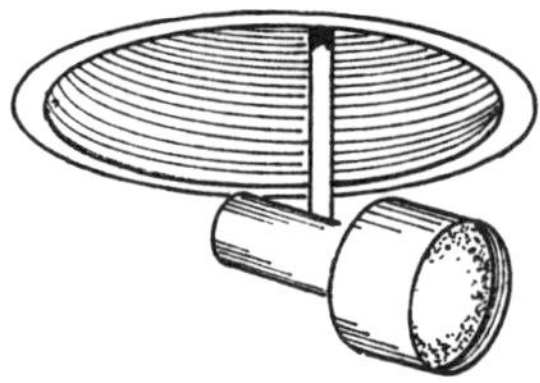

Downlights which are recessed or semi-recessed are normally used for accent lighting, supplementary lighting, or specific task lighting.

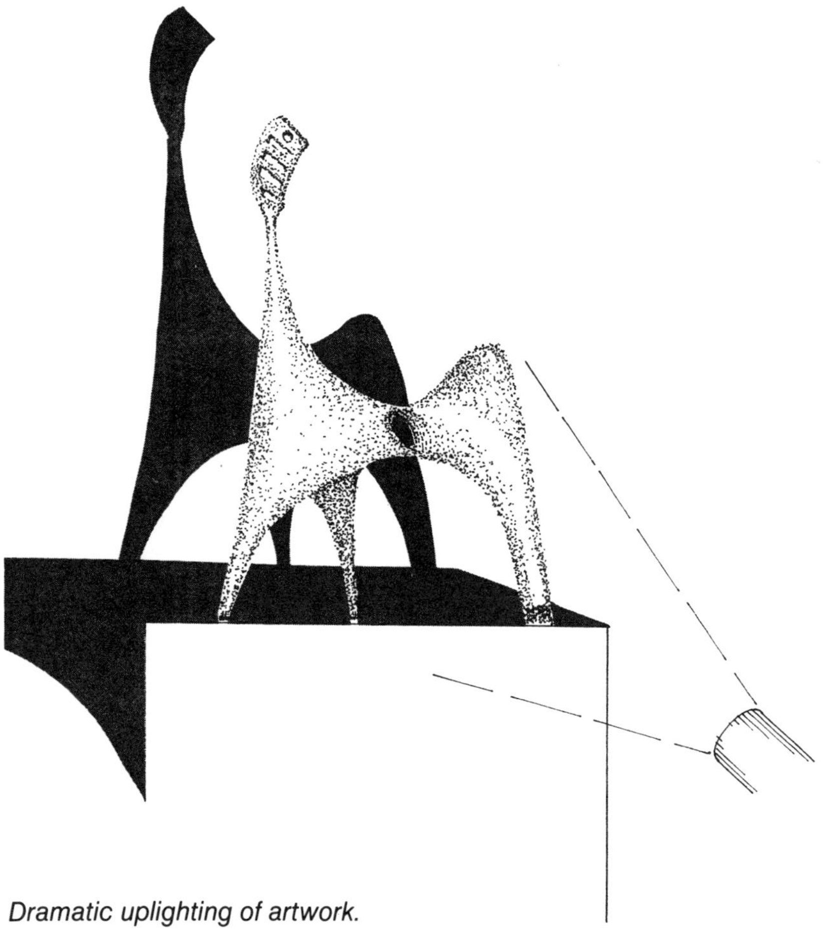

Dramatic uplighting of artwork.

A fixture built-in as part of the wall accents a sculpture.

General lighting for bedrooms can take many forms. Combinations of these examples are common.

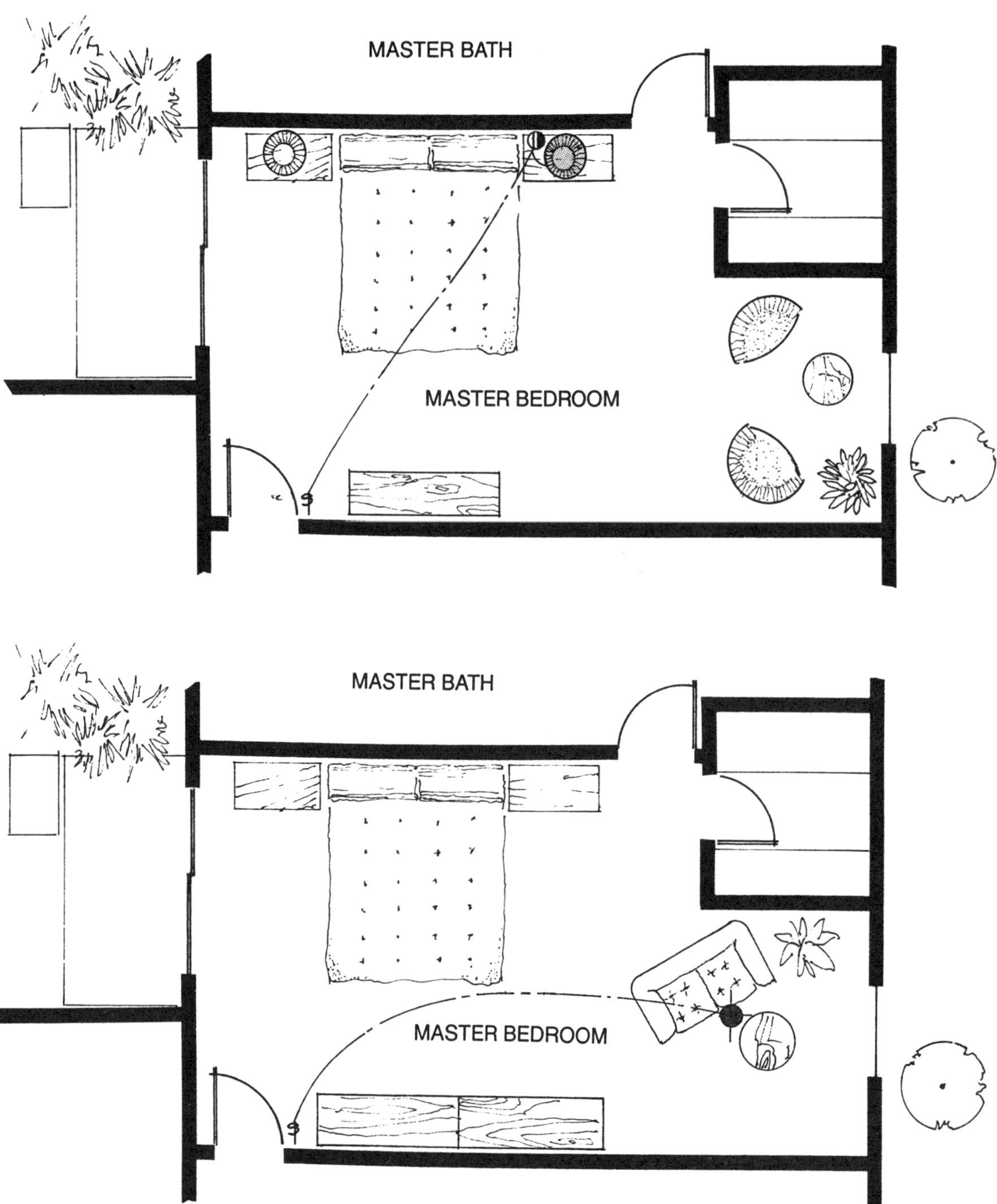

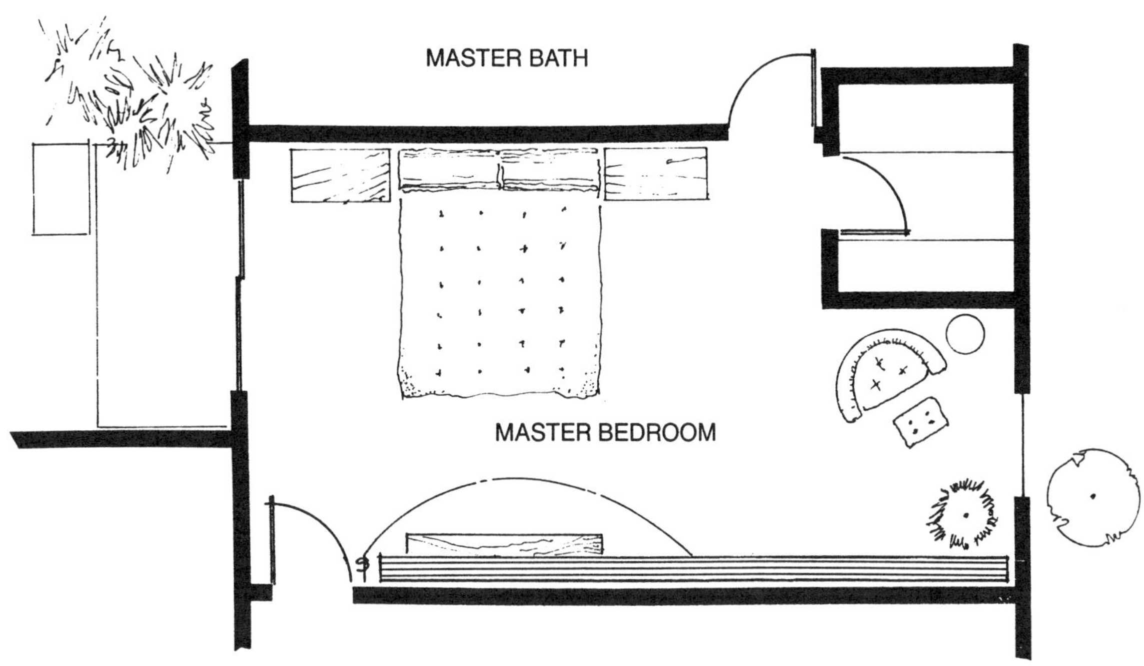

Vanity light.

Be aware of where you place light fixtures and mirrors in relation to each other. The glaring side of the fixture may be revealed in a mirror and spoil the effect of otherwise subtle area lighting. The lights at a mirror should be directed at the person and not on the mirror.

It Helps to Experiment

Try an experiment with your family or living room. Place furniture, plants, objects, etc. where you think best. Use portable lamps in different locations. Use the lamps, along with existing built-in lighting, trying various arrangements. Aim the light source in various directions. Change bulbs in the fixtures to

Lamps are available in a variety of sizes, shapes, colors, and wattages. Check proper wattage for each fixture.

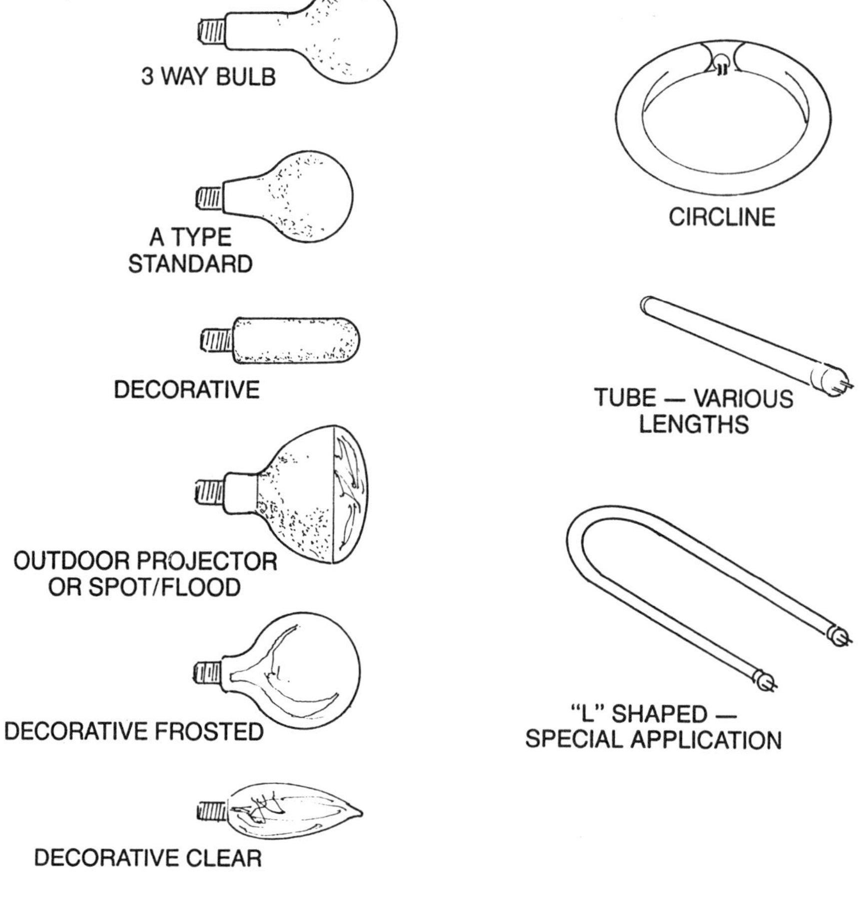

different wattage as necessary for the best effect. Before long you will have the arrangement that you think shows the room to its best advantage. This one small sample should show you what can be done with careful lighting design.

Good lighting working together with over-all design and furniture layout *is* worth the effort!

LIGHTING AND COLOR

Here is another quick, helpful experiment. Putting different colors under the same light will illustrate the importance of keeping room and furniture colors in mind when planning lighting. Dark colors don't reflect as much light as light colors. Depending on the type of lamps used (i.e., fluorescent, incandescent, metal halide, etc.), the same color will appear colder, warmer, or a different tone. Wall, ceiling, or floor texture will change under different lighting.

FINISH SURFACE

Matte finishes reflect light diffusely and therefore project the natural color of an object. Conversely, a smooth, shiny surface can reflect strong light so as to distort or obscure the color.

LIGHT SOURCES CAN HELP OR HURT

A poorly planned light source detracts from the overall atmosphere of a space. Surface blemishes in a wall or ceiling are emphasized by a certain type of lighting. For instance, a strong wash of light, especially daylight, coming from a narrow oblique angle, will accent a bad paint job or surface texture.

On the other hand, well planned light sources are a bonus and sometimes seem to *create the space itself.* In some spaces it's desirable to be aware of the effect of the light without being aware of the actual light source. In other areas, it might be acceptable for the light source itself to be a dominant design factor. This would occur with a sculptured

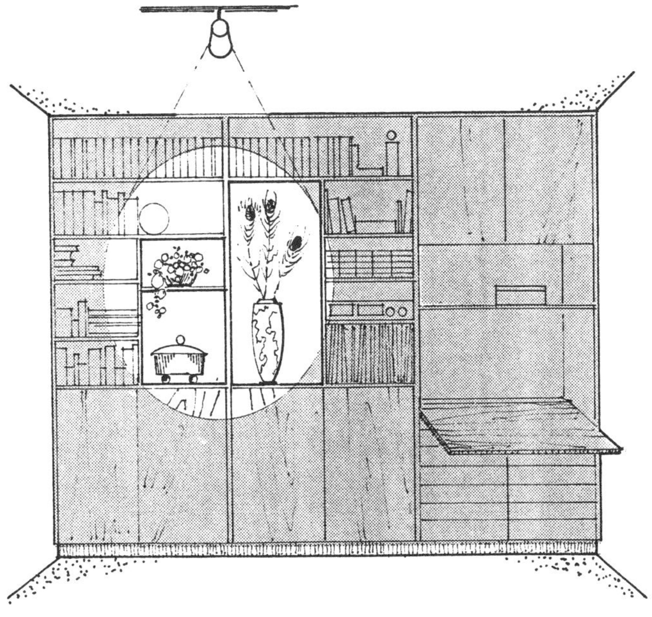

With directional lighting, areas of a room which are important to you can be accented, leaving less attractive areas in the shadow.

lamp, or indirect lighting which in itself forms an architectural feature.

Some lighting methods feature both the light source and its effect. An example would be stained glass in a window or skylight, or a beautiful lamp casting a well-placed glow.

APPLICATION

A licensed electrical engineer or licensed electrician should be consulted before actual electrical work is done.

Low Voltage Lighting

Low voltage lighting, which normally operates at 12 volts, is a handy application to keep in mind. Its unique features, some of which are noted here, might apply to your needs.

ADVANTAGES:

(a) Minimum space requirements.
(b) Good effect provided by low intensity.

With a nicely formed fixture the light source itself becomes a feature.

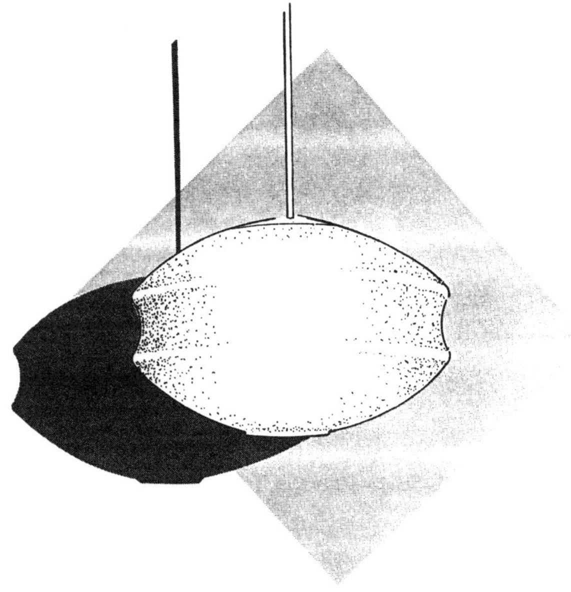

(c) Easy adaptation to existing structure or for exterior use.
(d) Safety — Safer for interior and exterior use.

DISADVANTAGES:

(a) Selection of fixtures is relatively limited.
(b) Switches don't match with regular house voltage switches.
(c) Dimming requires special low voltage dimmer controls.
(d) Transformers are required to change normal house voltage to low voltage.
(e) Replacement lamp cost is high and not always available in a typical neighborhood store.

INTERIOR

Low voltage lamps have a short filament which allows precise control of the light beam. They are useful for accent or decorative lighting.

The wiring usually is simple, small, and has less restrictive building code requirements. Therefore, low voltage lighting is useful especially in do-it-yourself remodeling.

Many bulbs are quite small and can be used with small fixtures for inconspicuous interior application.

Interior fixtures are available in various forms, such as recessed down lights, surface mounted, adjustable, and high intensity pin spots.

EXTERIOR

An advantage often considered by the do-it-yourself homeowner is that low voltage wiring is somewhat safer than 120-volt circuits. Therefore, it's often used with exterior landscaping. Exterior fixtures are available in many forms of accent lighting for trees, shrubs, walkways, steps, patios, buildings, pools, and fountains.

DIMMING

As with normal 120-volt circuits, dimmer switches are useful with low voltage lighting. In addition, lamp life usually is extended with the use of dimmer switching.

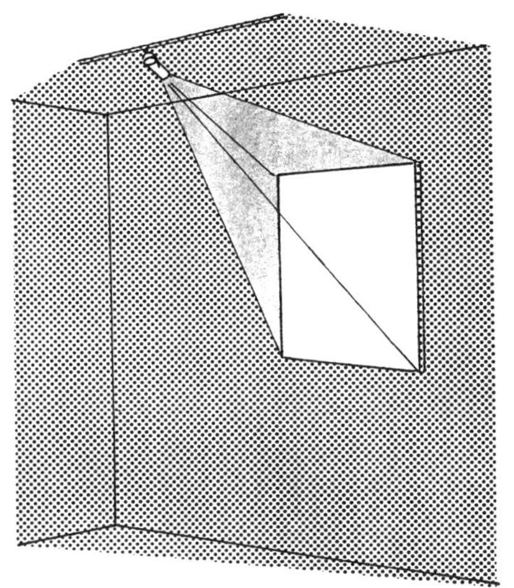

Low voltage fixtures make possible illumination of very precise areas.

Adjustable light beam focuses attention on art.

Glare on a shiny surface.

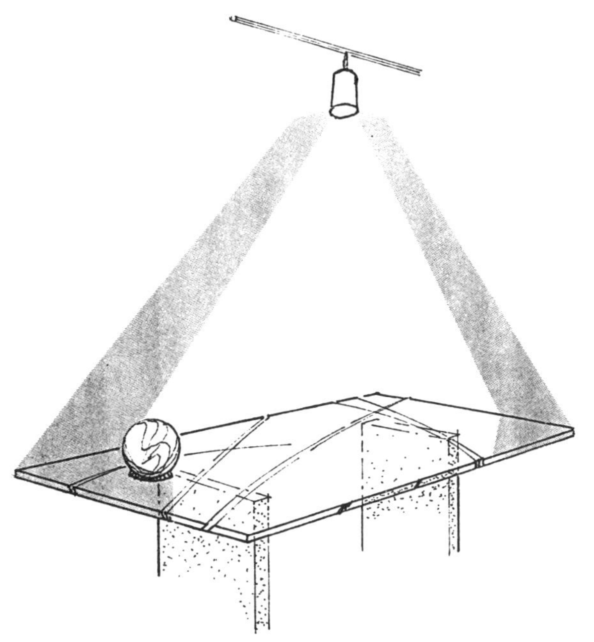

Reduce glare with a dimmer.

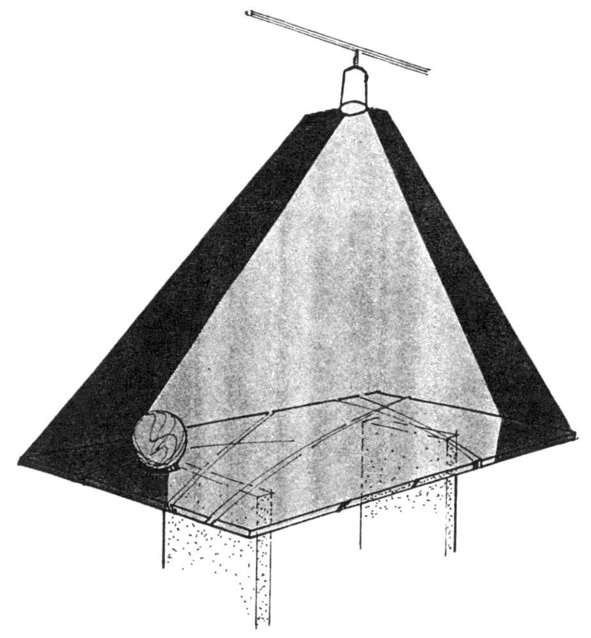

Skylights

Skylights are an option to satisfy the need for more daylight in a space.

The addition of one or more skylights, in the right place, can cheer up a room. Areas that frequently receive skylighting are: bathrooms, utility rooms, hallways, kitchens, laundry, etc. While adding to the aesthetic enjoyment of the space, skylights also improve function.

Skylights used in work areas provide supplemental task lighting. Small skylights in spaces without windows reduce the need to switch lights on and off for periods of short use.

ORIENTATION AND HEAT GAIN

In warm climates, care should be taken to locate skylights away from intense sun exposure. The exception is when skylights are used for solar heat gain in winter. In that case, they usually face toward the south. The same skylights then can be provided with some sort of protection from the summer sun. In addition, double dome and even triple dome skylights are available to reduce heat gain.

In cold climates, care should be taken to reduce the interior heat loss through skylights in winter.

SKYLIGHTS FOR VENTILATION

Operable skylights, which provide fresh air, can be purchased or made. Chapter 14, GETTING IT DONE, includes more information about skylights for ventilation.

SKYLIGHTS FOR NIGHTTIME

If the skylight occurs where the finished ceiling is some distance from the finished roof, a skylight shaft is required. At the ceiling, another lens can be added. The ceiling lens usually is plastic, but occasionally stained glass.

I often recess light fixtures in the side of skylight shafts, providing a night light source from the ceiling without need for

Continuous skylights provide general light where no windows are included in a room. (See Color Photo)

another fixture. Doing this allows you to use the same light source, day or night, to highlight a certain part of a room. This device is also effective when stained glass is used at the ceiling line. The artistic effect can be enjoyed both day and night.

Stained Glass

STAINED GLASS IN SKYLIGHTS

Using stained glass within or under skylights can be fun. Because of the infinite possibilities in design and color selection, any effect can be created: cheerful, somber, subtle, or wild.

CAREFUL DESIGN REQUIRED

Determine ahead of time what effect you want to create using stained glass, whether in a ceiling or wall, window, or door. Think how it will affect the room. A subtle effect or some added interest in one part of the room can be achieved by locating and designing the glass accordingly.

If you want a skylight to dominate a room, the size, design, and colors can be created to make it happen.

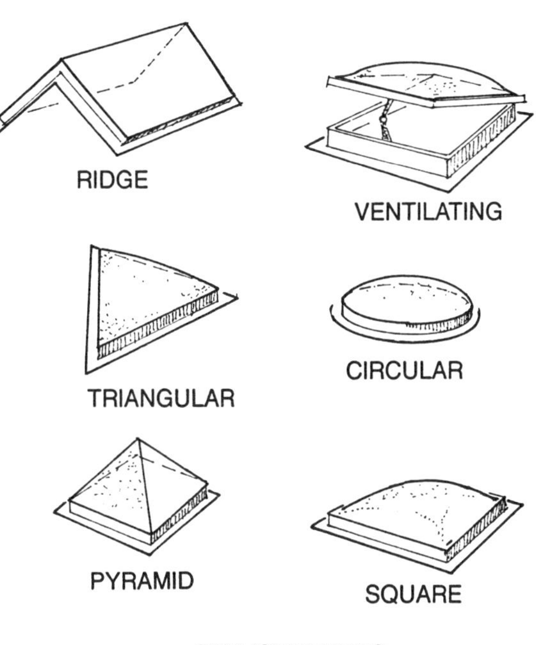

Skylights come in a variety of shapes and styles, either curb mounted or mounted directly on the roof. A single dome is standard, double domes are common, and a triple dome may be obtained for added insulation.

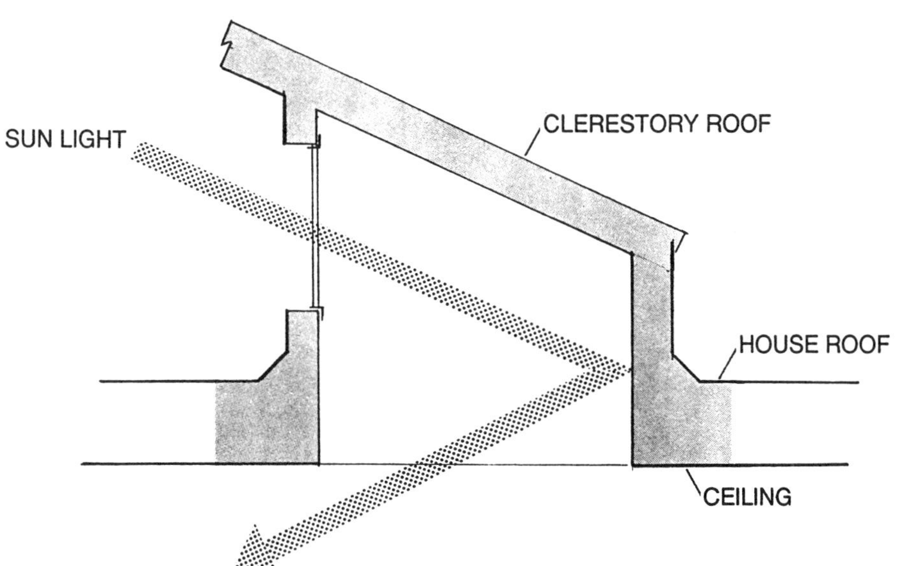

A clerestory skylight lets in the direct warming sun in the winter, and provides protection from the heat of the high summer sun.

An effective use of stained glass is to make it part of an eye-catching scene or focal point commanding attention upon entering (or leaving) a space or rounding a corner.

The many uses of stained glass to enhance a home make it a real consideration in any remodeling project.

Stained glass in a door panel.

Skylight with stained glass.

THE TIFFANY LAMP

The Tiffany Lamp, which is periodically revived, attests to the warm and interesting combinations possible with the combined use of stained glass and incandescent light. Years ago I designed a dining chandelier using an interplay of vertical sheets of stained glass suspended above the table with many small bulbs within. The finished product was so heavy that we had to penetrate the ceiling/roof and support it from several roof members, but it was worth the effort.

EFFECT WITH ECONOMY

Enjoying stained glass does not have to be expensive. Designed and installed by the craft person, it's usually done on a per-square-foot cost. Very small quantities in walls, doors, windows, ceiling, or whatever, may be used economically. It may be just enough to give a space that extra punch and spark of added interest.

Light, Color and Texture

COLOR

More light reflects from a lighter color than a dark color. It follows that lower wattage lights can be used in a light colored room than a dark colored room. This may be especially important with indirect lighting when you want to bounce light off a surface to provide light for an adjacent area.

Different colors and textures reflect different amounts of light and, in fact, react differently to the same light source. For instance, one color might look great under a certain lamp while the same lamp can make another color look awful. In addition, the *same* color will look different under different lights. The same material will appear one color shade in daylight and another under incandescent, and still another under fluorescent.

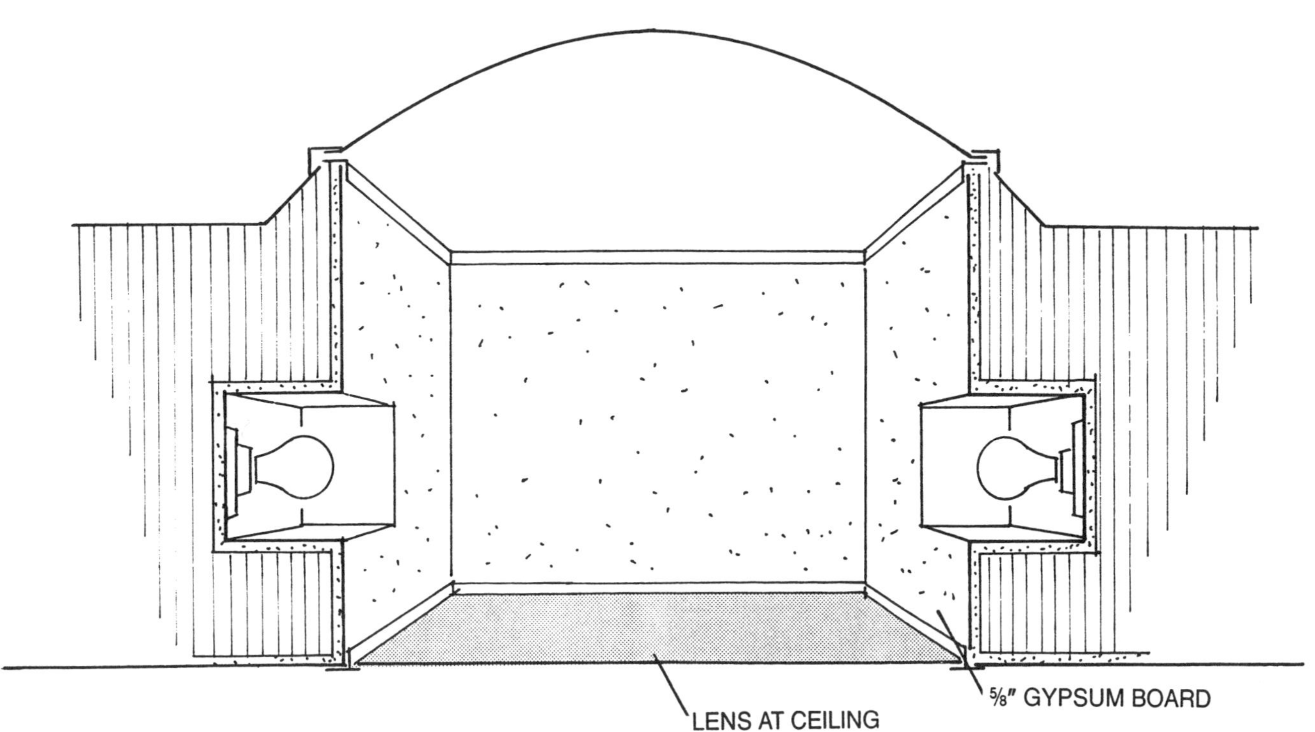

Recessed lights in a skylight shaft create a nighttime light fixture. Consult experts regarding building code requirements.

Pleasant affects are created with efficient use of stained glass used in small window area.

TEXTURE

Other variations take place with light and texture. The texture of a wall surface, floor, ceiling, upholstery, or whatever, will change with each different angle or intensity of the light source. Different textures reflect different amounts of the same light. A rough texture usually reflects less light than a smooth one.

The above is simply basic information and is included only as a reminder to think about when planning new spaces or altering old spaces.

Individual taste dictates that you make your own decisions about color, texture, and lighting. That could involve experimenting or maybe nothing more than being aware of exactly what you like or dislike. A possible starting point is to identify the best light source for your favorite color and texture and go from there.

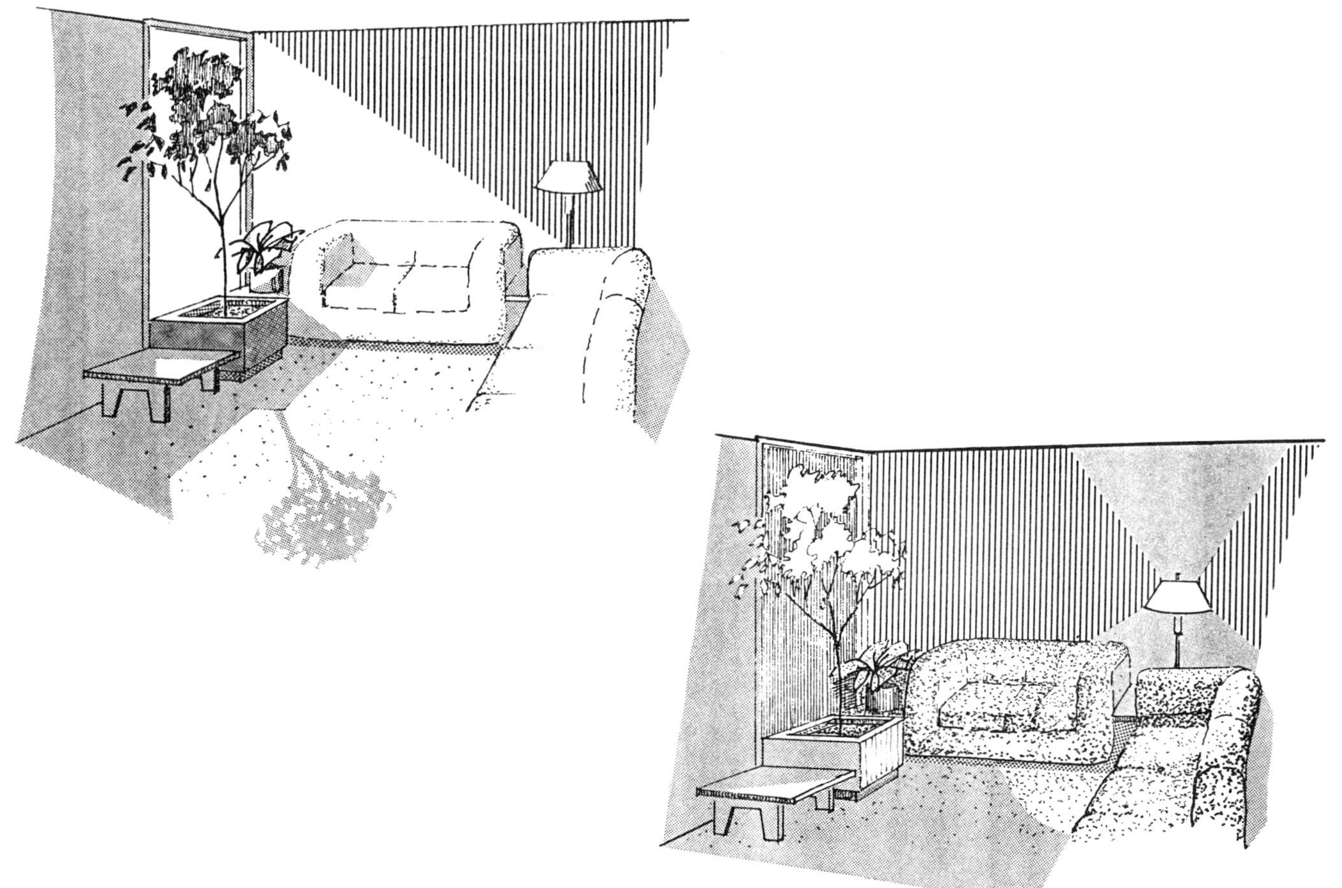

Textured fabric with subtle colors may be brilliant in natural daylight and become part of drab forms in the shadow of modest night lighting.

Landscape lighting doubles for security.

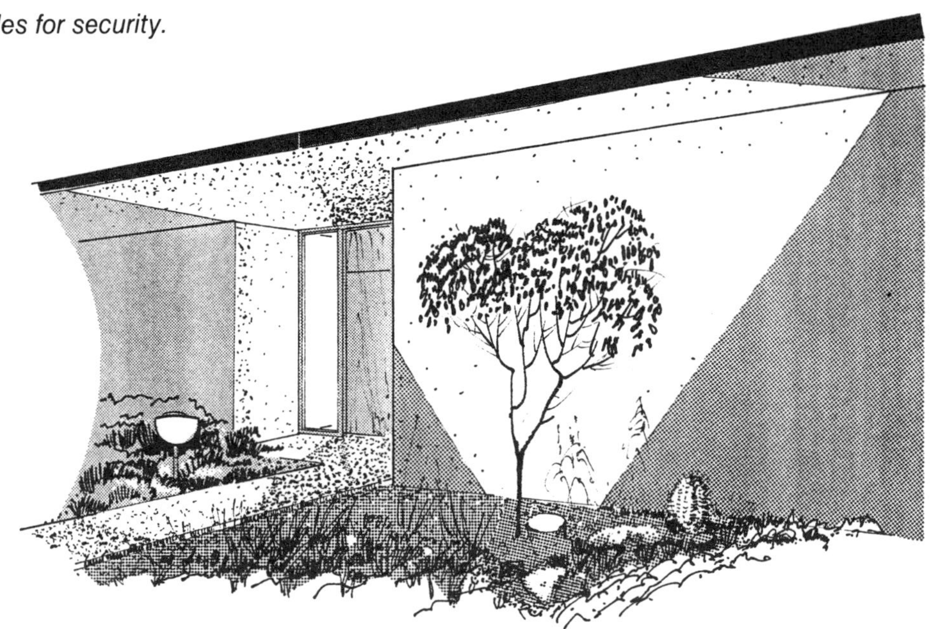

Exterior Lighting

PRE-PLANNING

The visual effect of exterior lighting is the after-dark introduction to your home. To make it a nice introduction, pre-planning is a must.

Outside lighting of most homes generally relates to function and is not planned for aesthetic effect. That's too bad because, for the same amount of money, fine aesthetic effects can be produced. Various lamps, from bright floods to soft downlights, can create patterns and feelings from subtle to brilliant. The choice is yours.

Pre-planning may not be enough. Sometimes experiments (trial and error) are needed to achieve the best result.

Usually, no changes in exterior building or landscaping are required. It's a matter of adding thoughtful lighting to existing conditions. For instance, a partial list of ideas might include:

(a) Low lighting of walkways and planter areas, with lamps below the line of sight.
(b) Up lighting of high shrubs or trees.
(c) Lighting of landscaping from above.
(d) Low voltage pond or fountain lights.
(e) Light washing on interesting wall surfaces.
(f) Backlighting for silhouette effect.
(g) Creating a design with the lights themselves.

Head-on flood lighting tends to make objects appear flat. More interest is achieved by lighting from two sides, with more light coming from one side than the other.

THE INTERIOR IMPACT

Well done outside lighting can visually improve the enjoyment of inside space. To look out at a well lighted scene in a courtyard, entrance or landscaped area is another plus.

Creating the Scene

Many times a nice scene is out there in the dark, just waiting to be lighted. On the other hand, an early benefit of pre-planning outside lighting might be the discovery that you have nothing of interest to look at. Not to worry — that can be corrected!

Creating something of interest to focus on can be done with landscaping, water, art objects, etc. (The daylight effect is improved at the same time, of course.) Also you may be able to play light on an interesting portion of the building.

Security and Safety

Basic security and utility lighting permits safe access, circulation, or congregation. It's something that varies with every home and every homeowner. Steps, ramps, parking, and driveway access are among areas that need to be lighted.

Be careful not to limit your design thoughts only to utility. Again, this is an opportunity to visually add to the immediate environment. Plan the lighting to enhance the landscaping or building surface affected.

MASTER SWITCHING

For the major indoor and outdoor security lighting, it's handy to provide switching in more than one part of the house. Master switching can be conveniently placed in the master bedroom, with alternate switching closer to the light source.

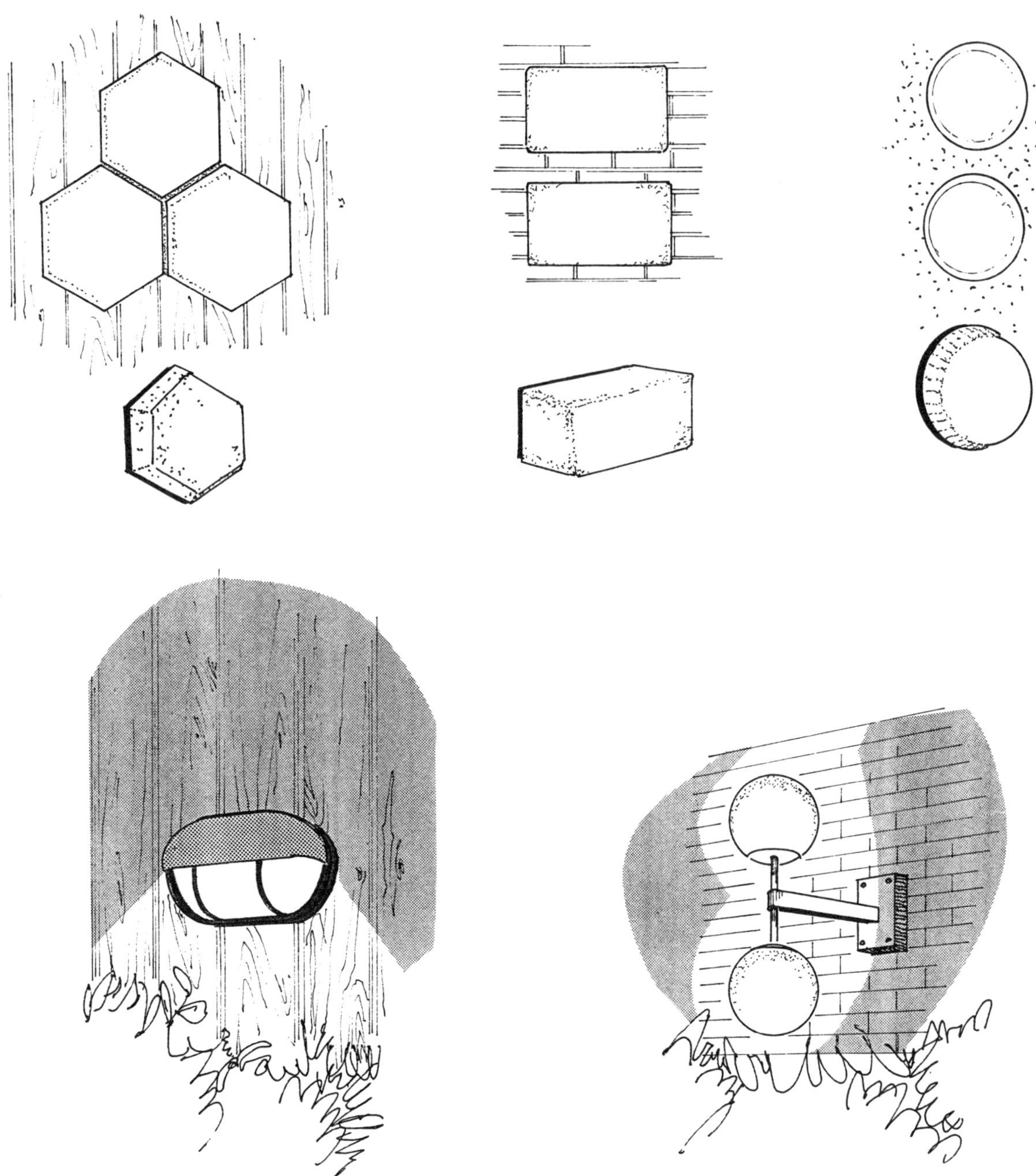

Wall bracket design has progressed from utilitarian access lights to crafted art forms.

Summary

Start paying attention to lighting in homes — your home and other homes. Make notes of what you like or dislike. Relate to quality (interest and atmosphere) as well as quantity (function).

In summary, I have included some lighting reminders for different rooms in your home. The list, not intended to be all inclusive, is to help you with the chapter check list that follows.

KITCHEN

a. Utility (to see what you are doing).
b. Warm and cheerful atmosphere.
c. Consider lighting needs in special places such as: sink and work areas; desk or telephone area; cookbook area; eating area.

DINING

a. Function and atmosphere. Light source can be from directions other than just overhead, such as wall mounted.

FAMILY & LIVING

a. Flexibility, function, economy, and atmosphere.
b. General lighting for ease of circulation and to make the room appear cheerful, comfortable, and well-balanced.
c. Reading areas.
d. Games and recreation.
e. Accent areas (plants, paintings, sculpture, etc.)
f. Power outlets in floor for mid-room lamp fixtures.

NOTE: Lighting required for accent or display might be enough for the atmosphere and general illumination.

Regarding indirect lighting: Look at the room critically. Will indirect lighting make the room more interesting, as well as contribute to general illumination? If not, then consider a different approach.

ENTRY

a. Inside and outside. Security, access, and atmosphere.

BEDROOMS

a. Master Bedroom. Do you want master switching here for areas inside and outside the house?
b. Low wattage night lights.
c. Wiring for intercom communication to bedroom and other areas.
d. Light fixture in center of ceiling is often not the best location. Alternate locations are:
   1. A light in front of a closet.
   2. Lights on paintings or decorative objects.
   3. Lights at reading chair or switch to lights at nightstand with 3-way at bed.
   4. Indirect lighting for getting around and atmosphere.

Check List

— Lighting/Interior —

Existing Interior Space	Lighting/ Atmosphere	Remarks	New Lighting Required, etc.
Entry	Too bright	Harsh	New fixtures when entry is enlarged
Family Room	Dull	Dark at fireplace end	Add skylights or windows near fireplace
Den/Study	—	New den to be added	General wall wash lighting and task lighting at desk
Living Room	—	Bad floor lamps	Replace floor lamps
Dining Room	Too dark	Poor light distribution	Replace fixtures
Kitchen	Not cheerful enough	Work area not bright	Add light to revised work area
Breakfast	—	Maybe add snack bar	Down lighting at snack bar
Storage/Pantry	Good	—	—
Bathroom (Common)	—	Add powder room	Down lights at mirror
Bedroom No. 1	Fair	Could be brighter	New floor or table lamps
Bedroom No. 2	O.K.	Poor	
Bathroom			

Example of How to Use the Check List

Sample

Note: You may wish to remove or copy the check list sheets for more convenient use.

Check List
— Lighting/Interior —

Existing Interior Space	Lighting/ Atmosphere	Remarks	New Lighting Required, etc.
Entry			
Family Room			
Den/Study			
Living Room			
Dining Room			
Kitchen			
Breakfast			
Storage/Pantry			
Bathroom (Common)			
Bedroom No. 1			
Bedroom No. 2			
Bathroom			
Master Bedroom			
Master Bath/Dressing			
General Storage			
Laundry/Work Space			
Recreation Room			
Basement			
Attic			
Special Purpose Room			
Other			
Other			

Check List
— Lighting/Exterior —

Existing Exterior Space	Lighting/ Atmosphere	Remarks	New Lighting Required, etc.
Drive	—	To be made wider	—
Carport/Garage	O.K.	None	None
Storage	—	Area to be redesigned	Add light to revised storage area
Work Shop	—	New shop to be added	Make sure adequate lighting installed
Entry Area	Harsh	New area to be added	New low post lights and wall bracket at door
Other	—	—	—
Other	—	—	—
Recreation	Dark	Add floods	Use pole lights with canopy for down-lighting
BBQ Area	Good	None	None
Other	—	—	
Security			

Example of How to Use the Check List

Sample

Note: You may wish to remove or copy the check list sheets for more convenient use.

Check List
— Lighting/Exterior —

Existing Exterior Space	Lighting/ Atmosphere	Remarks	New Lighting Required, etc.
Drive			
Carport/Garage			
Storage			
Work Shop			
Entry Area			
Other			
Other			
Recreation			
BBQ Area			
Other			
Security			
Patio/Courts			
Front Yard			
Rear Yard			
Side Yard			
Other			
Landscaping			
Decks			
Swimming Pool			
Other			
Other			
Other			

8

Special Purpose Spaces

In this chapter, "special purpose" refers to a space set aside for one use only. Your special purpose might be a luxury, like a sauna or gymnasium, or a necessity, like a work-at-home office.

In Chapter 1, I said that improvements which tend to increase resale value are the basic improvements, such as kitchen, bath, family room, etc. Special purpose spaces are less likely to increase the market value of your home. They represent a different form of investment.

Consider that you may live in this home a good part of your life. Think about personalized special spaces as *an investment in your pleasure* that occasionally might increase the market value of your home.

Also, while certain improvements might not be used by a new owner, the space alone may add resale value. For instance, a rumpus room or a billiard room easily can be converted to another use by a new owner.

Some special uses that might carry their value on resale are those requiring minimal space, such as a jacuzzi or wet bar.

Exterior improvements, such as a swimming pool, elaborate barbecue/ramada, or a greenhouse, add value to the right buyer, in the right climate. But don't count on it. Build it, if you do, for the pleasure it brings. *Enjoyment* of the special use should weigh heavily in decisions about what to include in your renovation.

Special Purposes

There are certain advantages to having a space customized for only one use, not the least being the atmosphere maintained. For instance, you are more likely to work at being a part-time artist if you have a studio exclusively for painting, potting, or sculpting. With the ideal layout and environment, you can leave your work, come back to it and take up immediately where you left off.

KNOW THE NEEDS

If you've decided to have a special purpose space, take your planning far enough to know minimum and maximum space requirements. Know what customizing (i.e., utilities, lighting, etc.) is required within the space. Having that information at hand, you can plug the space into the overall remodeling program. For instance, a darkroom can be closet-sized or as large as a bedroom. Thus, the extent of your work with camera and film development must be known to set your space needs. Then again, some functions such as billiards, require a *minimum size*

The interior of this home had an 8 foot by 8 foot open court opening off the living room. Nothing ever seemed to grow there. We enclosed it, creating a small gallery for the owner's sports photo collection. Natural light comes through a stained glass skylight.

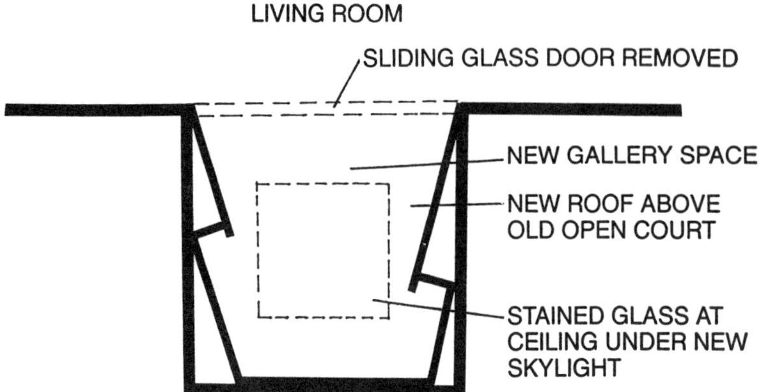

below which you should not go. (The minimum recommended dimension from billiard table to wall, or seating, is five feet.)

Items of Special Purpose

Special *items* (as opposed to *spaces*) are amenities requiring little or no space and limited construction change. Many have become commonplace in new home offerings and are usually accepted as attractive features. They include built-ins like intercom, sound systems, and security alarms.

Built-in items of this type become a permanent part of the house and often repay their cost at resale time, either in dollar value or as buyer incentives. On the other hand, items such as a sauna, built-in vacuum system, or even a partial solar system are relatively costly and may return only a small percentage of their cost, therefore, if built, the purpose should be for your personal satisfaction.

Other special items, such as custom stereo-video cabinets, become pieces of furniture and can be moved to another home.

The Luxury Myth

Luxury is defined by Webster as, "Something desirable, but costly or *hard to get* . . . that few can afford". Good planning and design can rewrite that definition. In remodeling, many well-done improvements that give the feeling of luxury and "the good life" are, in fact, relatively inexpensive and *easy to get.*

Also, what one considers a luxury is a necessity to another. In other words, priorities again come into the picture — becoming more clear as you complete the check lists.

KNOW THE COST

Get a realistic idea of costs before making a final decision about special purpose objectives. You may be surprised to find the cost less than expected. (It's equally important to know if the cost will be greater than expected.)

Expert Advice

Balancing desire with budget is where professional help can pay its way. Creative methods sometimes can be used to affordably get what you want.

Also, expert planning is a must for more sophisticated types of special purpose spaces. A music listening-and-recording room is an example. Other examples could be hydroponic gardening, wine and root cellars, or video theatres. Expert advice may come from a consultant or the study of information prepared by an expert. By

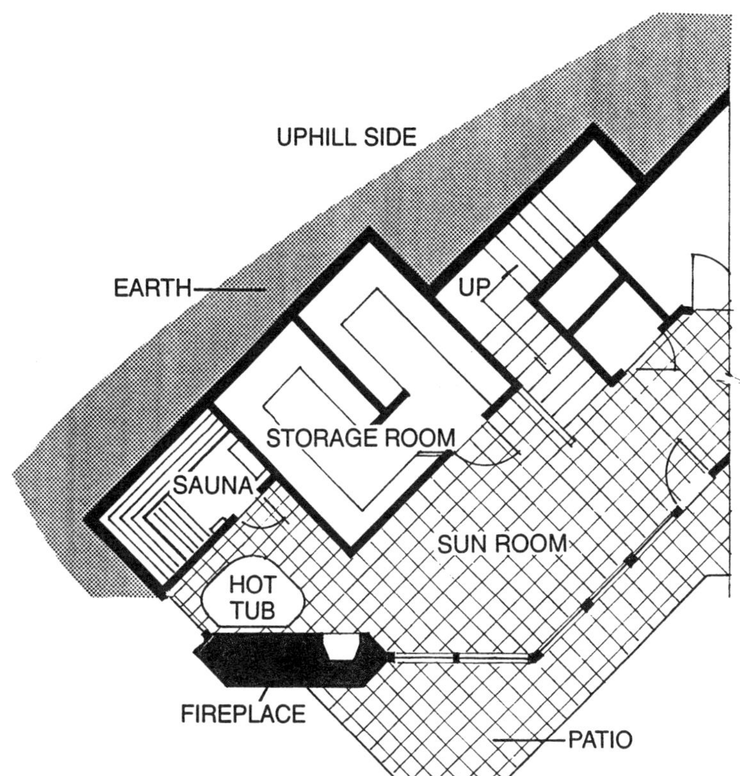

Multi-Special Purpose:

A sun room, sauna, and hot tub in the basement level of a cold weather home built on a hillside.

whatever method, thoroughly know your special purpose before planning its space.

A Wine Cellar

Your wine "cellar" can be a half dozen well-chosen bottles on the floor of a closet or a full-sized room containing a thousand bottles in a controlled environment. To store wine, you should meet three conditions: Fairly constant temperature, little vibration, and lack of strong light. Corked bottles, of course, should be stored lying down.

Much has been written about the ideal temperature at which to store wine. Precise controlled temperatures are suggested, generally in the 55 degree range. Do your own research and decide for yourself. My experience has shown that most wine can tolerate varying degrees in temperature (from 50 to 70 degrees) as long as the change is gradual. It will age faster at the higher temperature.

White wine exposed to sunlight can gradually oxidize to a brown-like color. Some sources claim that too much light affects the flavor, as well. As a general rule, white wine should be drunk fairly new anyway, so the cellar primarily will house the reds.

Vibration, with older wines, is a cosmetic consideration. Older wines usually produce a sediment and vibration tends to keep the sediment in motion. That makes for a muddy looking glass of wine. It also has been stated that vibrations damage the flavor of wine — a distinction lost on most of us!

Adequate wine storage conditions are not that difficult to achieve. So, if you want a wine "cellar", most likely it can be yours.

This small wine cellar got its start as an open wine rack under a stairway. It was later converted to a refrigerated cellar from spare parts and materials.

(See Color Photo)

LOCATION

A basement is a good place to look for wine storage space. Here you also can include food storage. Check along the north wall. Watch out for hot spots like pipes, furnace, hot water heater, heat ducts, etc.

If you want wine closer to the point of consumption, check the options within your total remodeling scheme. Convert the bottom portion of a closet or go under a stair. Use part of a base cabinet or put a wine cabinet on an unused wall.

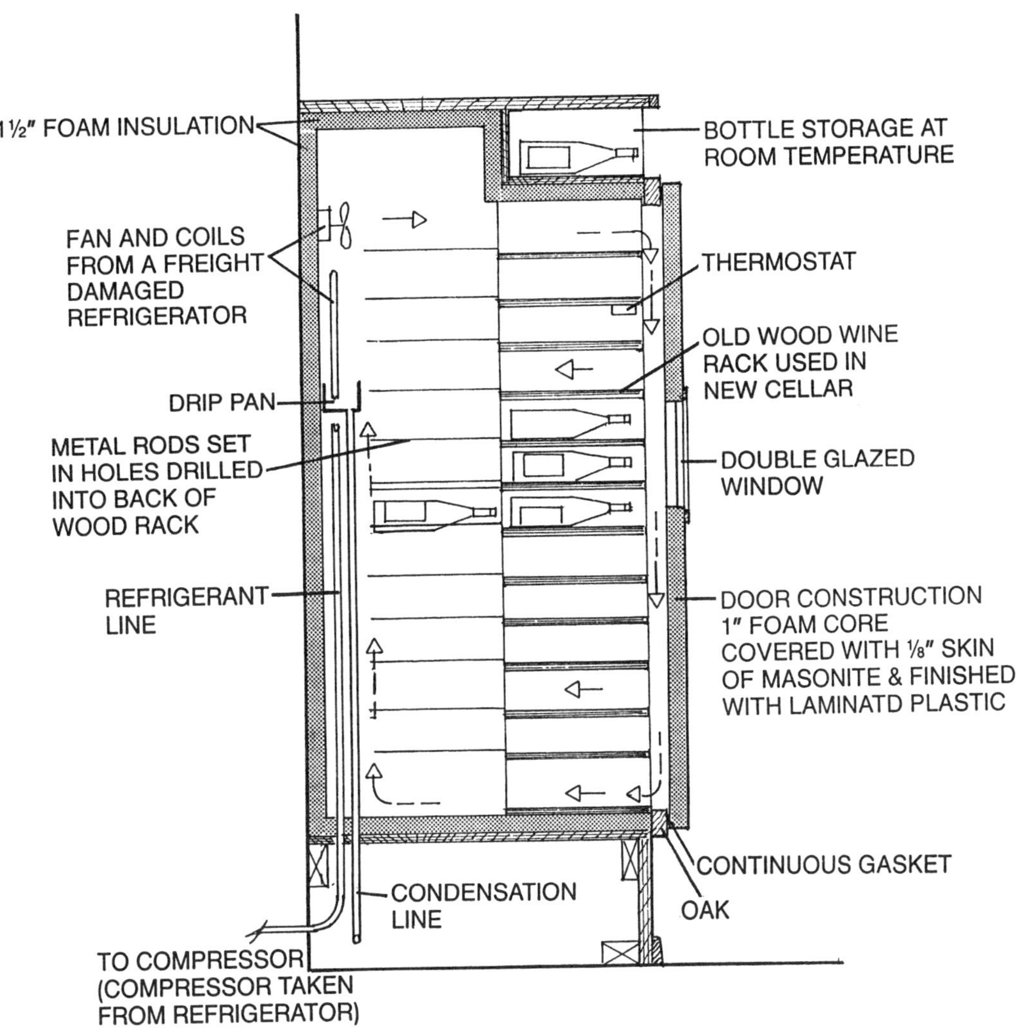

Section view showing wine cellar construction.

REFRIGERATION

You can buy a ready-made wine storage cabinet with a built-in refrigeration unit or make your own. Making your own might require help from a friendly refrigeration man, but it's a good way to get what you want, where you want it.

REMEMBER THE RULES: Constant temperature, relative darkness, lack of vibration. This is a fun project to do — and a joy forever!

An Indoor Garden

Indoor gardening can be the "planted-in-the-earth" variety, plants in pots or boxes, or both. Either way, you must solve the basic needs of light and water.

Natural light is preferred, but a combination of natural and artificial usually works fine. Many plants will grow in partial light. There *are* plants that grow in near darkness, but aren't much fun if you can't see them.

When planning your indoor garden, discuss it with a local plant specialist. Select plant types ahead of time and get advice about their care, feeding, and light needs.

PLANTING IN THE GROUND

One advantage to "in-the-ground" planting is the look itself — the natural feeling. Locate plant life convenient to a much used living area so the results of your labors can be enjoyed visually. If your climate does not include extreme temperatures, skylights can be used, further improving the visual effect. If ceiling height permits, you can grow plants or even small trees to a good size, and trees growing in a two-story space can be enjoyed from both levels.

Another advantage is that the ground retains moisture longer than pots or planter boxes so watering is less frequent. However, water must have a way of draining to keep the soil healthy.

A disadvantage to "in-the-ground" planting in existing space is the need to break out floor materials. Also, devise a means to prevent water from getting under adjacent floors and foundations. An expert should be consulted here.

GREENHOUSE

An addition to the house, doubling as a greenhouse, is a great way to create an indoor garden. A greenhouse is not only fun but, offers the chance to grow everything from orchids to onions.

A GARDENING ROOM

A gardening room with pots and boxes offers several possibilities. Plants within the space are nurtured and displayed in a controlled environment. From this room, you can supply potted plants for other areas of the house. One great advantage to having a gardening room, instead of planting in the ground, is the versatility it affords in the type and number of plants. Also, you can replace plants around the house as the mood strikes you.

Your gardening room must have proper floor material, drainage, light, water, potting bench, storage, etc. A lot of "how-to" gardening room literature is on the marketplace.

A DARKROOM

Darkroom needs vary with the depth of your photography and developing activity. If you only take family shots, but have a yen to do your own developing, then a converted closet will suffice. However, if photography is a hobby and requires sophisticated developing, a small room is needed. Your planning will include work surfaces, sinks, storage, equipment, lighting, a good exhaust fan and, of course, keeping out unwanted light from adjacent space. Again, consult with an expert in the field.

Helpful Hints

If you can adapt existing space instead of adding on, you probably will save money. Either way, many factors contribute to success. Following is a partial list of factors to keep in mind when planning a special purpose space.

1. What type of floor, wall, and ceiling finish should it have? Must they be hard and impervious, resilient, or have acoustical properties?
2. Will the room be kept neat or messy?
3. Will the space be private or have visitors?
4. How does the function relate to the rest of the house? For instance, how much would the space interact with family room, kitchen, baths, bedrooms, etc.?
5. Should it have private access to outside? Be near the front door?

6. Think about traffic flow. For instance, will it interfere with existing traffic flow to an important area?
7. Does the special purpose require precise temperature or humidity control? If so, it may need its own mechanical system.
8. Is plumbing or power affected?
9. How noisy is the new function? (Remember that sound insulation is obtained by proper sealing and with special materials, as well as physical distance.)
10. Are structural changes required? Is extra weight added to a floor above ground?
11. Will you need to introduce natural light by adding windows or skylights? If so, remember that it will change the exterior appearance of your house and affect heating and cooling.

When to Seek Help

Many types of special purpose layouts benefit from expert help. Don't be bashful about asking other people for helpful tips. Specialists normally are willing to give advice to someone who takes the time to seek them out.

Check List
— Special Purpose/Interior —

Special Interior Spaces	Existing Yes/No	Desired	Location	Remarks
Steam or Sauna Room	No	No	—	—
Jacuzzi or Hot Tub	No	Yes Jacuzzi	Master Bath	Replace existing tub in Master Bath
Gym/Exercise Room	No	Exercise space	Anywhere	Would be nice but not high priority
Child's Play Room	No	No	—	—
Billiard/Game Room	No	Yes Game Room	Existing Garage	Add new carport and new storage
Library	No	Yes	Several areas	Add shelving in Family Room and Master Bedroom
Music Room	No	No	—	Improve existing stereo system
Video Theater	No	No		
Potting Room				

Example of How to Use the Check List

Sample

Note: You may wish to remove or copy the check list sheets for more convenient use.

Check List

— Special Purpose/Interior —

Special Interior Spaces	Existing Yes/No	Desired	Location	Remarks
Steam or Sauna Room				
Jacuzzi or Hot Tub				
Gym/Exercise Room				
Child's Play Room				
Billiard/Game Room				
Library				
Music Room				
Video Theater				
Potting Room				
Indoor Garden				
Mud Room				
Dark Room				
Wine Cellar				
Wet Bar/ Soda Fountain				
Other				
Other				
Other				
Other				

Check List
— Special Purpose —

Special Items	Existing Yes/No	Desired	Location	Remarks
Smoke Alarm				
Security/Alarm System	No	Yes	2nd floor and stairway and first floor	Install 2 alarms
Intercom System	No	Yes	Doors and windows	Not high priority
Closed Circuit TV	Yes	—	—	Works fine
Built-in Vacuum	No	No	—	—
Built-in Music Speaker and Sound Control	No	No	—	
Built-in Intensive Care System	None	Yes		
Other				

Example of How to Use the Check List
Sample

Note: You may wish to remove or copy the check list sheets for more convenient use.

	Yes	—	—	New deck and seats in this area
Hot Tub	No	No	—	—
Greenhouse	No	No	—	—
Child's Play Equipment	No	Yes	South side	Approximately 10x20
Work Shop	Yes	—	East yard	O.K.
Other	Yes			
Other				

Check List

— Special Purpose —

Special Items	Existing Yes/No	Desired	Location	Remarks
Smoke Alarm				
Security/Alarm System				
Intercom System				
Closed Circuit TV				
Built-in Vacuum				
Built-in Music Speaker and Sound Control				
Built-in Intensive Care System				
Other				
Other				
Special Purpose OUTDOOR				
BBQ				
Swimming Pool				
Hot Tub				
Greenhouse				
Child's Play Equipment				
Work Shop				
Other				
Other				

9

Additions

With enough effort and ingenuity, you can dramatically change the appearance, feeling and function of the space within your home. About the only thing you can't do from within is make it bigger.

Check list results may describe changes needing more space than the house contains. If that happens, either reassess your priorities or give thought to an addition.

Or, it could be that you like everything about your home except that it simply isn't large enough. You must either add on or move. You choose to add on.

PLANNING PREPARATION

Adding space to your home means taking space from the yard. With that in mind, please review the following chapter, EXTERIOR IMPROVEMENTS AND LANDSCAPING, before making final plans for an addition. Determine what part of your outside space has high priority to remain outside space.

Will a particular outside activity take precedence over a planned inside function? For instance, there may be only one outside space large enough for a much wanted improvement like a swimming pool or special garden. You may choose not to diminish that space for a larger family room or to add a game room.

So, it's important that you first know exactly what part of your yard is the likely portion to build on. Listed below are a few suggestions:

a. Acquire a site plan showing your existing house, garage, storage sheds, or other structures located within the boundary lines. If you don't already have a site plan, have a surveyor do one, or you can draw it yourself. I explain how to do that in this chapter.
b. In most residential areas, you can't build on or next to the property lines. To allow for open space and separation between houses, all construction must set back a certain number of feet from each property line. Check with the building department that governs your area. Read the ordinance which tells you what the building set-backs are.
c. Does your house sit on a flat site or is it built on a slope? Flat lots are considered easiest, but, if you are on a slope, some interesting options open up for you! Depending on which way and how much the land slopes, you might end up with a step up, step down, split level, or two story addition.
d. Does your yard drain properly when it

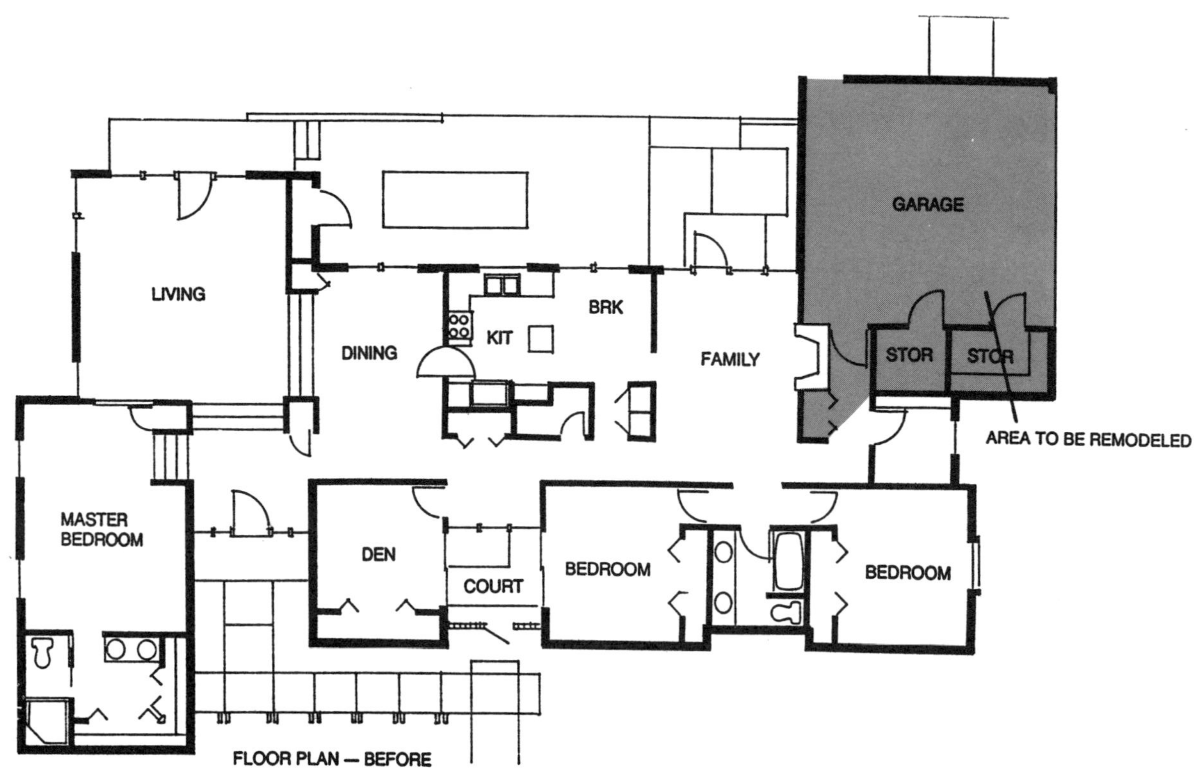

BEFORE *The number one priority for this family was to add a large general activity and recreation space. In addition, they desired the kitchen-breakfast-family areas opened up for a more spacious feeling.*

rains? All water should drain away from the house, with no ponding nearby. Suppose you have water ponding exactly where you want to put your addition — don't worry, it's usually correctable. During remodeling is a good time to correct a poor site condition.

There usually is more than one solution. Often the ground can be recontoured for good drainage. Maybe dirt fill should be brought in. Sometimes roof drainage has to be redirected, etc. I advise getting an expert opinion on drainage problems.

I recently finished a renovation that had a bad water problem adjacent to the house. Years ago a pool was added and the space between house and pool became a concrete deck. The contractor sloped the entire deck area from pool to house — with no provision to handle the water once it got to the house! The solution, not that difficult, was an expense that should never have happened. Pool and concrete are expensive to rebuild, so we installed a catch basin where the water collects and piped it to an area of lower elevation.

PROTECT THE GOOD INTERIOR SPACES

When planning an addition, it's a happy accident if the logical place to add on abuts an unattractive interior space. You can change the existing space in the process. However, if it occurs next to a favorite and delightful interior space, treat it kindly. Be careful how you create access from existing to new. Be aware of the nice rooms and good spaces and *try not to alter what makes them nice*. That point cannot be overstressed. It's

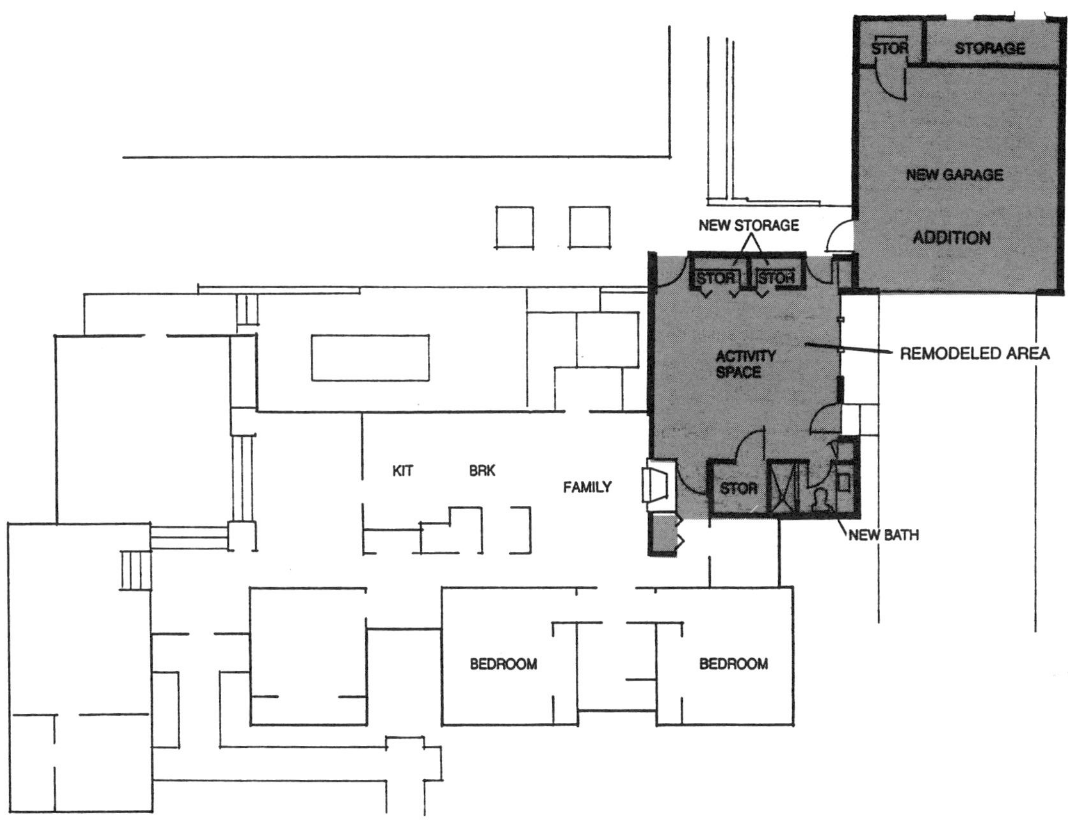

AFTER *Traffic flow to the new space is excellent. The space is well located for noise and access to outside activities.*

easy to forget that the atmosphere of a favorite spot *will change* when you: alter the light source, change the traffic pattern, enlarge the space, etc.

Here's another plug for the "design program." Master planning a total remodeling is especially important when it comes to adding on.

THE SITE PLAN

Before planning in depth, have a site plan showing all existing construction on your lot. With the "as built" site plan you can quickly and accurately determine the space available for additions and changes.

With luck, you will have a site plan left by the builder or previous owner. If you strike out there, the options are:

a. Draw it yourself.
b. Have it drawn up by someone else.

Drawing It Yourself

YOUR PROPERTY LINES

Finding your property lines is one of the first steps. In some neighborhoods, they are

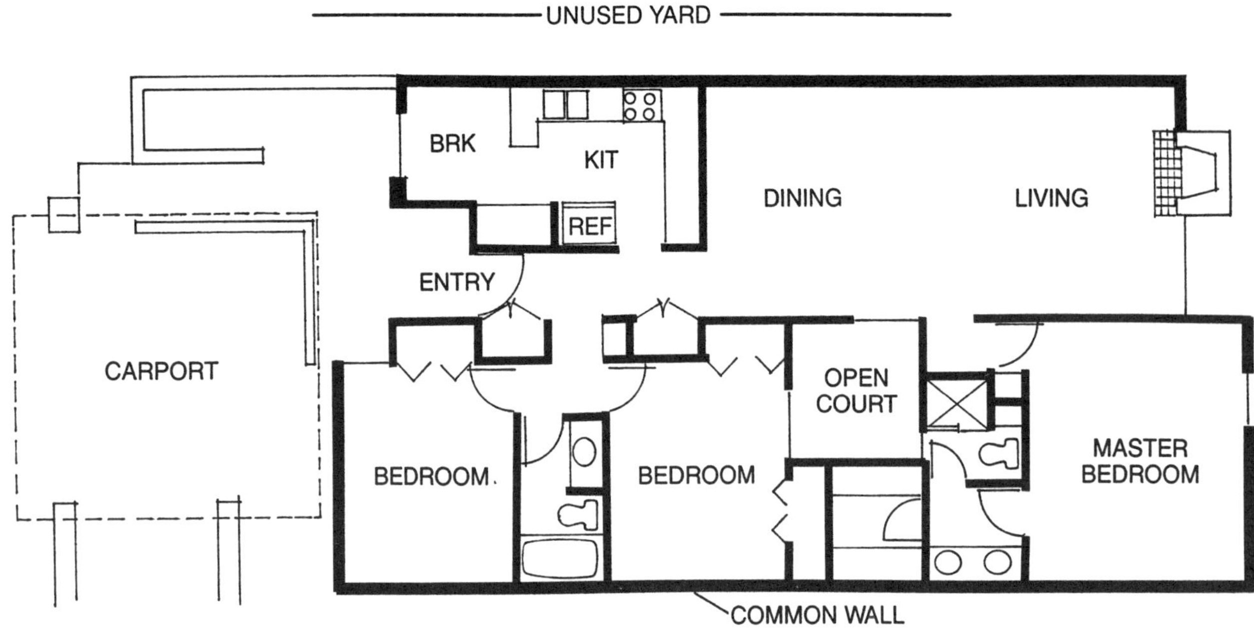

BEFORE *A couple with two children bought this condo on a relatively large corner lot. It contained a side yard that was unused and unseen from within. Inside they wanted a new master bedroom suite, a den/office, and revised kitchen opening to a large new family room.*

AFTER *The side yard allowed room for expansion. The new space opened up to outside activities. A much needed shop, laundry, and storage area was added. The unused interior court was converted to a desired gallery. Each member of the family benefited from the renovation and additions.*

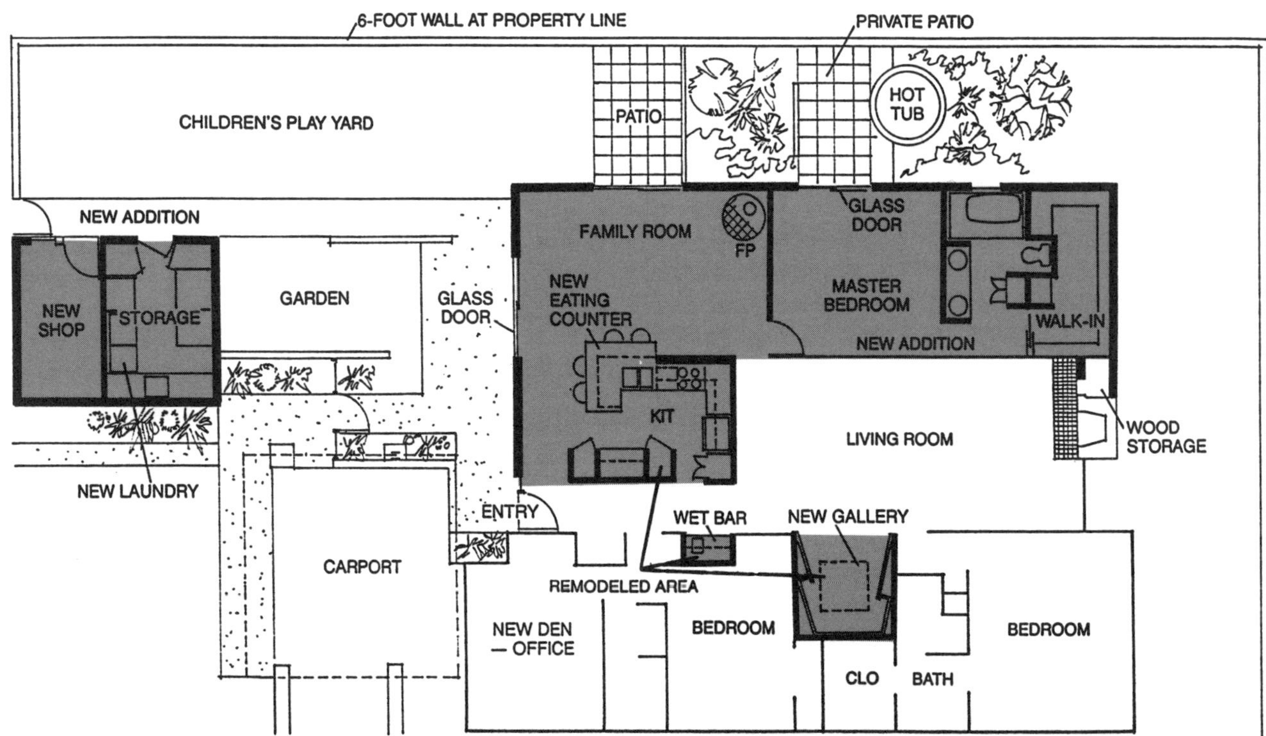

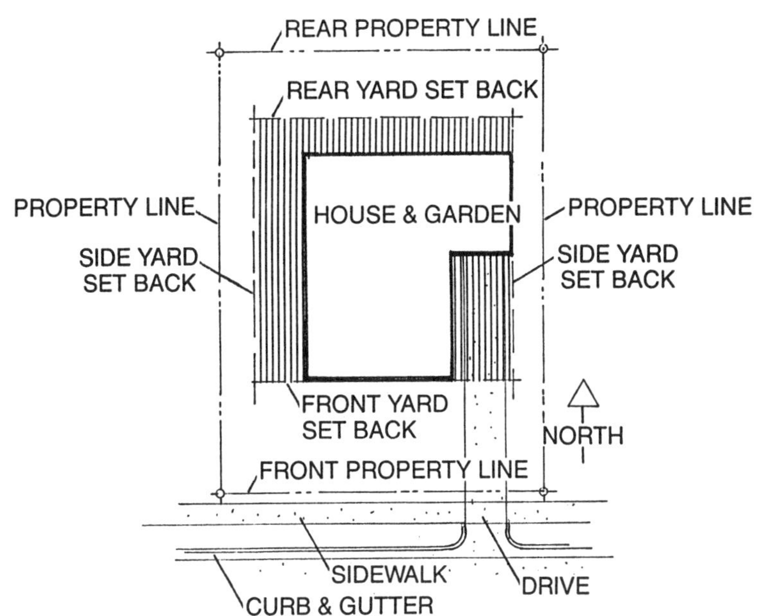

Typical site plan.

established by existing walls, fences, and utility lines. (Utility lines usually run on an easement that straddles the property line.) Sometimes you can find the corner stakes. Corner stakes, or pins, are normally steel bars about 3⁄4″ in diameter driven into the ground with a portion sticking up. (If you are not positive that any found walls, fences, or stakes reflect the accurate property lines, have your property surveyed.)

In drawing your site plan, use the same type of paper used for the floor plan — 1⁄4″ graph lined tracing paper about 18″ × 24″. Select a scale appropriate for your lot size. For example, a scale of 1 inch equals 10 feet means that 1⁄4″ on the graph paper equals 2½ feet. Or, at a scale of 1 inch equals 20 feet, each 1⁄4″ on the graph paper equals 5 feet. Select the scale that will give you the largest drawing and still fit on the sheet.

With your property lines drawn on paper, add the set-back lines. With information obtained from local building and zoning officials, determine what the building set-back requirements are. The set-back lines are then drawn inside the property lines. The area left inside the set-back lines is for construction.

You are now ready to draw in the house, garage, walls, patios, trees, walks, and drive, etc. In essence, show all existing features within the boundaries of your property lines.

DRAWING THE PLAN

Each time your property lines meet and turn a corner, there should be a metal pin or stake. Run a string between the corners. The string becomes your lot lines. Measure the distance from your strings to every existing improvement on your lot. Draw the improvements (house, garage, pool, sheds, etc.) in the correct place. In this way you will complete the site plan. One necessary caution: Without surveyor instruments you will not be able to attain total accuracy. For *total accuracy* you should have your property surveyed and a plan drawn by a registered surveyor.

The Addition

An addition is not necessarily more difficult than rearranging interior space, but

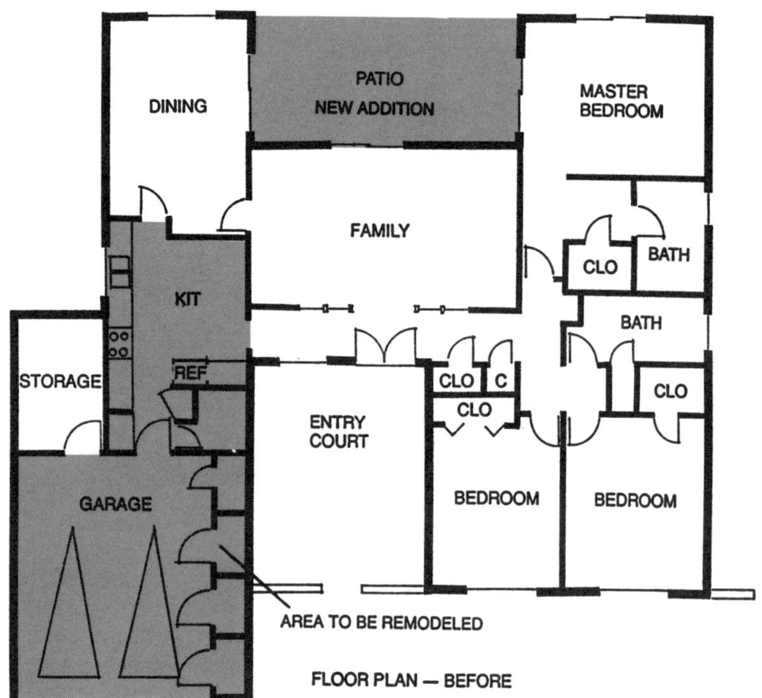

BEFORE *A family of four needed more space for family activities, a partial kitchen renovation and a new game room.*

AFTER *The new game room is well located for noise isolation from other spaces.*

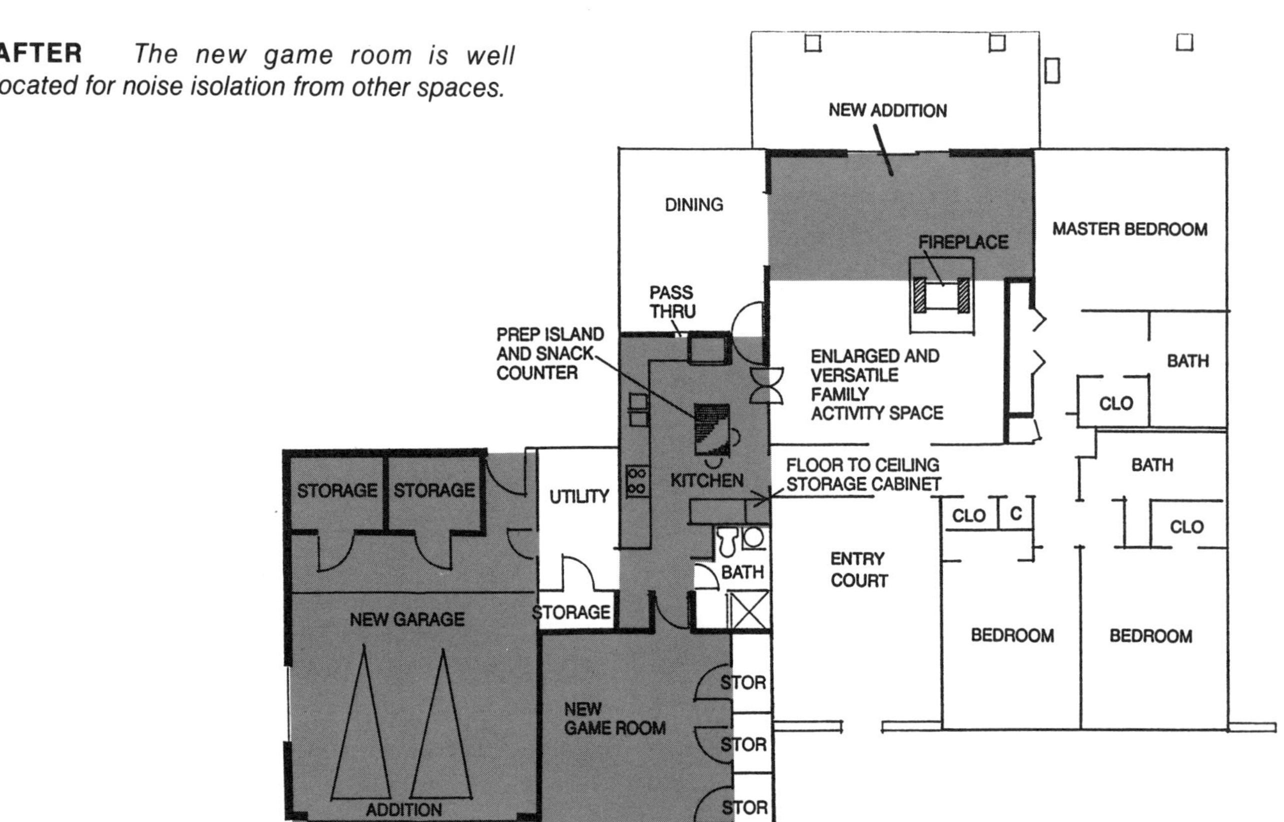

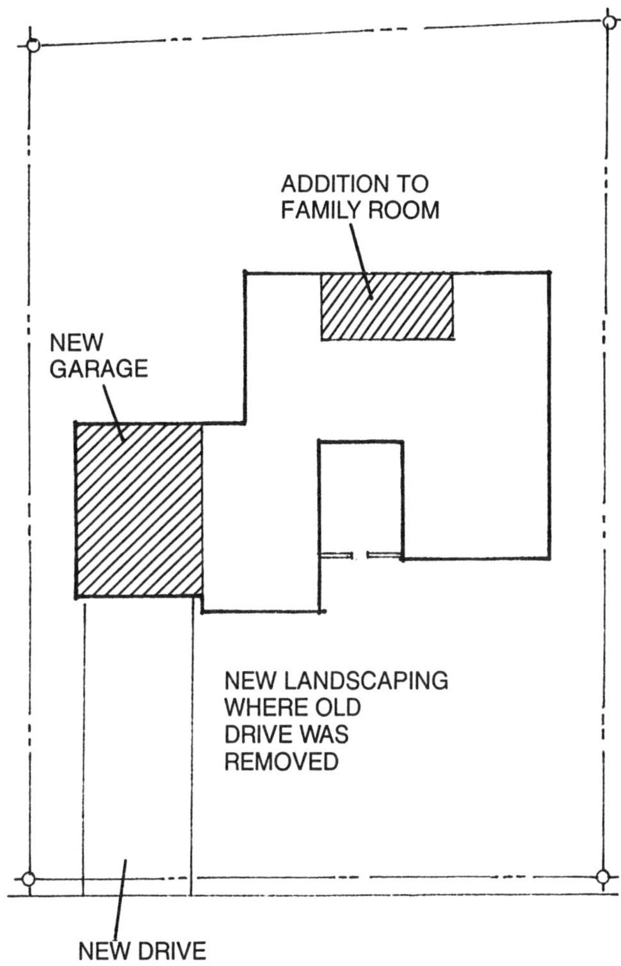

Site Plan. The lot was large enough to add a garage adjacent to the existing. A new driveway was added.

it is more immediately visible. The addition must aesthetically compliment and become a natural part of the house — *looking as though it was there from the beginning.* Achieving that look is not always easy.

A casual drive through a strange neighborhood can prove the above statement. Look for additions. If they're all done well, you won't find any. Usually you can find them.

One of the most common is easily, but seldom, corrected. It's the garage or carport which became an interior room. The conversion often looks fine, but the driveway, instead of being re-done, is left running up to a blank wall.

THE NATURAL LOOK

Integrating a well designed addition can help a drab looking house come to life. The marketability of your home may become greater. With rare exception, it's possible to design an addition which blends in harmony

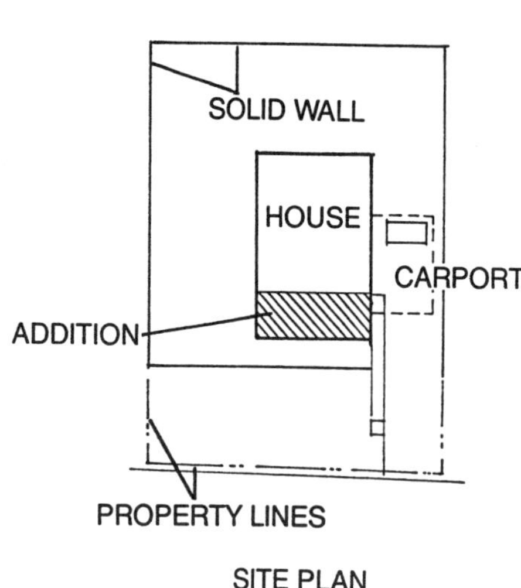

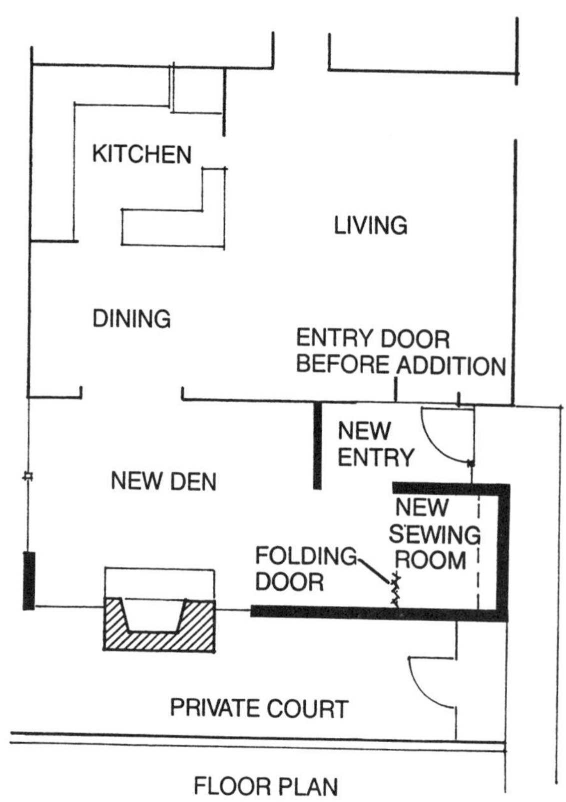

The owners of this small home set, as their first priority, the addition of a small adult area for conversation and entertaining. Another need was a small sewing space which was integrated with the design of a new entrance. The addition aesthetically tied in with the existing house.

with the original. In fact, it should be your goal to so design the addition as to aesthetically and functionally *improve* your home. You may need to retain a consultant for help with this effort. If you do, check their work and find one with a good track record in home additions.

ADDING A SECOND FLOOR

A common question is "can we add a second floor to our one story house?". The answer is usually that you can go up, instead of out, but there are more things to consider. Listed below are a few advantages to building new space above, followed by some of the pitfalls.

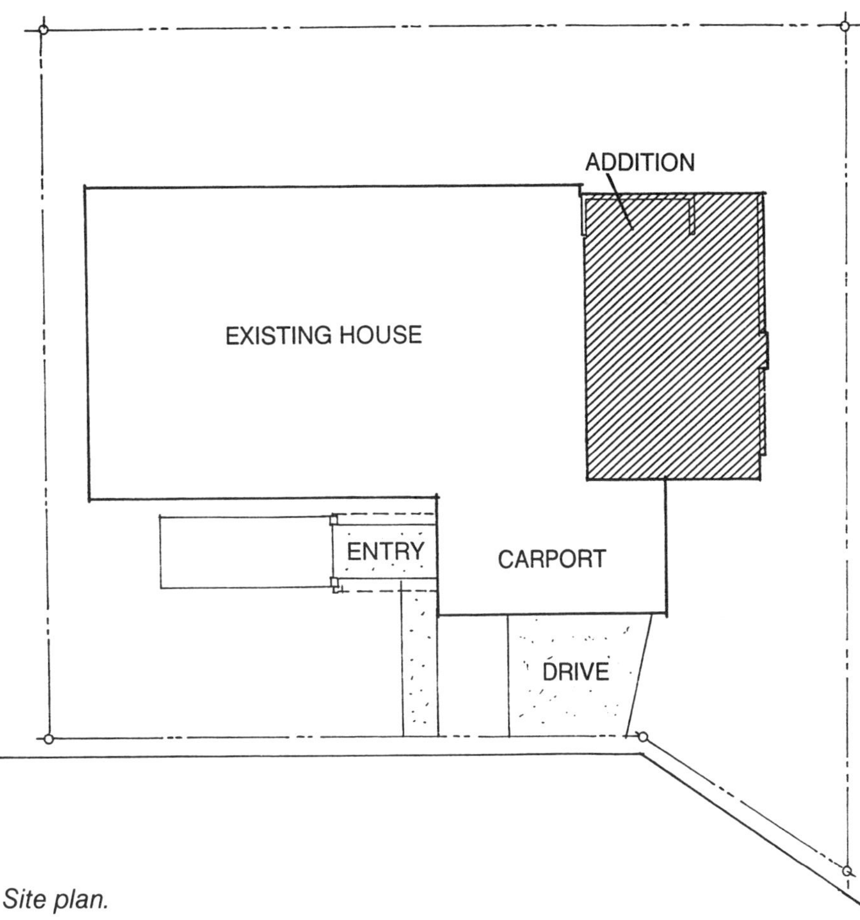

Site plan.

ADVANTAGES:

a. If well designed, the entire home can become more interesting, inside and outside.
b. Going up instead of out saves space on your lot for other things such as patios, decks, pool, BBQ, recreation, garden, and landscaping.
c. Function can be improved. Some spaces work better with the over-all scheme if isolated on an upper level.
d. Going up may give you more flexibility with design and rearranging space.

DISADVANTAGES:

a. Adding a floor usually is more expensive then adding the same amount of space at ground level.
b. New space must be served by heating and/or cooling systems. Normally, it is easier and cheaper to do it well if all space is on one level.
c. Adding a second floor is a highly visible change. Creating a natural and pleasing appearance requires abilities usually beyond those of the average person.
d. Single story houses are seldom built to accommodate a second floor. Adding above generally means building, or rebuilding, from the foundation up. Professional help should be obtained.

The very first step is to check your local zoning laws and your property deed restrictions. Be sure you are allowed to build over one story.

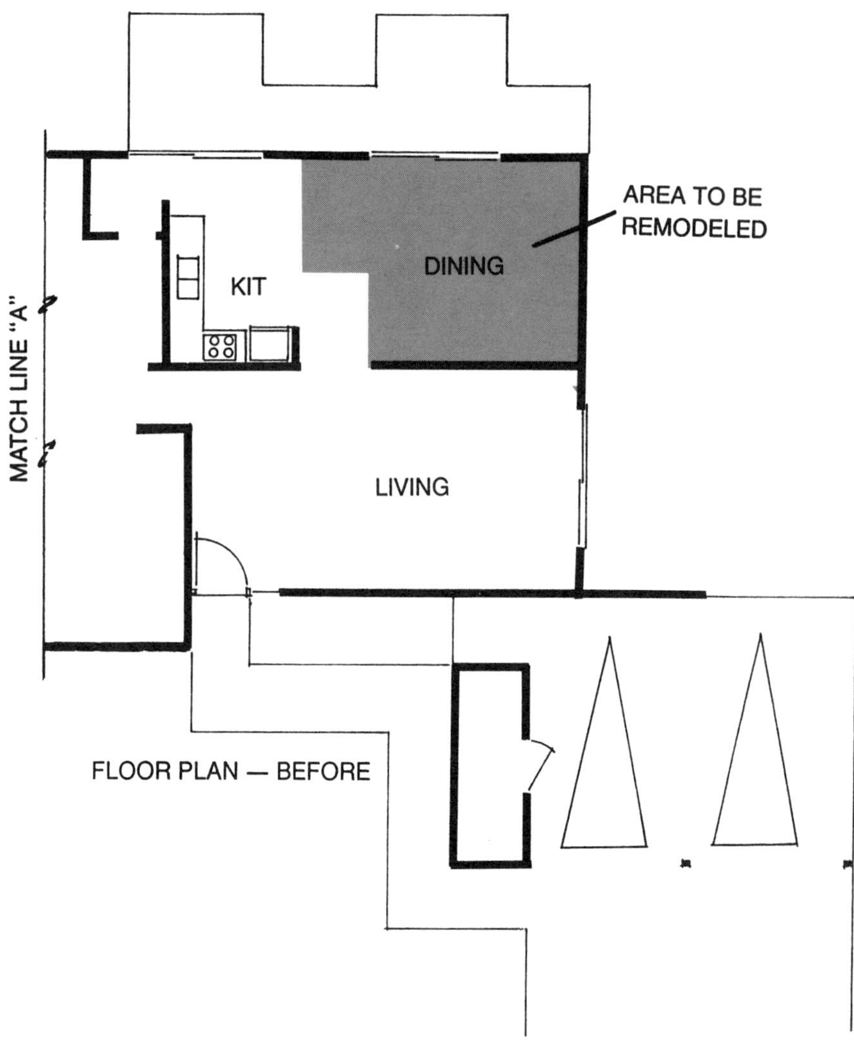

FLOOR PLAN — BEFORE

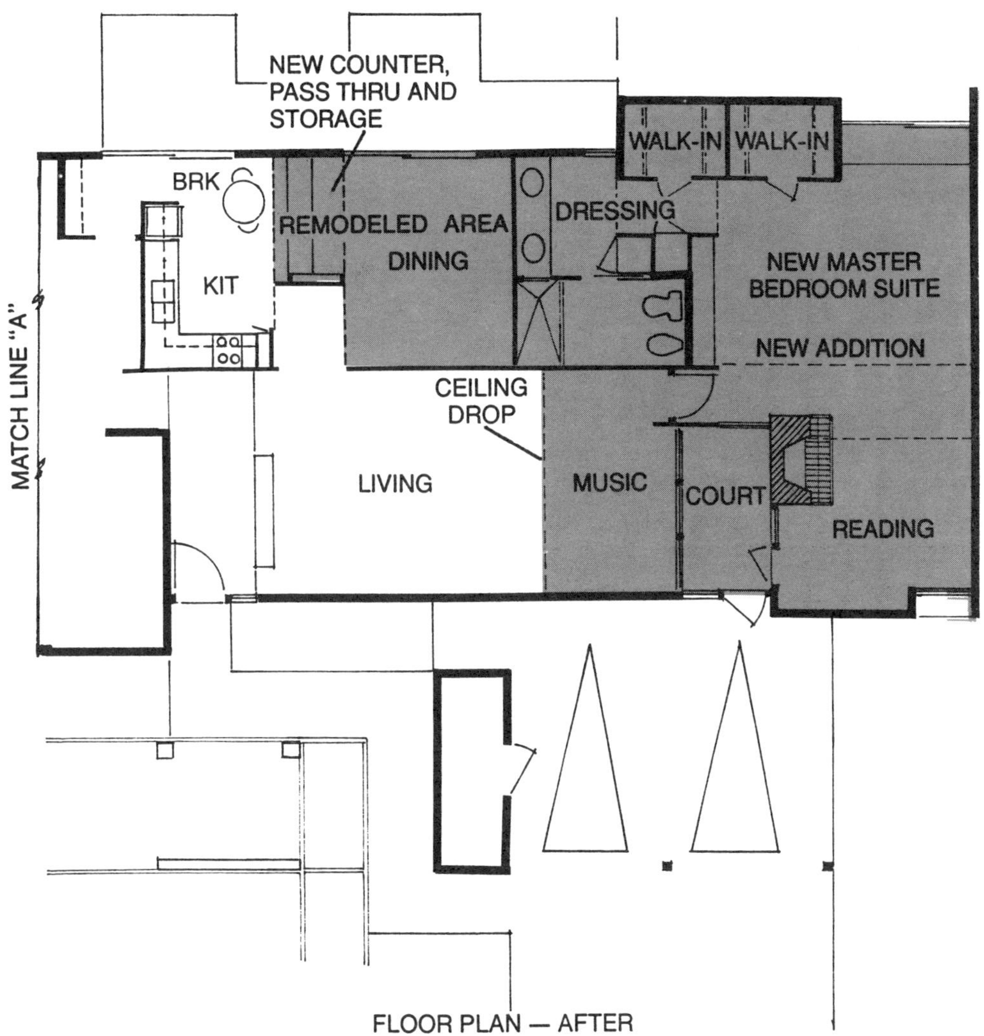

FLOOR PLAN — AFTER

AFTER *The owner's priority was a new master bedroom suite which would, in turn, make theirs available as a needed extra bedroom. Designated areas for music and reading were also required in their lifestyle. Another priority was a more effective use of kitchen-breakfast-dining space, with a semi-private dining area.*

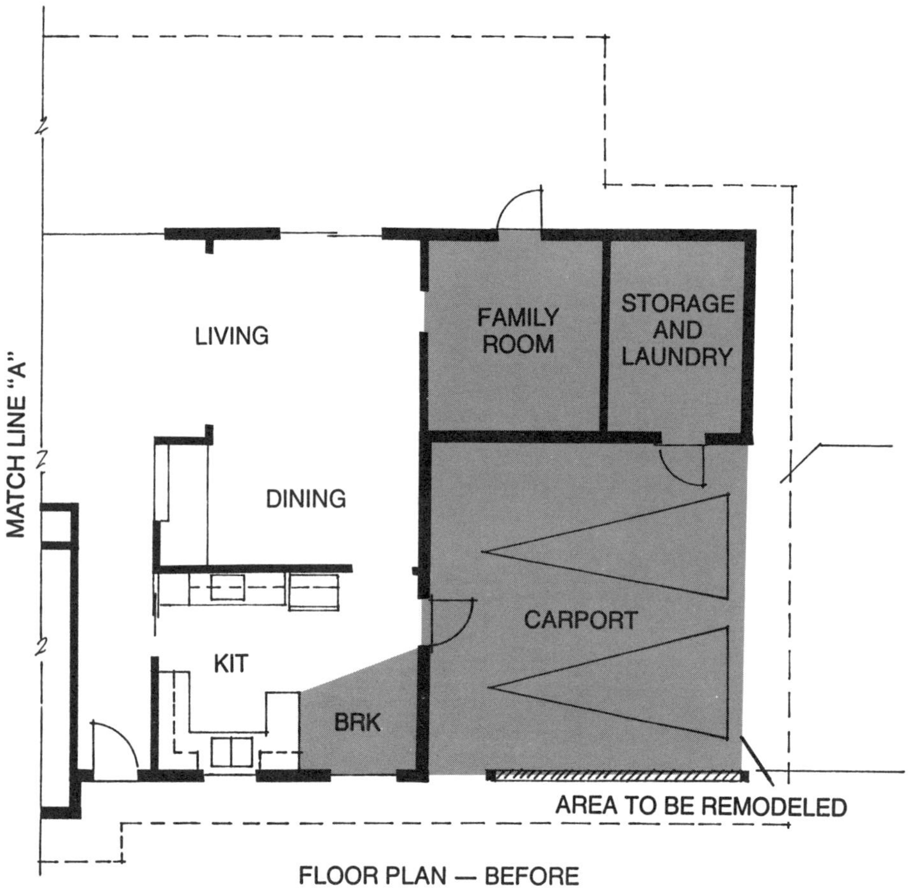

FLOOR PLAN — BEFORE

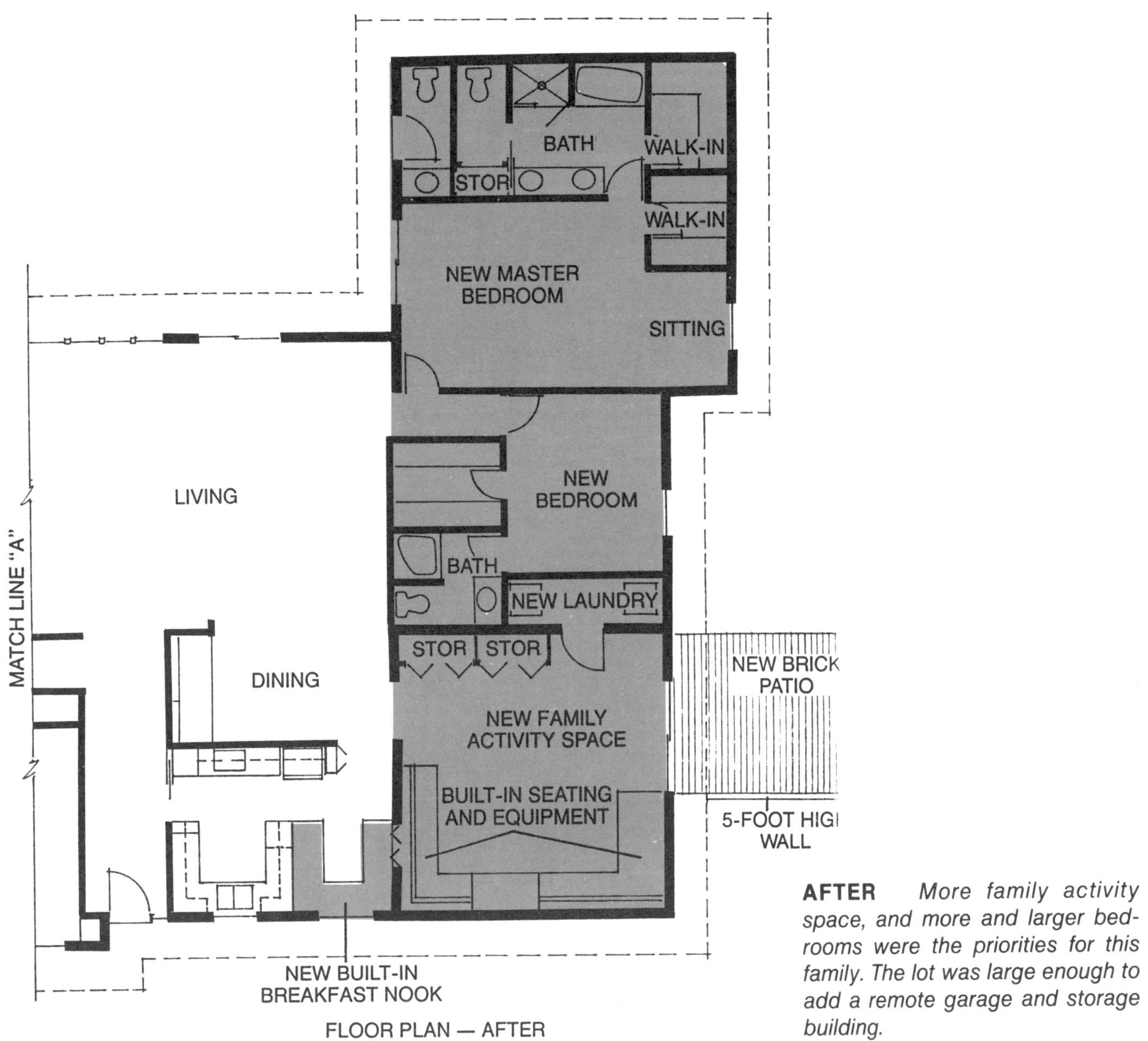

FLOOR PLAN — AFTER

AFTER *More family activity space, and more and larger bedrooms were the priorities for this family. The lot was large enough to add a remote garage and storage building.*

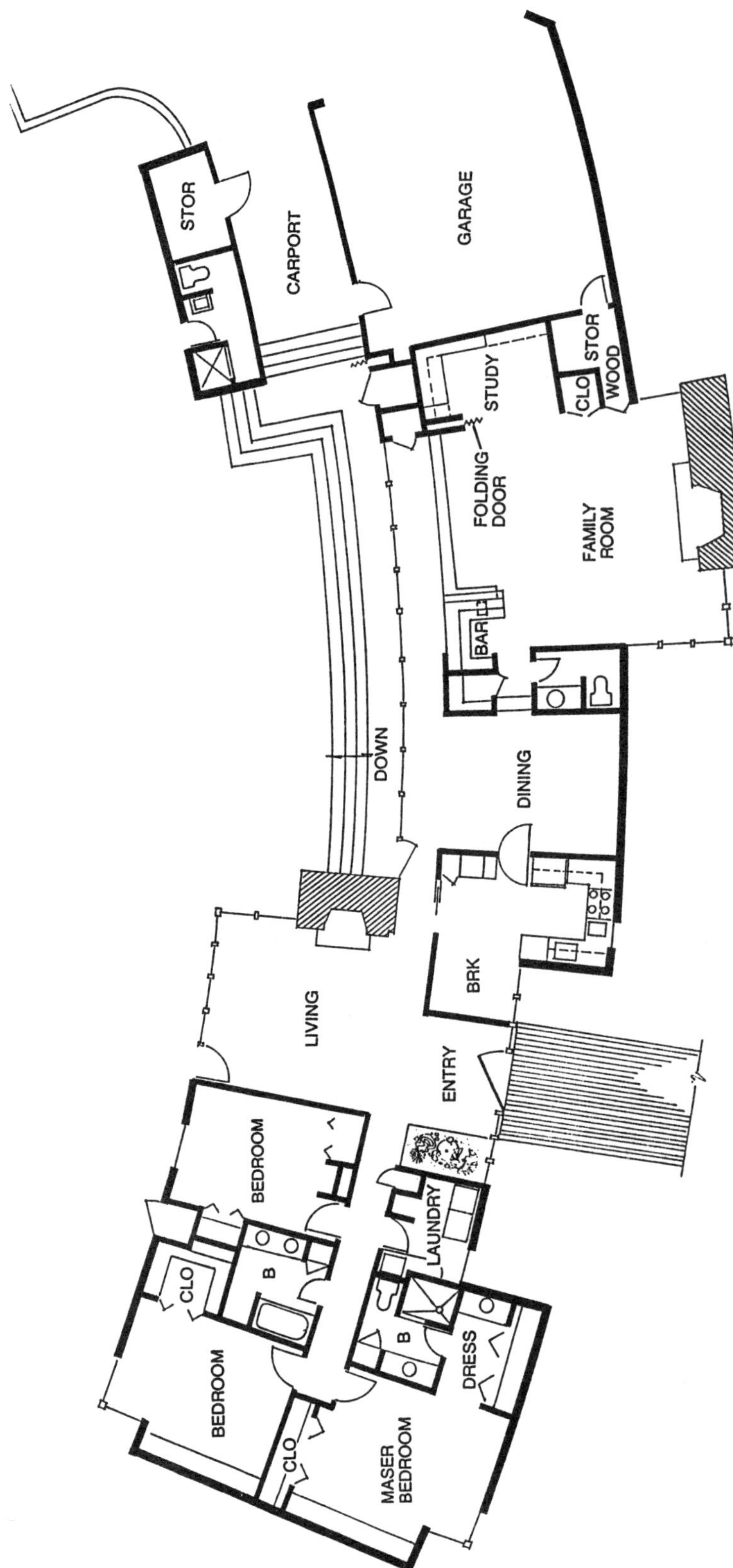

FLOOR PLAN — BEFORE

BEFORE *This house was designed with three bedrooms to accommodate an average sized family. With the arrival of a family of seven, an addition to the bedroom wing was the high priority. The family also wanted a children's activity space central to their bedrooms.*

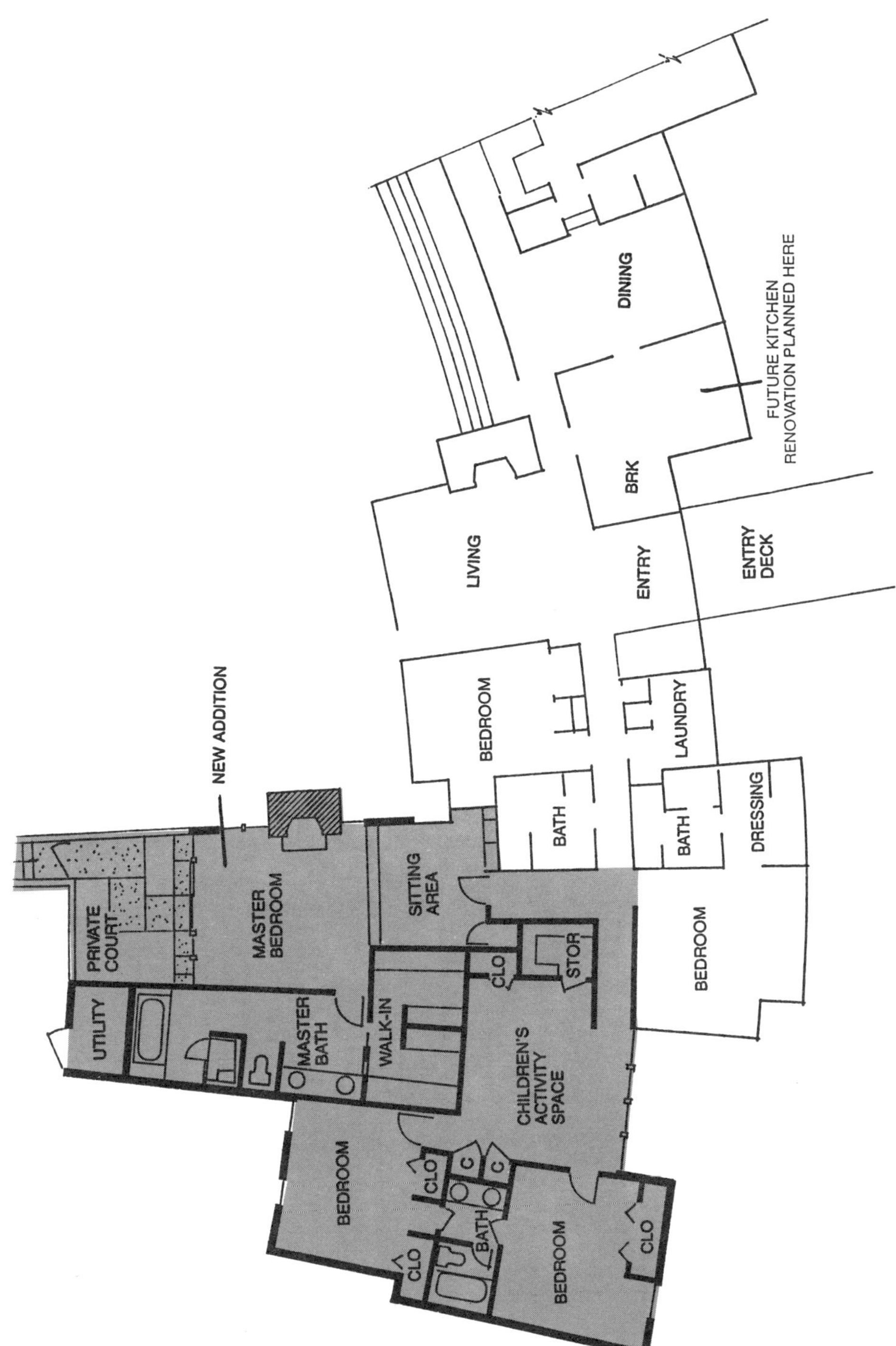

AFTER *The addition worked well with the interior flow of the house. Aesthetically, the addition became a natural part of the exterior appearance. This is possible to achieve regardless of the size or shape of a house.*

Market Value

Additions are probably the most common form of renovation. Also an addition may have the most impact on the enjoyment of your home. A word of caution is due, however, about it's effect on market value: Additions generally are the most expensive form of renovation. It's a rare addition that will increase resale of a home equal to the cost of the addition.

For that reason, if you plan to move in the near future, an addition, in a marketing sense, is not cost-effective. Some additions, if not well done, can actually hinder resale!

Family rooms and bedrooms are popular additions. Surveys have shown that, typically, about half the cost of construction is added to the resale value.

Adding a full bath, especially in a three bedroom, one bath home, is a better investment risk. It normally adds a higher percentage of its cost in resale value.

A swimming pool in cool climates will add little of its cost to the resale value. In warm climates, however, a pool may return most of its cost on resale.

Reaction to patio or deck additions is similar to pools. Percentage of return is slight in cold climates and higher in the Sun Belt states.

Garage conversions compel another addition — the addition of another garage or at least a carport. While you may not mind parking outside, many potential buyers could be turned off without covered parking.

Garage conversions, with the addition of a new garage, make sense if you have the room to add the extra building. Coupled with adding indoor space is the opportunity to add storage in both converted and new space. In fact, you can take care of storage requirements for the entire home with this particular renovation.

THE BOTTOM LINE

Don't count on getting your money back. As with all renovation work, plan it and build it if you intend to stay awhile and want to increase the enjoyment of your home.

NEW ENTRY
COURT
SETBACK
EXISTING HOUSE
PROPERTY
LINE
ADDITION
FUTURE POOL

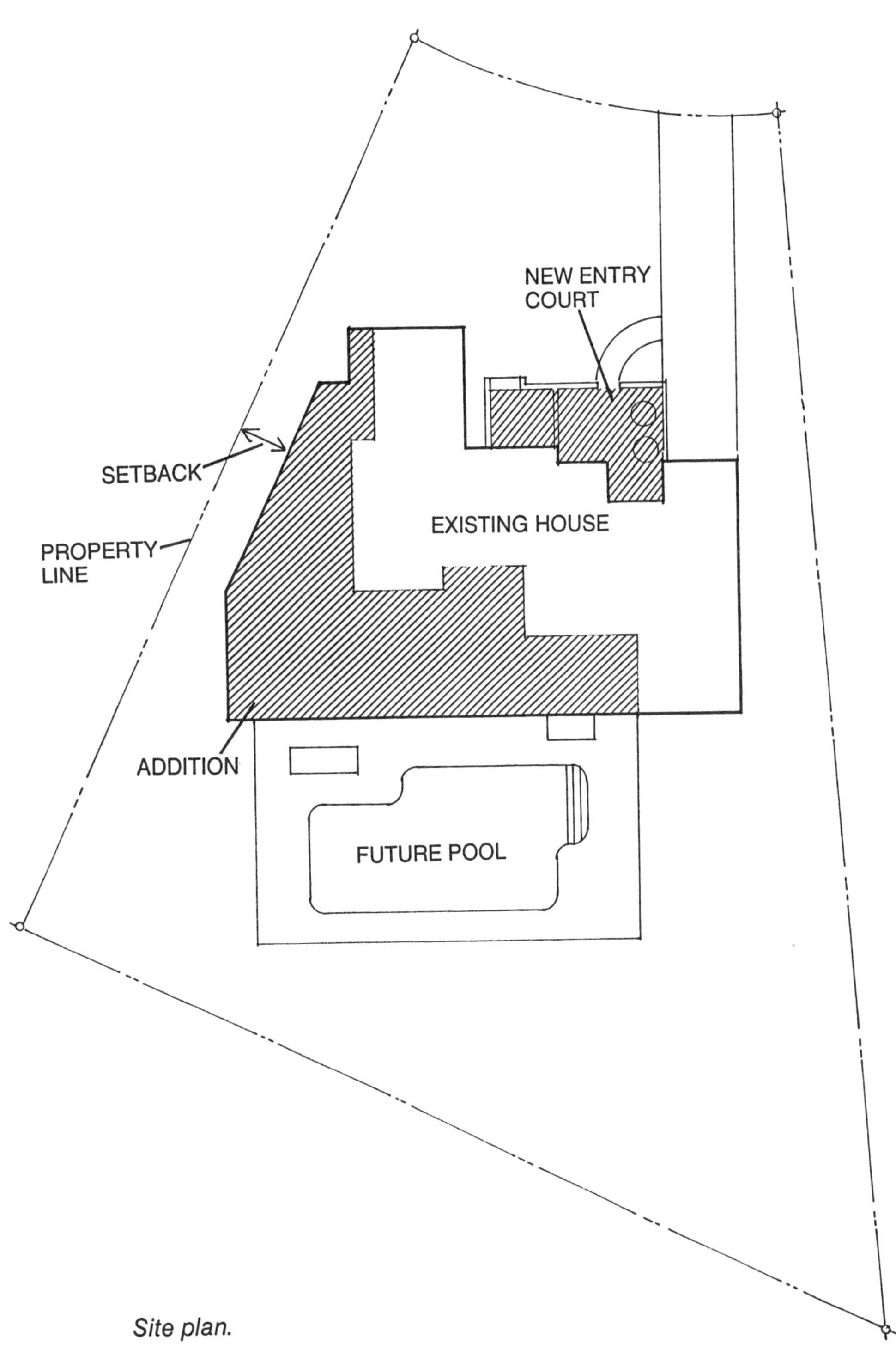

Site plan.

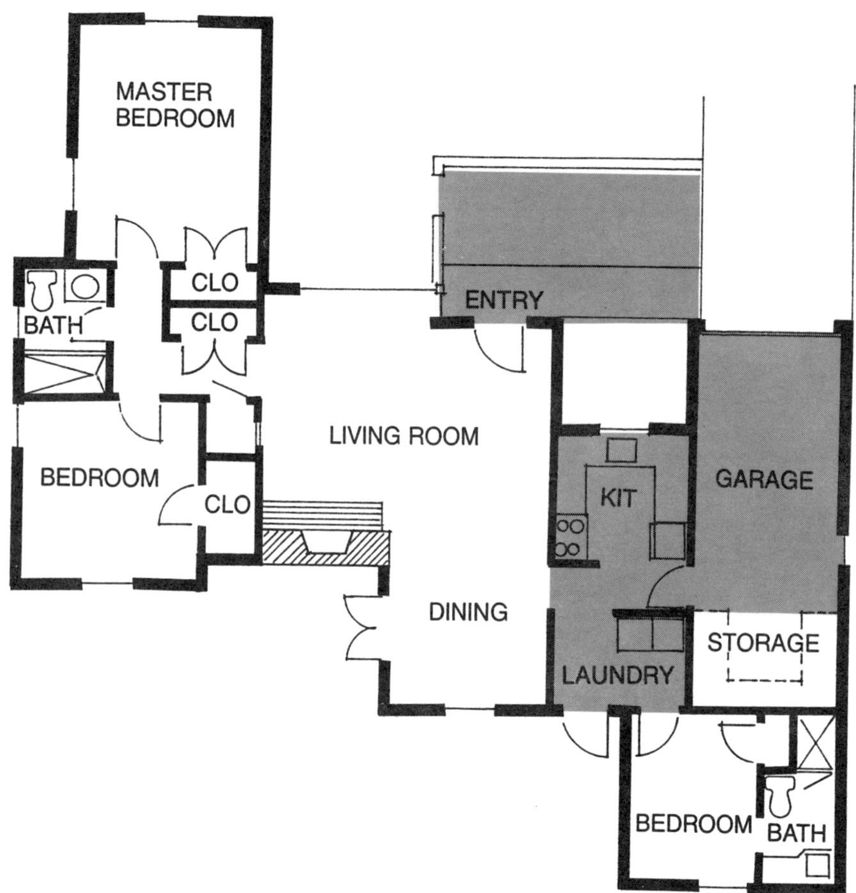

BEFORE *This old house was too small for the owners' lifestyle. Priorities established by the family were:*

1. *Add a large family activity space.*
2. *Increase kitchen capacity with a small eating area added.*
3. *Add a new master bedroom.*
4. *Indulge the owner's hobby with a wine cellar.*
5. *Add a pool in the second remodeling phase.*

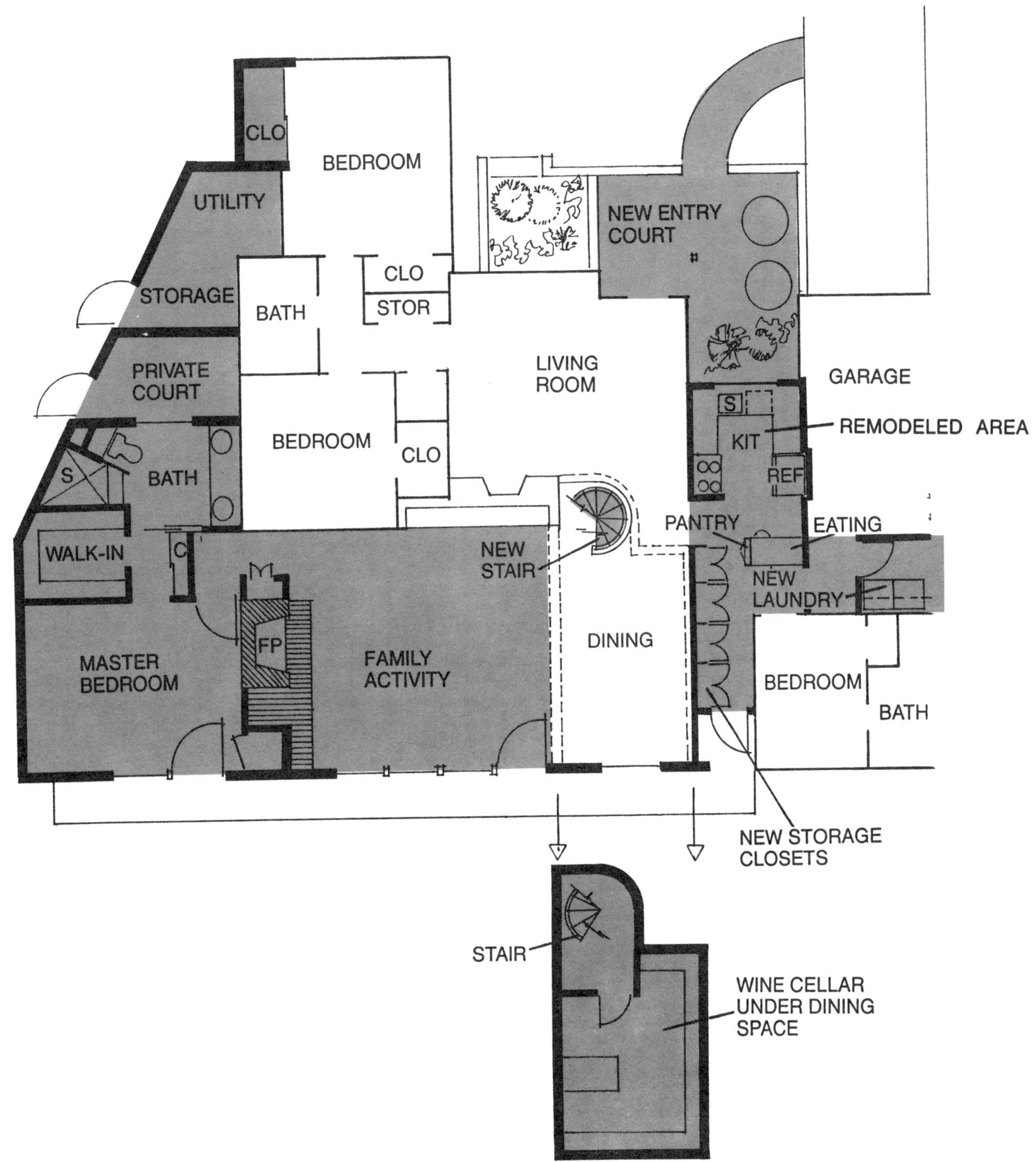

AFTER *The owners planned to remain in the home indefinitely and were not concerned with overbuilding. Renovation of the small kitchen would possibly return its cost on a sale. On the other hand, the value of the underground wine cellar should be considered for its increase to the owner's pleasure.*

BEFORE *A young couple, ready to start a family, wanted to upgrade, and increase the size, of this old home. Their high priorities were to improve the kitchen and bedrooms, add a master bath, and a den/family area.*

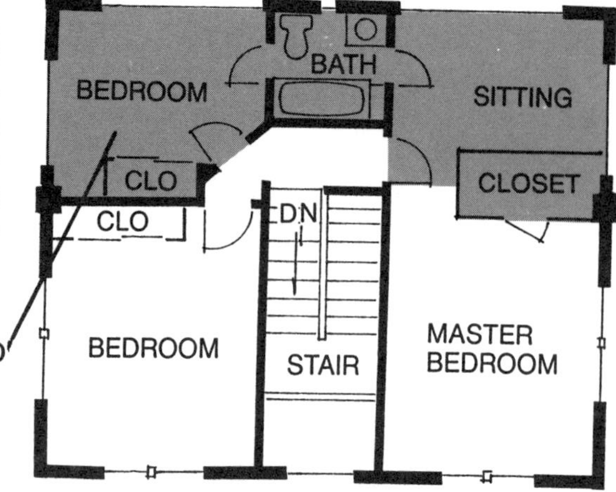

SECOND FLOOR PLAN — BEFORE

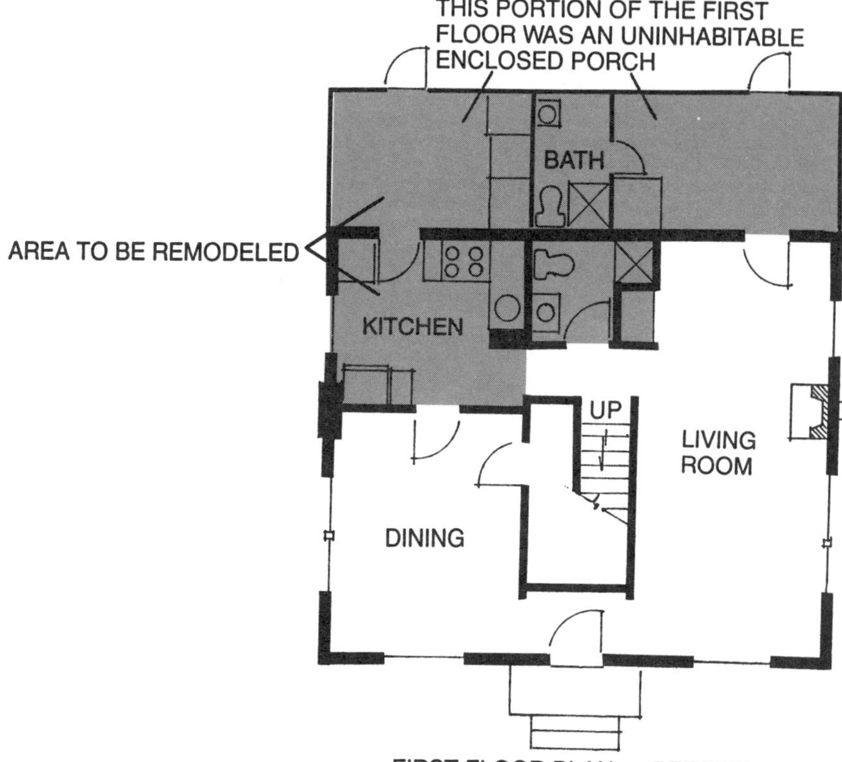

FIRST FLOOR PLAN — BEFORE

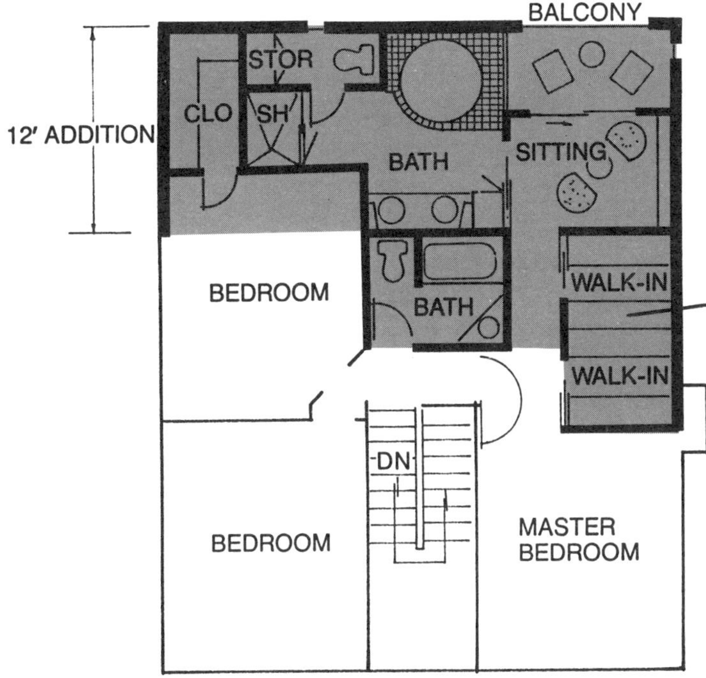

AFTER *Second Floor Plan. Second floor improvements included new walk-in closets, enlarged second bedroom and closet space, a new balcony and spacious master bath. The improvements included with the addition to this home are the type that have a probability to return a substantial percentage of their cost on future home resale.*

REMODELED AREA

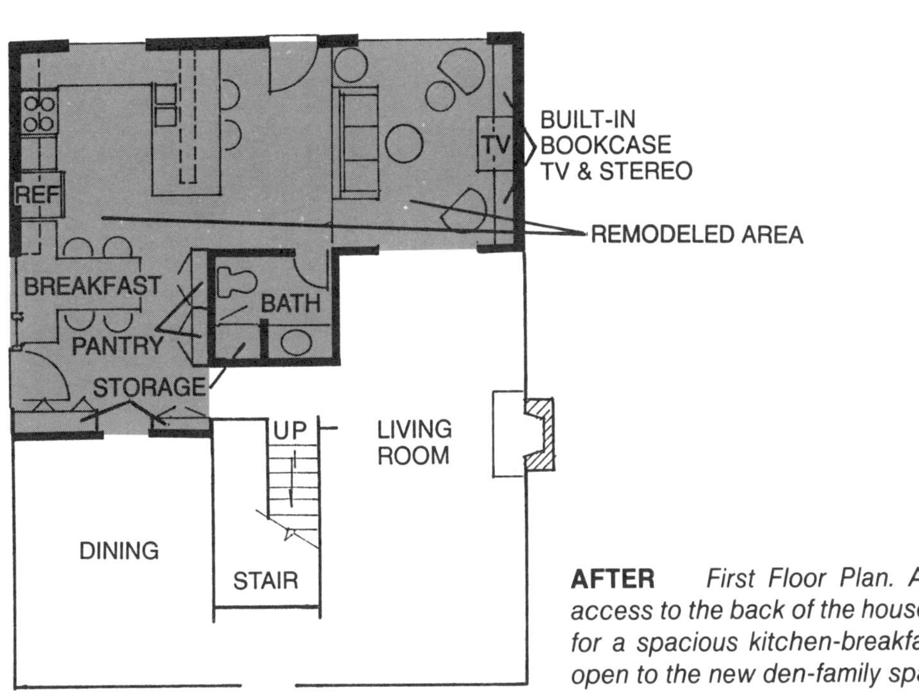

FIRST FLOOR PLAN — AFTER

AFTER *First Floor Plan. Adding 12 feet access to the back of the house allowed room for a spacious kitchen-breakfast-pantry area open to the new den-family space.*

Check List
— Additions —

Interior Space	Existing Yes/No	Size	Is New or More Area Desired?	Is Space Affected by Add-On?	Remarks
Entry	Yes	O.K.	No	No	
Family Room	No	—	Yes	—	Add new room - tie in with Kitchen and Liv. Rm. Need yard master plan.
Living Room	Yes	O.K.	No	Yes	Fireplace location creates awkward furniture arrangement. Change.
Dining	Yes	O.K.	No	No	—
Kitchen (Breakfast)	Yes	Too small	Yes/New	Yes	Kitchen very poor. Add new kitchen, pantry, breakfast area.
Bathroom (Common)	Yes	O.K.	No	No	—
Master Bedroom	Yes	O.K.	Yes	Yes	Need more closet space. Add reading area and balcony if possible.
Master Bath	No	—	Yes	Yes	Add master bath. Want separate shower and spa tub.
Bedroom No. 1	Yes	O.K.	No	No	
Bedroom No. 2					

Example of How to Use the Check List

Sample

Note: You may wish to remove or copy the check list sheets for more convenient use.

Check List
— Additions —

Interior Space	Existing Yes/No	Size	Is New or More Area Desired?	Is Space Affected by Add-On?	Remarks
Entry					
Family Room					
Living Room					
Dining					
Kitchen (Breakfast)					
Bathroom (Common)					
Master Bedroom					
Master Bath					
Bedroom No. 1					
Bedroom No. 2					
Other					
Other					
Other					

10
Exterior Improvements and Landscaping

For simplicity, I separate exterior improvements into two types: (1) utility and (2) pleasure. They do interrelate, of course. Improving utility often increases pleasure. The separation here is one of convenience.

Utility and Functional (Improvements)

MAINTENANCE

Exterior maintenance is easy to forget. One day you look carefully and notice peeling paint, sagging gutters, and a worn out roof and wonder when it all happened.

Some materials last for generations, but they never seem to be the ones in your house or mine. Maintenance is needed to preserve a good appearance and to keep us feeling good about our homes. Proper maintenance also helps retain value. It certainly increases value in times of inflation.

Feeling good about the way a house looks seems to draw attention to the entire outside area. Lawn, trees, shrubs, flowers, rocks, walks, courts, and walls all seem to get more attention when the house itself is kept looking good.

In a similar way, when interior remodeling is being planned you begin checking the outside to see what should be done to round out the project. If you're an average homeowner, the outside repairs or maintenance required won't break the budget. But, give some thought to improvements as well. This might be the time for positive *changes* to the house exterior.

MATERIALS AND METHODS

Certain brick material can, when not maintained, regress to a shabby looking state. The look can be changed. Pointing the joints can improve appearance. Or, if brick never did seem right for the house design, that too can be changed. Painting or plastering will each create a different look.

Then again, you may be unhappy with walls that are already plastered or painted. Sand blasting, to reveal the character of the old brick, is a device used to transform the outside appearance. Use it, though, only if it makes sense for the character and style of the house.

The above examples are rather extreme measures to "maintain" or cosmetically improve the appearance of a home. They illustrate an event, however, that frequently occurs with maintenance. The event being that materials preservation and cosmetic improvement are often mutually beneficial.

Let's consider that point as it regards the goal of getting the *most value* for the money spent.

METHODS AND VALUE

Before simply repainting your home the same color, or re-roofing with the same material, give it the once-over with an eye toward improvement.

What are the best features of the exterior design? What lines are the most pleasing? What is it about the house that's not pleasing and detracts from the appearance. If you can answer these questions, you're a step ahead, because you can then accent the positive areas of the design and try to neutralize the negative.

Maybe the worn-out roof material never did look right for the house. And the fascia boards or shutters that need replacing — should they be visually accented (to visually stand out) or diminished (to visually diminish)? The list goes on, each house being different. Think about yours. While repairing and maintaining to preserve the materials,

Adding a small indoor-outdoor sculpture studio gave the owner the inspiration to develop the outdoor space. A simple layout was the approach taken. Freeform pool gives the feeling of more space.

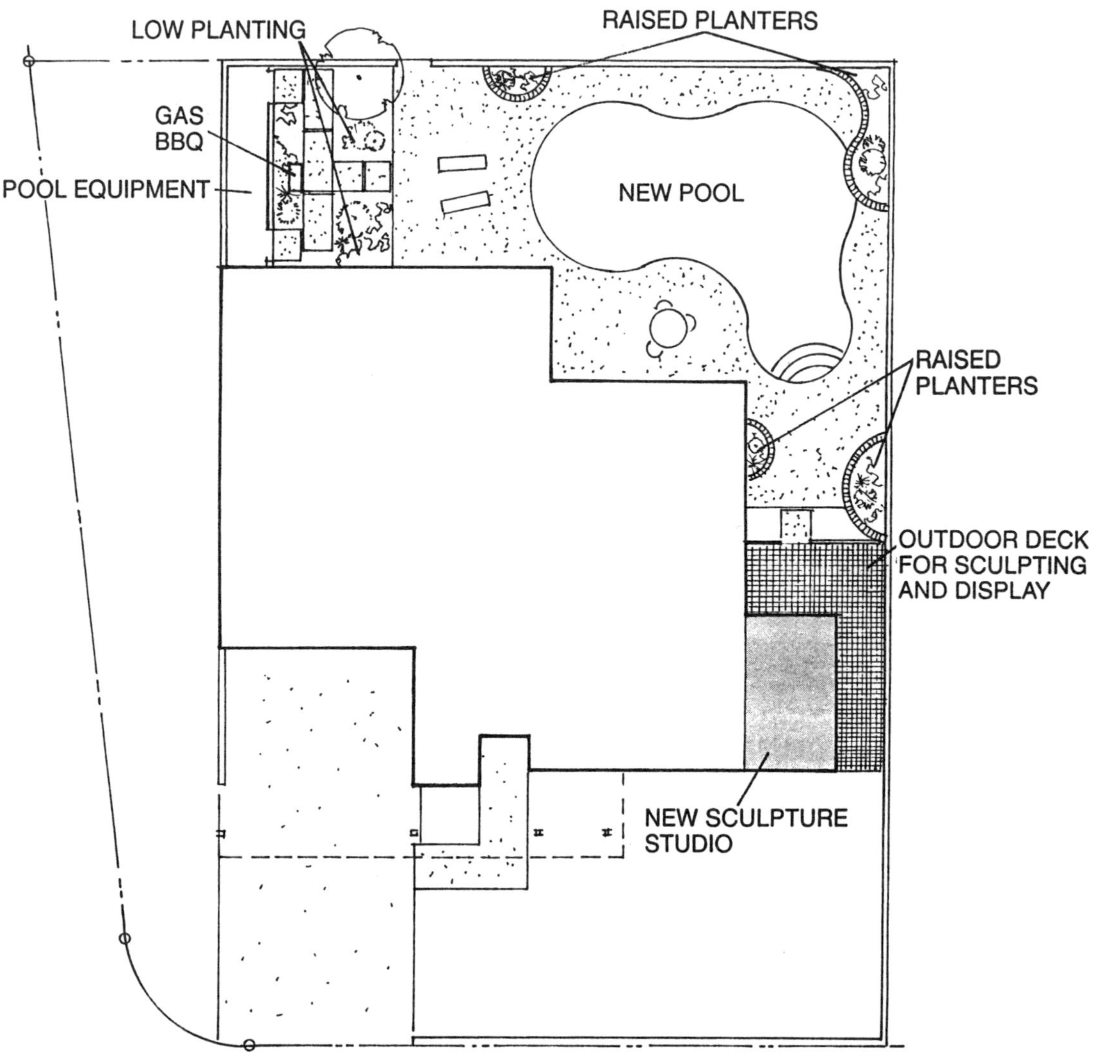

try for an aesthetically balanced effect to complement the whole.

The above is written assuming your budget will not allow a redesign which would change the entire appearance of your home. That may be the ultimate solution for some houses, but few of us can afford it. Hence, the approach just described is for the greatest benefit at the least cost.

ROOF STRUCTURE

Changing from a light to a heavy material on the roof may cause an overload on the structure below. An example would be changing from asphalt shingle to clay tile (light to heavy). Have a structural engineer check it out first.

OUTSIDE STRUCTURES

Outside activities are cause for outside improvements. Shelters, decks, gazebos, BBQ and entertainment centers, to name a few.

In Chapter 9, ADDITIONS, a Site Plan was developed. The same plan can be used to work with all kinds of exterior improvements, from swimming pools to rose gardens. The site plan gives you the chance to plan (using overlays of tracing paper) various

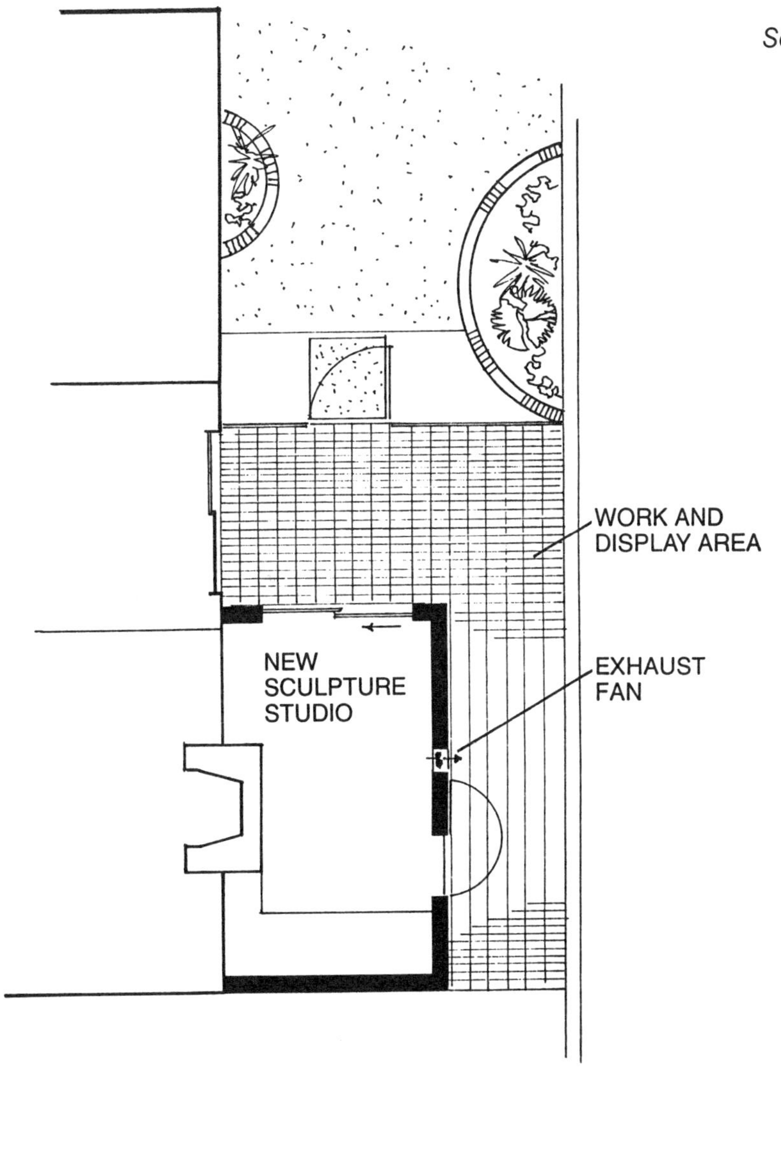

Sculpture studio addition.

schemes for optimum use of the available space. It becomes your outdoor master plan.

The check list process, deciding priorities among your needs and wish list items, works equally well outside the house.

OTHER NEEDED SPACES

Exterior storage areas, short-changed in most housing, are probably noted on your want list. Enclosed or sheltered space for work projects is another common need. Many hobbies or second income activities are done outside the house itself and need space. Guest quarters can be in a separate building if space and zoning laws permit. Again, the list is endless.

Your exterior space deserves careful thought. Look over this chapter's Check List. Add to it freely.

When sketching overlays on the site plan, keep things in scale (to the proper dimension). Otherwise, you'll fool yourself about the space consumed by your planning. You won't really know what space is left to use.

Don't forget to plan for the flat areas, such as drives, walks, and patios. Show new walks and planters at their proper size.

If you create a new drive, widen a driveway, or add car parking, be realistic about the space it requires.

Outdoor Pleasure (Landscaping)

The desire to create areas for outdoor fun and aesthetic pleasure further increases the value of an exterior master plan. Landscaping is one of the tools used. Aesthetic pleasure and good landscaping go hand in hand.

No attempt is made here for a how-to with landscaping. It would be superficial at best and, therefore, not much help. You can consult a professional or some of the many books devoted to that subject. My hope is to convince you of the *value* of good landscaping and stimulate you to go further. Make landscaping a part of your exterior master plan.

LAST SHOULD NOT BE LEAST

Landscaping is typically the part of a renovating project left until last. Often the money runs out before planting begins. The result is a couple of spindly trees, some one gallon shrubs and a little ground cover. The total exterior suffers with this common scenario. Make landscaping improvement a *part of your renovation budget.* Calculate a realistic cost estimate and set that amount aside.

ENERGY EFFICIENCY AND COST FACTORS

Energy savings, in hot climates, result from shrubs and trees that provide shade for your home. In colder climates deciduous trees, that provide summer shade, lose their leaves to let the winter sun shine through. Another savings occurs with plants and trees that require less water than others. Also, if you don't like yard work, select plants that require little maintenance. Competent nursery or landscaping people can advise you.

Cost control in landscaping means getting *the best effect for the least money.* Again, I'm whistling the same tune — to do this, do some *planning.* Plan it on paper. That always appears to take so much time and yet saves time *and* money once you learn to do it.

Landscaping is not just plants, of course. There are rocks and boulders, patios, decks, walkways, walls, terraces, earth mounds, ponds, fountains, wood in all forms, etc., etc. Depending on your talent and ambition, you can do much or all of it yourself. If you have pre-planned the exterior so it all blends together, the physical labor seems less a chore because it looks better with each step.

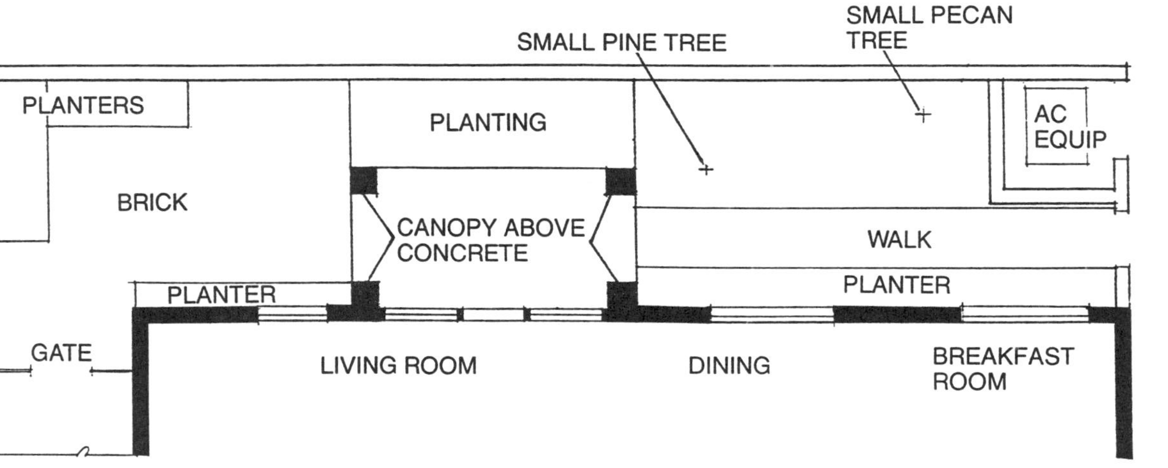

BEFORE *This townhouse has an 11 foot wide yard off the primary living spaces. The before plan shows an uninspired layout. The space was seldom used.*

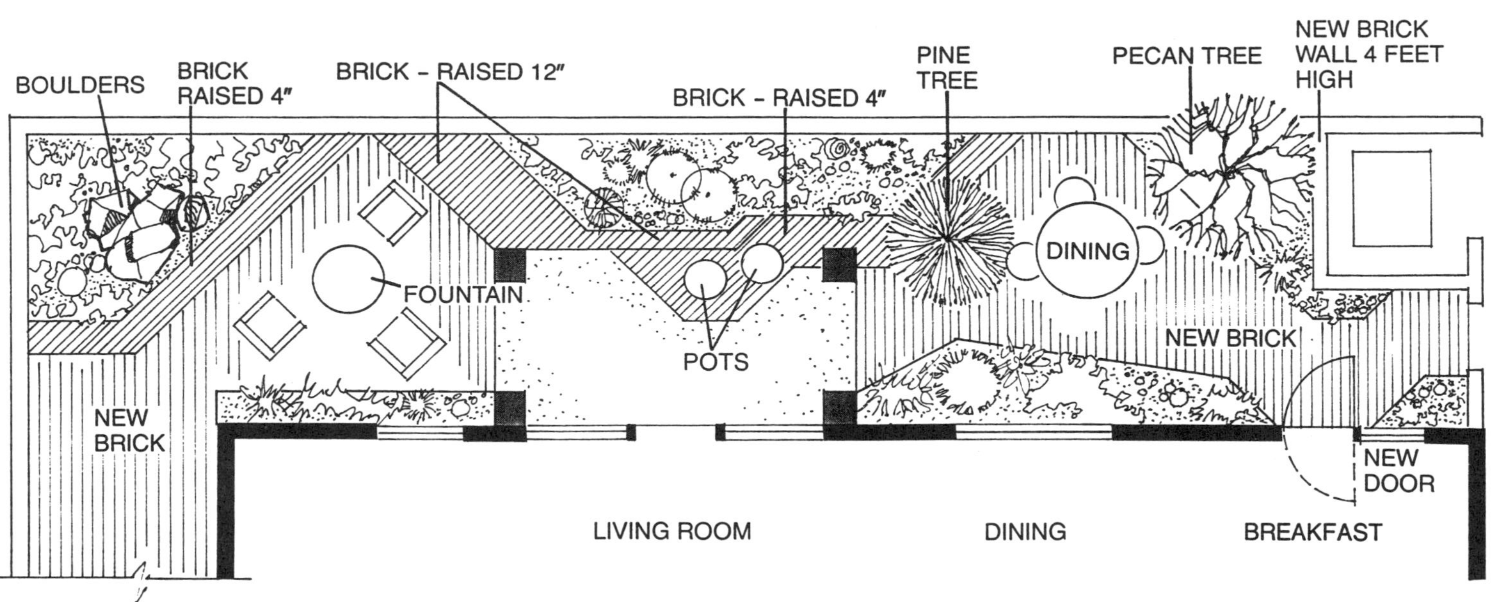

AFTER *The renovation plan creates an interesting blend of brickwork, boulders, fountain, and plantings, with room for conversation, lounging, and dining.*

Now, that sounds a little far-fetched — but I think it really works!

DESIGN IS THE THING

Think about the yards, or grounds, you have seen and remembered for their beauty. One thing they usually have in common is that everything seems to work together. Every space is carefully thought about and executed. The relationship between each area, one to another, seems complete. Surface treatments, recreational areas, and features — plants and trees, courts and walls — all flow together naturally.

This home is located in a relatively flat, open area. The need was to create an outdoor activity, recreation, and entertaining space, walled-in for privacy, and visually enjoyable from within the house.

The owners wanted a portion visible from the entry court, adding to the atmosphere of arrival.

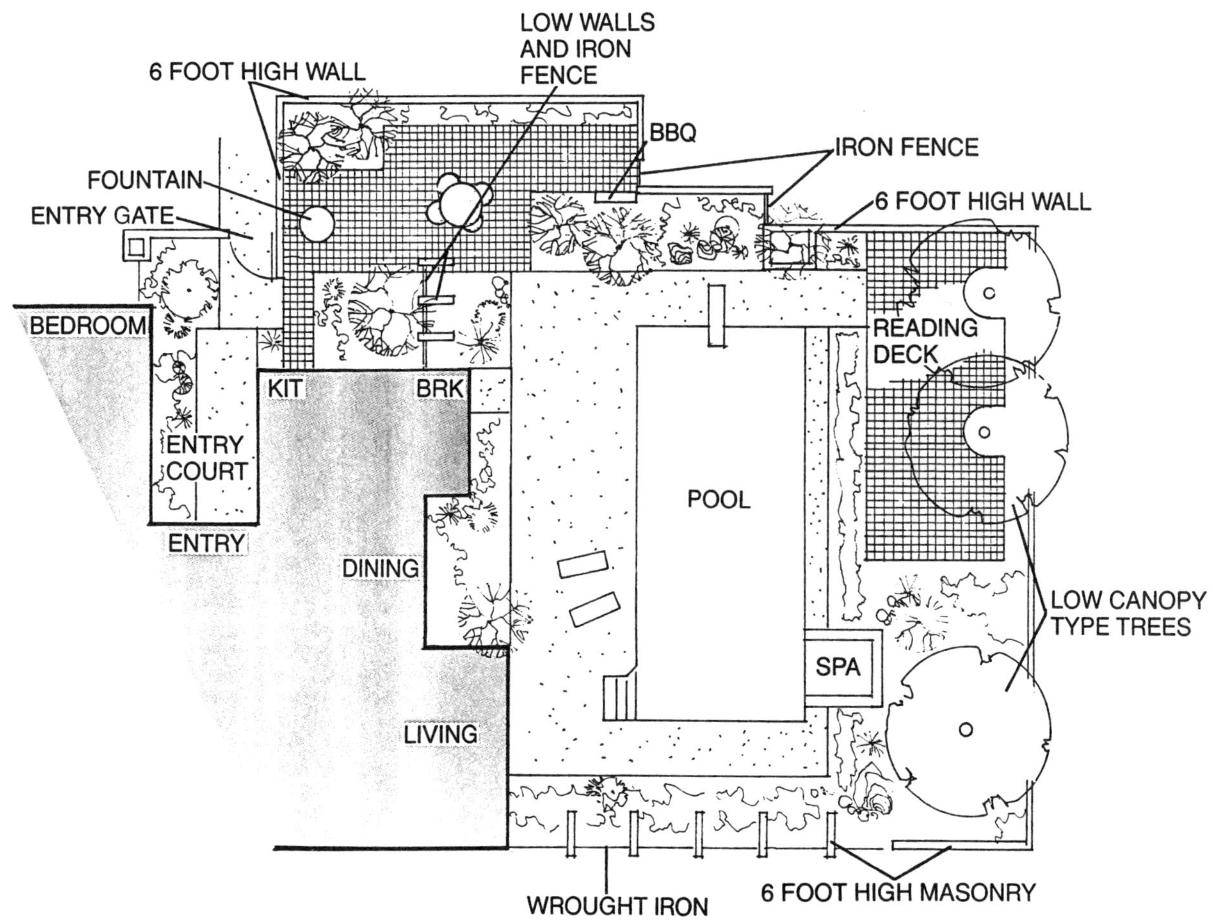

The above paragraph describes a successful exterior design, assuming that it also has a degree of delight, repose, and beauty. You may decide to retain help for the complete design, but try it first yourself. You could surprise yourself and come up with a real winner. If you do get help later, your input to the designer will be more valuable for your own earlier attempt.

THE ENTRY SETS THE TONE

The entrance to your home is not the front door. It begins with the first thing visible. Whether it be yard, walks, plants and trees, or creating an entry court — it becomes a silent statement about you and your home.

Even if your front door is practically in the street, do something distinctive with what you have to work with.

The approach to your home, I believe, should be the pleasant beginning of that pleasant environment — your *total* home.

The entrance way to this small home is dramatized with carefully selected plants and shrubs. The redwood decks, walkways, and open framing above, complement the landscape to create an elegant entrance, enhancing the appearance of this modest home.

Check List

— Maintenance & Repair —

Area	Existing Material	Condition or Quality	Changes Desired	Remarks
Foundation	Concrete	O.K.	None	—
Building Walls	Brick and Frame	Brick - O.K. Siding - Poor	New siding of better quality	New color scheme for siding
Trim	Wood	Good	None	—
Windows/Doors	Wood	Fair	Repair and paint	New color scheme
Overhang/Soffit	Wood	Good	None	—
Fascia & Gutter	Wood Fascia	Good	Add gutters at north and east	Repaint
Roof				
Other				

Example of How to Use the Check List

Sample

Note: You may wish to remove or copy the check list sheets for more convenient use.

Drive	Concrete	O.K.	Clean	—
Walks	Concrete	Good	None	—
Patios	Concrete pavers	Fair/Uneven	Change to Brick	Match brick color with house
Freestanding Walls	Masonry	O.K.	None	
Garage/Carport	Brick and Frame	Good		

Check List

— Maintenance & Repair —

Area	Existing Material	Condition or Quality	Changes Desired	Remarks
Foundation				
Building Walls				
Trim				
Windows/Doors				
Overhang/Soffit				
Fascia & Gutter				
Roof				
Other				
Other				
Other				
Other				
Drive				
Walks				
Patios				
Freestanding Walls				
Garage/Carport				
Storage				
Pool				
Game Areas				
Other				
Other				
Other				

Check List
— Landscaping —

Space or Area	Condition	Quality	New Features, Alterations or Additions Desired
General	O.K.	Fair	General design only fair. The quantity should increase
Entrance	Fair	Poor	Redesign completely at entry
Yards:	O.K.	Fair	Add new plant material to enhance existing
Front	Poor	Fair	Improve lawn. Improve watering system.
Rear	O.K.		

Example of How to Use the Check List

Sample

Note: You may wish to remove or copy the check list sheets for more convenient use.

Check List

— Landscaping —

Space or Area	Condition	Quality	New Features, Alterations or Additions Desired
General			
Entrance			
Yards:			
Front			
Rear			
Side			
Side			
Other			
Other			
Other			
Other			
Other			

11

Furnishings

This chapter will focus on the *importance* of furniture and accessories and provide hints about selection and value.

Furnishings reflect your personality, tastes, and lifestyle. Unless your house interior is architecturally unique, the furnishings in any one space will probably create the strongest visual impression.

When furnishings do not reflect the owner's individuality, it's when a decorator or salesperson incorrectly exerts influence on selection and arrangement. When that happens, the end product is at odds with the personality of the owner/occupants. Seeking professional help in selection of furnishings is fine, but you should be comfortable with the final selections.

The Selection Process

Take your time. Too often, furniture is selected in a hurry. You will probably keep it for a long time. Some families keep furnishings for generations.

Don't select furniture because it's trendy, or appears to represent a certain period. It may not relate to real needs or the aesthetics of your home. Trendy design, like "pop" art, or "post modern" architecture, represents fads that are usually short lived and become tiresome. Furthermore, those pieces can be difficult to work in with a total layout.

Select furniture because it is well-designed, well made, and complements your planned arrangement and architectural space.

A well-designed piece of furniture is good looking and functional. It can stand alone in a space and look good, or work-in with other furnishings. It fits with many different surroundings and you don't tire of looking at it.

COST

This chapter contains cost savings ideas in furniture selection. Some of the ideas suggested are:

a. *Under-furnish* instead of over-furnish.
b. Select based on lasting value, i.e., aesthetics and quality.
c. Carefully plan on paper to reduce chance of selecting wrong or unneeded furniture.
d. Plan the use of some built-ins. This process may be cheaper than buying manufactured products.
e. Establish a budget.
f. Tips on where to buy.

Habit and the Existing Plan

Unless your home was custom designed for you, or you were just lucky, furniture was arranged to fit the plan, rather than by your design. Orientation of rooms, existing walls, windows, doors, and traffic patterns dictated options for furniture arrangements. Type and size of furniture (i.e., rigid in lieu of casual or small rather than large) is compromised, because what fits the room might not be your first choice.

Following the direction of this book, you should develop a new approach to interior design. Placing furnishings in the paper planning phase is an important step in that process.

Furnishing the New Rooms

Keep it simple! A common mistake with furnishings is to do too much. Most homes are over-furnished — many to the point of clutter. As it is with any artistic composition, the good features of a furniture layout (i.e., beautiful sofa, table, lamp, etc.) are enhanced because of empty space around them. Also, by eliminating some furniture and rearranging the balance, you can often create space for that occasional multi-use activity. So you save two ways, buying less furniture and creating more space.

PLANNING AHEAD TO SAVE

Whether you furnish spaces with new or old furniture or a combination of each,

Texture and color in art work (stained glass and Navajo rug), accessories and furnishings, work together to create a warm atmosphere.

the process remains the same. First, determine your needs and then survey what you have. You may require very few, if any, new pieces. Old, but well-designed and well-made furniture can be refinished and fit well in newly-remodeled space.

Following are things to keep in mind when planning furniture selection and arrangement:

a. FUNCTION: How will it be used? This relates to size, durability, type of material, comfort, and construction.
b. TRAFFIC: Review the expected traffic flow throughout the rooms. Don't let your furniture arrangement interfere with *logical* traffic flow! A slight interference may work, but more than that will be a constant irritation.
c. LIGHTING: Plan your lighting to complement furniture, art objects, and basic room planning. Some lighting might be built-in, such as ceiling spots, wall washing, or general illumination. Other lighting will be part of the furniture, such as table and floor lamps, or maybe wall-mounted fixtures. See Chapter 7, LIGHTING.
d. COLOR, TEXTURE, AND FINISH: Color, texture, and finish in furnishings help establish the desired atmosphere. For instance, some deeply textured finishes make materials appear darker than smooth surfaced materials of the same color. Colors chosen, warm or cold, lights or darks, etc., all affect the mood of a space. Therefore, the selection process should take place when choosing the finishes and colors of the room itself. A side benefit here is that you won't wait until the last minute and make hurried choices.
e. ACOUSTICS: Floor covering, seating, wall coverings, and ceiling material all act to either increase or dampen the noise level in a space.

Choose Carefully

We often buy furniture in a hurry. Don't rush it! Let *value* be your guideline.

VALUE

Value comes in many forms. To some it means furnishing an entire room for the price others might spend for a chair. To another it can be just finding that one piece of furniture that you have been looking for — at a price you can afford. In any case, value should mean getting what you want at a fair price.

Good furniture is aesthetically pleasing and well made. You don't have to compromise with the selection. If you develop a plan and know what is needed, acquire the pieces gradually, selecting carefully. By doing the furniture plan with the remodeling plan, you will have time to order it, if necessary. It's sometimes the only way to get the right color, fabric, wood finish, etc., to complement the whole. (An important point! Delivery time from factories is notoriously slow.)

CARPET AND FLOOR COVERINGS

Chapter 14, GETTING IT DONE, includes helpful information on floor covering materials.

Sources

If you find the right pieces in familiar stores — great! If not, don't give up — there are other sources. Here are a few ideas:

a. Check the better office furnishing stores. They often stock chairs, sofas, lamps, and other items applicable for home use. Get on their mailing list for sales.
b. Check out independent home furnishing stores that stock high quality, well

This is an example of built-in place design elements. Sunken area and sofa create a built-in space. Curved wall, fireplace opening, and round flue housing complete the customized look.

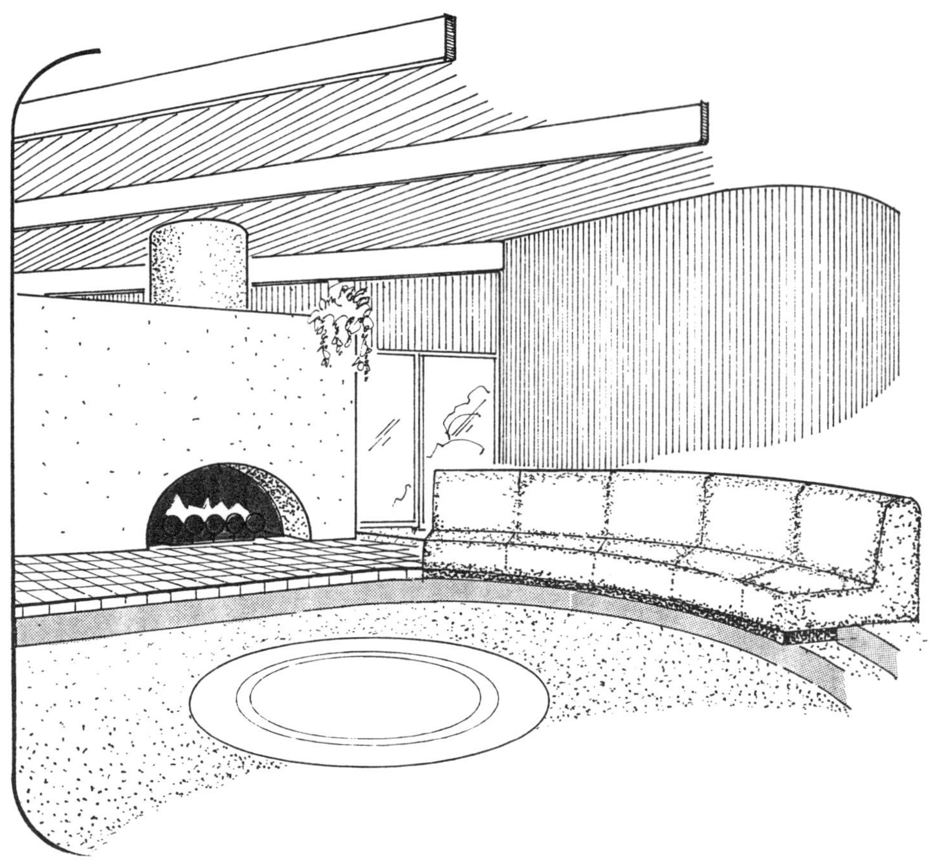

designed pieces. Some are small and you may have to search them out. Ask to be placed on their mailing lists, and to be notified of upcoming sales.

c. Consider ordering from catalogs of fine furniture. A salesperson in a good store will often work with you from their library of catalogs and fabrics, or you can work with a designer.

d. If you select an independent designer, your range of choices might be greater. A good designer will have knowledge of what is available and where to find it. Get specific about their fees, furniture costs, and your budget.

e. You can have a fine piece of furniture hand made, rather than buying a ready-made piece. This way you get exactly what is best for the room, and often at a lower price. For best results, some furniture should be designed and drawn up on paper. Common items to acquire this way are: bedroom furniture, stereo and TV cabinets, bar units, tables, and most other things made of wood or metal. Seating areas also can be designed and custom-made, bid, and built-in with the remodeling construction.

Built-In Furniture

Built-in furniture is a handy way to save space and, sometimes, money. Consider that approach. Another advantage is that furniture will be in place when construction is complete. A disadvantage is that the custom and fixed-in-place arrangement is hard to change and might inhibit resale of the home with certain people.

Furniture Budget

As always, be realistic about the budget. If you work with a designer, establish at the outset what you can spend. If you have a small budget, there are options. You can:

a. Furnish your space with low-cost items.
b. Partially furnish new spaces, selecting the best value, and acquire the balance on a planned schedule.

I prefer the latter method if all items can be purchased in a reasonable time period.

Above all, remember the statement made in Chapter 1. You can furnish the same room on a shoe-string or spend many thousands. With *either* budget, it can look ordinary, or great. The key is *planning ahead* to develop a good scheme of furniture and accessories — *before you buy one piece*!

Art and Accessories

Some form of art objects are present in almost every home. It's a special treat to acquire something and look forward to seeing it on the wall.

It is possible to acquire fine works of art at a reasonable cost. Don't misunderstand. I don't mean great works of art. That's in a class by itself and requires a lot of money. Most of us have to be satisfied with visiting museums to see great art and that is possibly the way it should be, anyway. But good art objects are obtainable, although it does take some looking. A few typical sources are listed below.

a. ART OR CRAFT GUILDS: By whatever name they call themselves, these groups can be found in almost every town. Check with your local museum or the yellow pages.
b. ART GALLERIES: Browse through them. Ask to be put on their mailing list. If you can't afford original prices, check out the prints and poster art. Reproductions can be purchased at a reasonable cost. In fact, a good frame for a print can cost more than the print itself!
c. COLLEGES AND UNIVERSITIES: These are *fertile areas* for original art at a good price. Watch for exhibits of student or faculty work. Don't stop looking after seeing one show. There will be a constant production of new work from new people.
d. THE ARTIST: While looking around, you might discover one or two artists whose work you particularly like. Don't be shy about contacting the artist directly for a custom piece to fit that special wall or niche in your home.

The check list will help you estimate a budget allowance for furniture, art, and accessories.

Plan the Arrangement

The furniture arrangement within remodeled or added space should be part of the basic renovation design. Don't wait until construction is complete and then shoe-horn in the furniture. The arrangement goes with the space and should be laid out, on paper, as the room is planned.

If you aren't happy with your existing furniture layout, don't be discouraged. It's not always easy to express your true taste and lifestyle in the type and arrangement of furniture. Look around your home. Does the existing floor plan dictate the furniture arrangement? Sure it does. And, even though there is more than one way to furnish any space, the selected arrangement and type of furniture will influence the way you use the space. In renovation, decide first what you want to use the space for. Then plan the space and furniture layout together to make it happen.

Furnishing Layout

Using the method described in Chapter 1, draw each new or remodeled room to scale and start living in it on paper.

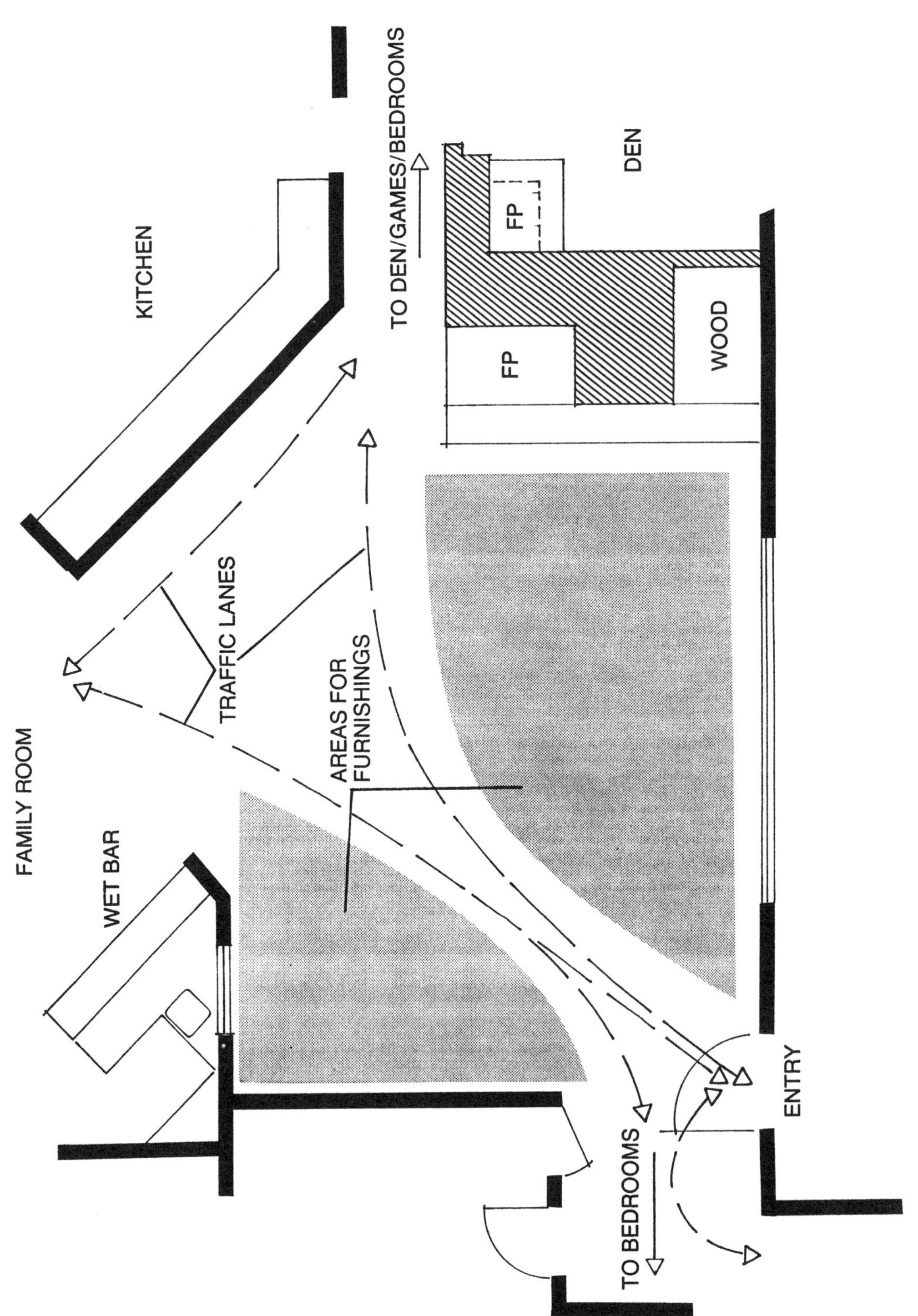

Existing floor plan shows general traffic patterns and spaces left to develop furniture groups.

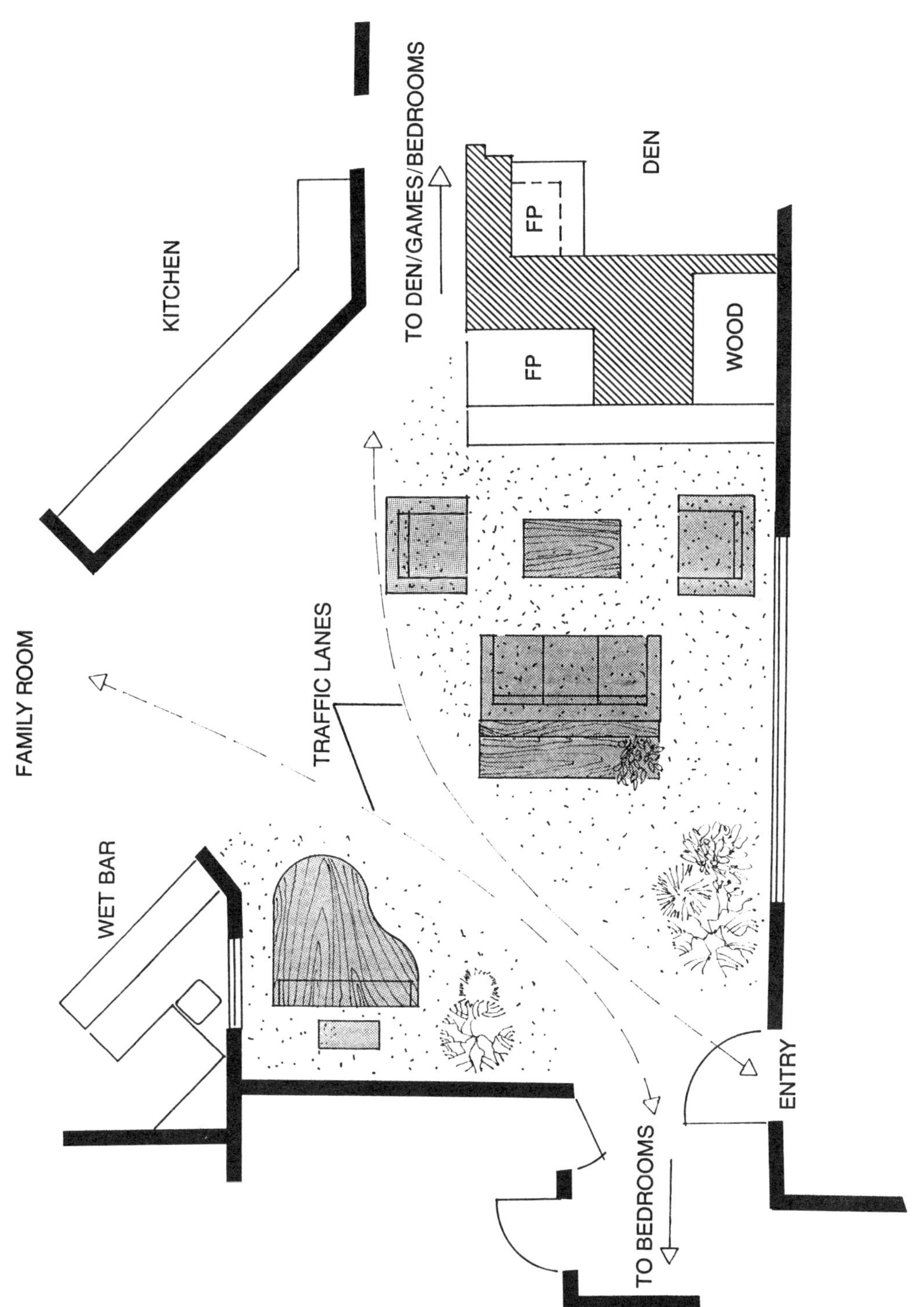

Furniture and interior plant-scope complement the space function.

As an example, imagine a new family room. Within it are fireplace, wet bar, TV/stereo, game table, and assorted seating. There will be at least one interior door entering this room and maybe an exterior patio door as well as windows placed for light and view.

The location of all fixed-in-place features such as doors, fireplace, wet bar, and large pieces of furniture (i.e., game table) begin to establish traffic patterns. Placement of movable furniture items (TV, seating, etc.) will complete the pattern. Leave space for that favorite hanging or painting.

Throughout this book, I remind you to sketch "*to scale*" always. There is good reason. With furnishings, for instance, if they're not to scale on a drawing, you won't be sure until everything is built and bought if space and furniture are right for each other.

IF THE ROOM IS TOO SMALL

The following scenario is not uncommon, particularly with multi-purpose spaces:

No matter how many ways you plan the furnishings, there seems to be two or three things trying to occupy the same space. Several options are open:

a. The obvious one — omit some furniture.
b. Find furnishings that are smaller. There is a big difference in overall size of furniture that is used for the same task — from seating to pianos, pool tables, and TV. You can simply select items to a scale to fit the space.
c. Make the space larger.

Another discovery is that door placement and door swing can either increase or decrease the space needed for traffic and circulation. Pocket or folding doors may help a space problem.

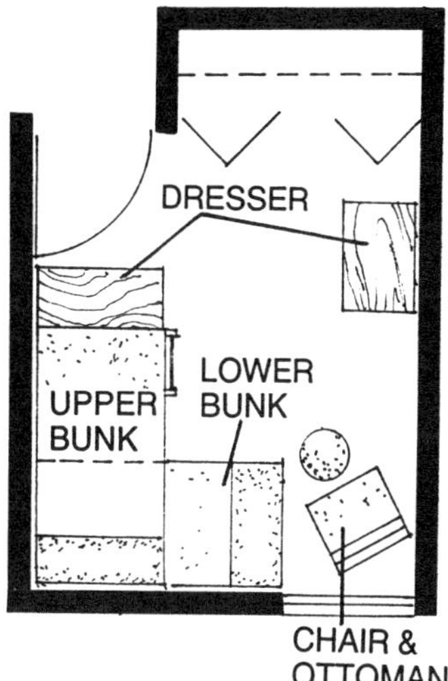

Small furniture in a small room. An 8′ 8″ × 10′ 0″ child's room for one, is converted to a room for two. Bunk beds, either stacked or at right angles, combined with small dressers and seating.

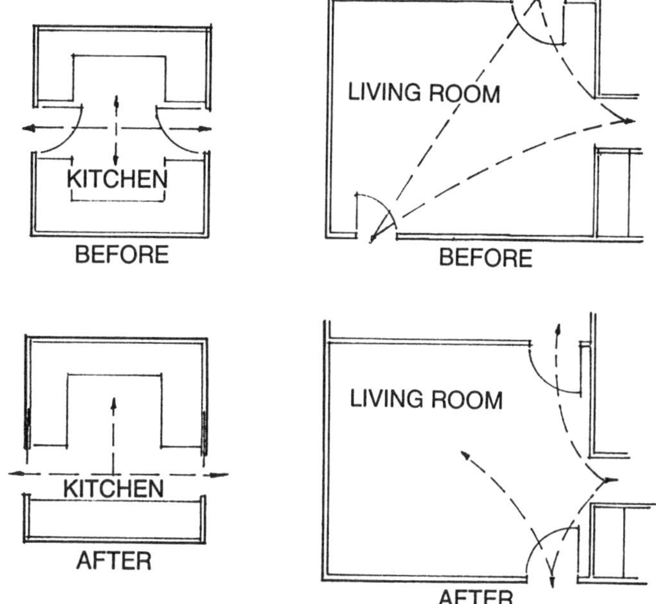

Room plans showing improved function and traffic flow with changes in door type and location.

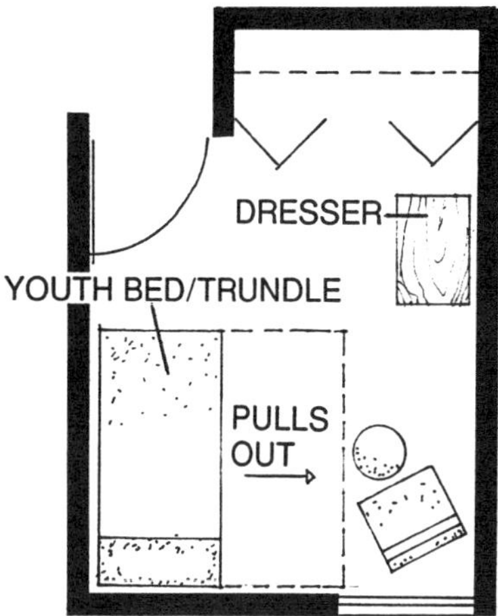

Another option, useable but less efficient, for double occupancy.

ACHIEVE A BALANCE

Try to have a happy marriage between the traffic pattern set up by the fixed-in-place features, movable furnishings, and the functions taking place in the room.

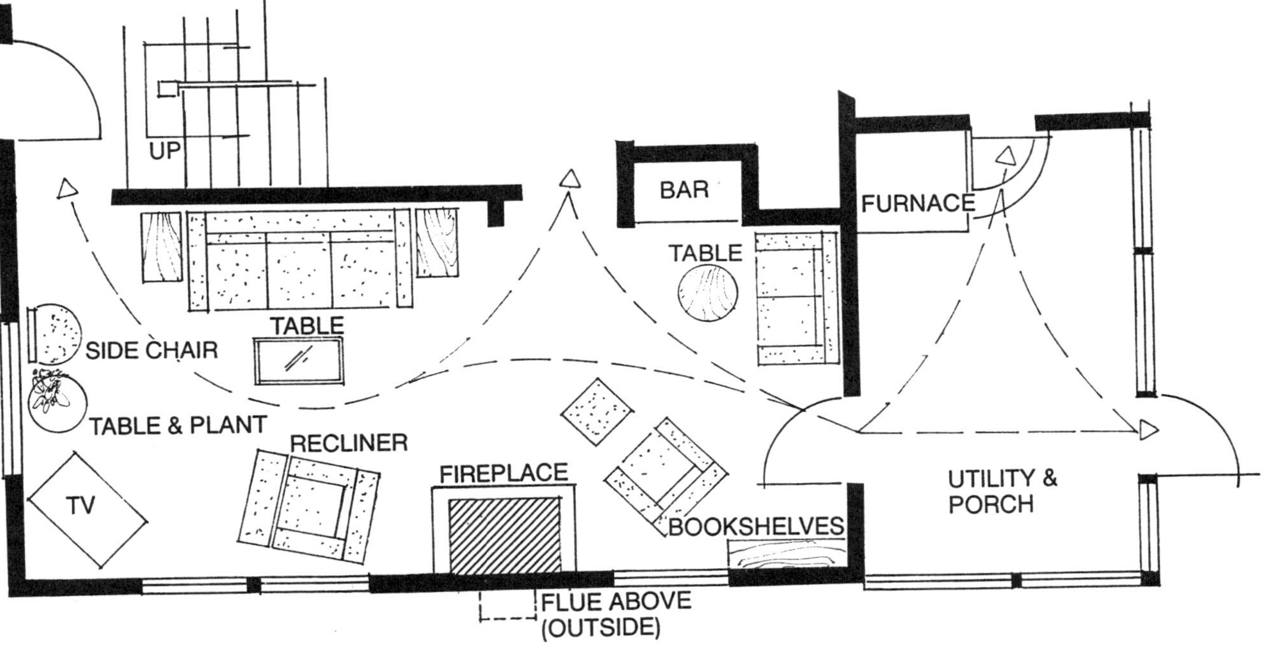

BEFORE *This existing floor plan is an example of a poor furniture layout and architectural elements creating problems. Problems are:*

1. *Fireplace intrudes into the room space and has little aesthetic value.*
2. *There is no real conversation area.*
3. *Traffic is forced through middle of room because of furniture placement and small door to porch.*

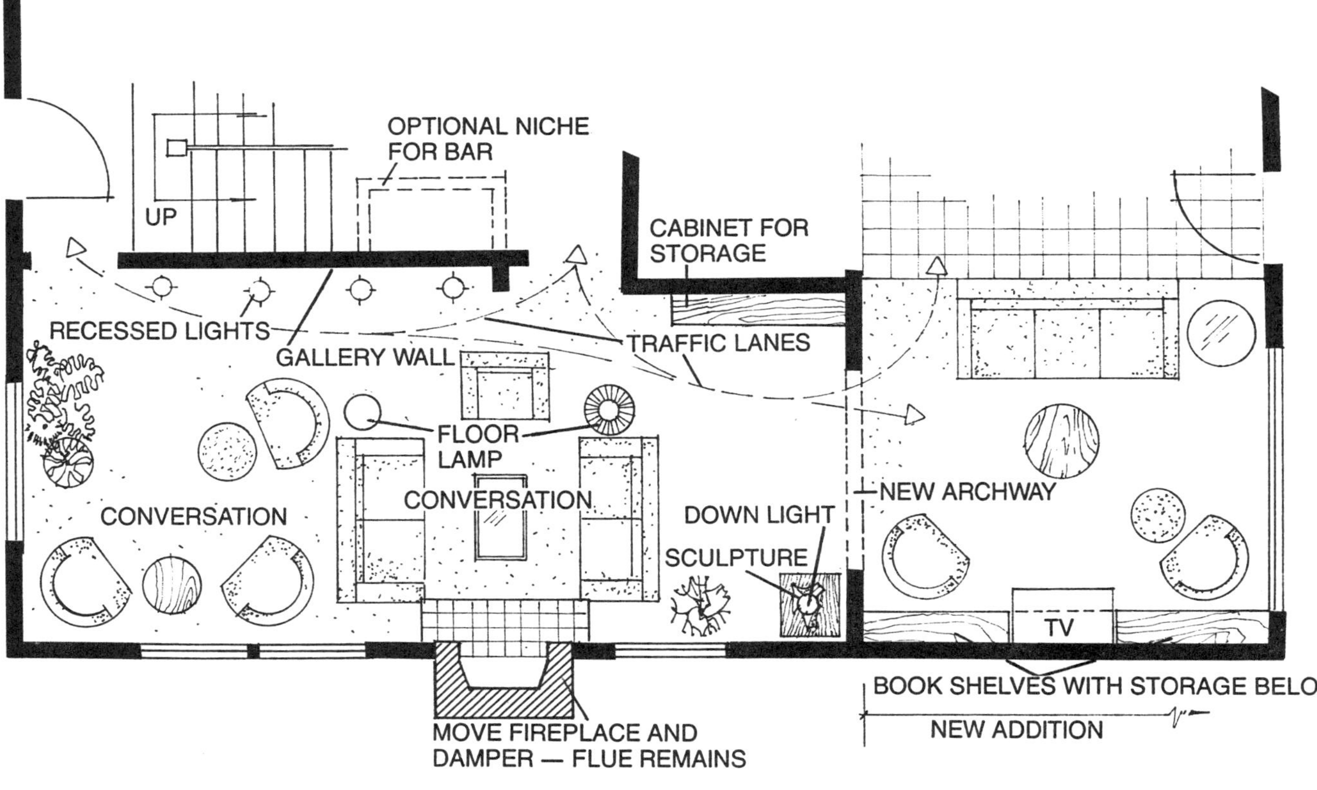

AFTER *Moving the fireplace and creating a new furniture layout provided many improvements. Adding-on where porch was allowed separation of functions. Improvements are:*

A. Separate TV or reading area.

B. Two conversation areas.

C. Ability to enjoy fireplace.

D. Wide archway to addition helps improve traffic flow and integrate new space with living room.

E. Improved traffic lanes don't interrupt room functions.

F. Art gallery wall, sculpture, and new lighting add interest to space.

G. Plants complement space and function.

Check List

— Furnishings/Interior —

Rooms	Existing Furniture	Existing Artwork	Items Desired	Remarks
Entry	None	One print	Add art work and potted plants	Increase entry size
Family Room	Sofa, chairs and tables	Prints and hangings	Recover seating New coffee table	Layout O.K.
Den/Study	—	—	New desk, chairs, lamp, clg. spots	Add new study w/ built-in shelving
Living Room	—	—	—	—
Dining Room	Table and chairs	One painting	New light fixture	—
Kitchen	—	—	—	—
Breakfast	—	—	Snack bar seat & hanging plants	Verify adding new snack bar
Storage/Pantry	—	—	—	—
Bathroom (Common)	—	—	Wall hanging in new powder room	—
Bedroom No. 1	Bed, dresser desk and chair	Photos and Posters	Lamp and small, comfortable chair	—
Bedroom No. 2	Bunk beds w/ drawers and desk	Posters		
Bathroom				

Example of How to Use the Check List

Sample

Note: You may wish to remove or copy the check list sheets for more convenient use.

Check List
— Furnishings/Interior —

Rooms	Existing Furniture	Existing Artwork	Items Desired	Remarks
Entry				
Family Room				
Den/Study				
Living Room				
Dining Room				
Kitchen				
Breakfast				
Storage/Pantry				
Bathroom (Common)				
Bedroom No. 1				
Bedroom No. 2				
Bathroom				
Master Bedroom				
Master Bath/Dressing				
General Storage				
Laundry/Work Space				
Recreation Room				
Basement				
Attic				
Special Purpose Room				
Other				
Other				

Check List
— Furnishings/Exterior —

Rooms	Existing Furniture	Existing Artwork	Items Desired	Remarks
Entry Area		—	Table/2 chairs, art, potted plants	Add new walled entry court
Patio/Courts	—	—	—	Add court and patio deck
Front	—	—	See entry area above	See entry area above
Side	—	—	Dining ht. table and 4 chairs	New wood deck being added
Side	—	—	—	—
Rear	Lounge/chairs at pool area	Metal sculpture	—	—
Other	—	—	—	—
Yards				
Front	—	—	—	—
Side	—	—	Sculpture or Fountain	
Side				
Rear				

Example of How to Use the Check List

Sample

Note: You may wish to remove or copy the check list sheets for more convenient use.

Check List
— Furnishings/Exterior —

Rooms	Existing Furniture	Existing Artwork	Items Desired	Remarks
Entry Area				
Patio/Courts				
Front				
Side				
Side				
Rear				
Other				
Yards				
Front				
Side				
Side				
Rear				
Other				
Other				
Decks				
BBQ Area				
Swimming Pool Area				
Balconies				
Other				
Other				
Other				
Other				

12

The Budget

Unless money is no object, establish a budget early in your renovation planning. Make it realistic and comfortable. A budget figure is not cast in stone, but it's good to have one in the back of your mind in the early planning phase.

The "back of your mind" is the key phrase. Don't let it constrain your initial thinking. Too often, good planning ideas are rejected before they can be developed because they *seem* too expensive. In reality, they may represent good value. So let the whole planning picture unfold before deciding upon priorities.

In the last paragraph, I'm not talking about free spending. Just the opposite. A major thrust of this book is to provide guidelines for value, to "get the most for the money." The important thing is that you spend the money in the right places. To do so requires that you first determine the order of importance of your objectives. Compromises — or stated another way, carefully selected priorities — come in final planning, when using the check lists.

The Big Idea

There's another way to reinforce my point that too much early emphasis on budget restrictions can inhibit planning ideas. It's better to scale down from a big idea than never to have had one.

"Big Idea" is a little hard to describe. It's the result of total planning and inspired thinking which springs from developing the *design program*. It results from knowing that a home renovation should enhance both the function *and* pleasure derived from your home. It is also the result of imagination — no small point.

When it comes time to compromise, it should be a matter of deleting those items, in a good plan, that are least effective. Delete enough to achieve your final budget objective. If that is not possible, another option is to remodel in phases, which is discussed later in the chapter.

Factors to consider when arriving at a budget:

1. Your design priorities.
2. Cost savings: Short term and long term.
3. Cash available.
4. Borrowing and pay back ability.
5. Future resale value.

Cost Savings — Short Term and Long Term

This book deals with cost effective

planning, which means both meeting the budget and getting value for money spent. Meeting the budget relates to the short term. Getting value for money spent concerns short *and long term.* Both short and long term expense should be weighed when renovation and construction are being considered.

Basically, short term expense involves the money spent on the renovation itself: construction, finishing and furnishing. Long term expense relates to maintenance and replacement costs of materials and products put into your renovation.

Let's look at a few areas of your home where you may be faced with a choice between short and long term cost savings. (Cost *savings* being the result of less expense on one end or the other.)

FLOORING

A hard surface material such as ceramic tile or a good grade of carpet, usually is easy to maintain and is long lasting. But, they are relatively expensive. In other words, higher short term costs, but less cost down the road for maintenance or replacement.

Looking at the other option, an economy grade of resilient tile or carpeting will save money initially, but may be harder to maintain and will be replaced sooner. The extra cost, therefore, is in the long term.

EXTERIOR WALLS

Another comparison is with masonry products. A material with integral texture and color, such as brick, is long lasting and, in most climates, relatively maintenance free. A concrete block that requires painting will require repainting periodically. The painted block, however, is less expensive than brick for the initial installation.

HEATING AND COOLING EQUIPMENT

One important difference between various types of heating and cooling equipment is *relative* efficiency. Furnaces or air conditioning equipment with a high efficiency rating will use less energy and cost less to operate in the long term. The initial purchase price, however, is usually higher.

INSULATION

Many materials, involved with the short term/long term cost analysis, are hidden from view. Included among them are plumbing piping, electrical work, and insulation.

Insulation is easy to illustrate. We understand that eight inches of fiberglass insulation costs more than four inches. Equally obvious is the fact that with eight inches the insulating value is improved, thus reducing the on-going costs to heat or cool your house. Thus, short term expense for long term savings.

ROOFING

There is a wide range of roofing materials, from cheap to costly. Generally, the life span of each is greater as the cost goes up. For instance, a relatively expensive clay tile roof will last much longer and require less maintenance than a low cost built-up or shingle roof. Again, the trade-offs are obvious.

CONSIDER EACH PRODUCT

It's *not always* the case that the expensive product lasts longer or vice versa. Often a product or type of material that is relatively inexpensive to buy and install will be long lasting with low maintenance. Selecting the right one is a matter of taking the time required to research and gain the knowledge.

IT'S NOT ALWAYS THE COST

It's appropriate to underscore a point about design. Selection of the finish material should be based on the sense of what best fits the design or ties-in with existing finishes. Never lose sight of the need to base selections on consistently good design. In so doing, it still occurs frequently that *more than one material will work* and the short term/long term cost analysis comes into play.

Survey of Materials

Most materials used in your remodeling should be selected by the time the design is complete.

CHECK LIST

Keep a list of all materials selected from ground to roof, inside and outside. Before they are noted on the final drawings, review the cost of each material. Is there something else that would do as well for less money?

Remember, there are two steps in judging the cost of a building material. The first is the cost to buy the material and have it delivered to your site. The second cost is installation - the cost in labor to put the material in place and apply whatever finish is needed. No small item, this. Some materials are tedious to install, while others go in place quickly. Ask a good builder, or your architect, for information. Labor is too costly to ignore.

At the same time, consider the short and long term cost factors.

All this may seem like a lot to think about — like maybe I'm making materials selection a chore instead of a pleasure. Not really. If budget is not a major concern, you won't be going through the process I have outlined here. On the other hand, if money is a primary care, the procedure becomes a natural part of the selection process and well worth the small effort.

Remodel in Stages

Establishing priorities is a great help should you decide to remodel in stages. It allows you to make good use of a master plan for total renovation of home and surroundings. If your budget is necessarily low, to remodel in two or more stages is possibly your only choice.

Deciding to remodel in stages also allows you to *master plan your budget* (as well as the renovation) and provide a timetable for future improvements.

I recommend consulting a professional with a good track record in home renovation, if you plan to remodel in stages. One advantage to phasing your improvements is learning from mistakes made during the first stage.

Financing

Two vital factors in budget planning are: (1) cash available and (2) the ability to borrow and pay-back money. There are many ways to finance a remodeling project. I won't name them all, but lets look at a few of the options.

A SECOND MORTGAGE

To acquire, or "take-out" a second mortgage means borrowing the required amount from a lender such as a mortgage company or bank. This is a secured loan, which means that the lender receives a guarantee (usually your home) as collateral for the loan. Second mortgages are a popular form of home improvement financing. Lenders usually are open to, and competitive with, this type of loan. And, typically, the larger the loan the more competitive they become.

REFINANCING

You might refinance your home with the lender who holds the existing mortgage. With this method, the existing mortgage will be "re-written," or cancelled, and a new mortgage established. The new mortgage includes the balance due on the original mortgage plus the additional amount for remodeling. You pay the fees required for a "first" mortgage, making this a relatively expensive way to borrow.

Refinancing is not as common as obtaining a second mortgage. Typically, avoid the process in times of high inflation when the interest rate is higher than the rate set for the existing mortgage. Conversely, when rates are significantly lower, refinancing is worth considering.

CAUTION: Determine if your existing mortgage contains a prepayment penalty clause. If it does, your cost to refinance may include paying a penalty fee.

LENDERS' FEES

Be aware of lenders' fees in the mortgage process. There is a definite, and substantial, expense involved when you refinance or obtain a second mortgage. Remember the old axiom, "He who has the gold makes the rules." In addition to gaining interest on money lent, lenders charge fees for the loan itself. A portion of the fee, plus miscellaneous charges, is normally paid in the loan application process — before you actually receive the loan. They don't all charge the same fees, so shop among the *reputable* lenders. Ask for a complete list of their fees, plus other charges such as processing, appraising, credit report, etc. Lenders are in the business of selling money and should be competitive with their product.

PERSONAL BORROWING

You might be able to obtain an unsecured personal loan. Such a loan is granted without collateral (i.e., no lien or second mortgage on the house). It is given essentially on your good credit and ability to repay. Of course, having money on deposit doesn't hurt your case. A substantial unsecured loan might be difficult to obtain, so let's look at some other options:

a. If you have a savings account with a bank or savings and loan, or a money market account with a stock or mutual fund company, you often can borrow against it. The account, of course, will become the collateral.
b. Borrowing money on a life insurance policy is possible. The face value of the policy is likewise reduced until the loan is repaid.
c. You can throw all caution to the wind and borrow from relatives!
d. Borrowing on credit cards is a way to get cash. Personally, I would put off remodeling before using that method.

CASH

If you have the available funds and don't want to add to your debt, paying cash is a still practiced method. Available funds don't necessarily mean cash in the bank. It could mean cashing in stocks, selling other property, etc.

OTHER OPTIONS

The options mentioned above are not intended to be all inclusive. I am not a financing expert. This section was included simply to illustrate that many avenues are open to you. Explore them. Ask your accountant, insurance agent, attorney, and financial adviser for ideas and advice.

A WORD OF CAUTION: Remember the two vital factors mentioned at the opening of this section. Ability to borrow is one. Your ability to pay back is equally important. Make that a definite part of budget setting criteria.

13 Working With An Architect

Some people retain a consultant for minor alterations. If you feel the need, that's the right thing to do. Others wait until more complex planning is required. Most never consult anyone.

One condition that always calls for the services of a professional is when safety is concerned. When the structure of a building is involved, or if safety of people in and about the home is affected, you should retain a consultant. Also, changes in the electrical, plumbing, or mechanical systems in a home should be done by experts in the field.

Finding the Right Help

I'll be the first to admit that I have no tested method of finding a good plumber. I'll confine my guidelines to the selection of an architect.

Don't take the easy way out by choosing a friend or relative. If the renovation is important to you, invest a little time in the selection process. What remodeled houses do you like and who was the designer? Check around, make calls, and compile a list of architects who do remodeling work. Ask the architects for a list of projects they have done, with owners' names. Call the owners and look at the homes if you can. It's important to see enough to make a judgment on quality, owner satisfaction, and your own reaction to the work.

Meet with architects, discuss your project, ask questions, gauge reactions, and check out the chemistry. You will be working together and it's important that you get along.

Agree on the Fee

When you find an architect whose work and personality you like, it's time to discuss the fee. The traditional method of payment for an architect's service is a percentage of the project construction cost. It can be difficult to do renovation work with this method. To use this method, it's necessary that the extent of the architect's work can be determined and the construction cost reasonably estimated.

In my experience, it's difficult to determine the amount of work required (as in: how much time will it take) in the initial stages of a remodeling project. One reason is because all the elements of the house are in place and usually hidden from view. Questions about structure, electrical, plumbing, and mechanical can only be *approximately* answered.

Precise answers come with possession

of accurate as-built drawings, or by physically uncovering the elements. The latter method is typical. In addition, the need to retain other consultants can't always be determined in the early discussion period. Services of electrical, mechanical, or structural engineers may or may not be needed.

Another payment method is a fixed fee that is established at the beginning of the project. As with the percentage method, it's necessary that the architect can determine the exact scope of the project to calculate a fixed fee. After the point of agreement, if changes are made to the scope or size of the project, the extent of the architect's work also changes. For that reason, a fixed fee doesn't work well with many types of renovation projects.

HOURLY METHOD

Providing services at hourly rates is a commonly used method for home renovation work. The rates vary, but normally include a basic rate for actual time spent, plus an amount to cover the architect's employee-benefits, overhead, and profit. This method is often called a Multiple of Direct Personal Expense.

A combination of two payment methods is occasionally done. The hourly method is used in the early stages to define and establish extent of the work. After that a percentage or fixed fee method is employed to complete the project.

PLANNING AND DESIGN

When an agreement is signed and the architect begins work, your participation is essential. To get the best results for the money, be helpful, straightforward, and open minded.

Give the architect *all* the information you have, including your financial budget for remodeling. The architect is the last person to be coy with about available funds. No one is in a better position to help you spend them wisely. To mislead any consultant about the amount you will spend means wasted efforts and final results that are less than they could have been.

Hopefully, you have completed the check list summary. This program of space requirements is the starting point for a design. Add to it all bits of information accumulated in the process. Include input on your likes and dislikes about everything, such as: finish building materials, colors, textures, lighting, etc.

It's not necessary to attempt rough planning and design sketches of your own. A good designer can develop ideas based on your priorities and desires expressed in the design program. In this regard, it's better not to become attached to an early design attempt of your own. To do so might inhibit your ability to accept a good, but completely different scheme presented by the architect.

UNDERSTAND THE DRAWINGS

When the architect presents design sketches, you must have a clear understanding of what is intended. You have an obligation to ask the architect to clarify *anything* you don't understand.

Ask for reasons behind any portion of the drawings not clear to you. This is not the time to be bashful or too proud to admit less than total comprehension. Many people have difficulty interpreting all aspects of design drawings. Don't let the architect go merrily along thinking you understand and approve the design if there is a part of it you don't grasp. The architect is not a mind-reader. So, communicate!

SEE THE SPACE

It's worth noting that the method described in Chapter 1 for visualizing the space can be employed now in reviewing architect's drawings. Imagine yourself in the redesigned rooms and spaces. "Walk" through them. Understand the where-and-why of doors, windows, built-in furniture, room sizes, etc. Communication between you and the architect should be comprehensive, with no questions unanswered. Review each element and explore all means to get the most out of construction dollars. Time spent at this stage helps to avoid future surprises and changes. The next stage converts design ideas to construction drawings from which your renovation is constructed. Changes made after that time usually cost time and money.

The Construction Drawings and Specifications

Once you're satisfied with the final design, work begins on construction drawings and specifications. The architect will handle this phase of the work, working with draftsmen and structural, mechanical, and electrical consultants, as required.

During this phase, you will review progress and answer questions presented by the architect. They may pertain to things like kitchen appliance selection, final choice on a finish building material, plumbing or lighting fixtures, etc. It's a good time, as well, to make furniture selections, if needed.

It should now be apparent that the more input you give the architect during the initial meetings, prior to and during the planning phase, the more cost effective his efforts should be.

BIDDING THE WORK

The drawings and specifications construct your project on paper. But it's still only paper. The next step is to bid the project and select a contractor to actually build it.

Together with the architect, carefully select the contractors to bid your remodeling. Select contractors of similar, high quality. Prequalify their capabilities *before* asking them to bid. When bids are returned you then can feel more assurance about selecting the lowest bidder.

Bidding time depends upon the complexity of your project, but is typically two or three weeks.

SELECTING THE CONTRACTOR

If you have selected the bidders wisely, you normally accept the lowest bid. Your architect and attorney can provide assistance in contractor selection and awarding the contract for construction. Also, at this time, consult with your insurance advisor for owner's protection during the building process.

CONSTRUCTION

After signing the agreement with the contractor, the final phase of your project begins. Success during and after the construction phase depends in large part on earlier decisions. Construction progress and completion provide the ultimate appraisal of the design program and design process.

The process of communication continues to be very important. Ask your architect to outline the events forthcoming in the construction phase. Discuss in detail, with the architect and contractor, procedures to follow during construction. Have a clear understanding of the responsibilities of each party — owner, architect, and contractor. Guidelines presented in Chapter 14 concerning the construction phase should be of interest here.

In spite of all attempts to avoid changes or "extras" occurring during construction, there usually are a few. It would be a rare thing to find: a perfect set of drawings; an owner who doesn't want something different; a contractor who doesn't suggest a substitution for a different material or method of construction. It is wise to have a contingency fund available beyond the exact amount of the construction contract sum.

There is no such thing as a guarantee of success in your relationship with consultants or the construction process. However, as with all things, the basics apply: common sense, fairness, mutual trust, understanding individual responsibilities, and constant communication — always communication.

14

Getting It Done

Home remodeling is excitement and the fun of creativity — not just in seeing the finished product, but using it on a day-to-day basis. Sure, it means mess, money, and effort, but the satisfaction of time and money well spent is a good feeling.

This chapter ties it all together. Now it's time to complete the master check list in Chapter 1 which will set priorities for final decisions and give you guidelines to get the job done.

Deciding Priorities

Look at the Chapter 1 check list. Please note the next to last column wherein you assess the importance of remodeling ideas. At this stage, the most important step toward cost control is proper planning. Good planning means to make cost effective changes — get the most for the money. Poor planning, or no planning, results in changes that add little to the enjoyment and value of your home.

If cost is no object, you might elect to do everything noted on the check list. However, establishing priorities is all important if you have a fixed budget or intend to remodel in phases.

Economic value should not be the *total* concern. Your home is your *most important environment.* Amenities enhancing this environment are also important. The *total worth* to you, of a finished remodeling, should be *greater than just the economic value.*

CHECK OUT FUNCTIONS

Remodeling often stems from a major functional problem in the home — or a lot of little things adding up to general dissatisfaction.

A functional problem could be having two bedrooms when you need three, a cramped kitchen, or not enough bath rooms. Relieving such problems can easily be your number one priority. Sometimes problems are not so well defined and choices become more arbitrary. They might be "wants" instead of "needs." If you have trouble deciding what is most important to you, go back to the check lists and discuss objectives.

What do you want to achieve? How will adding this or that enhance your life style? What change will make the home better for the entire family? You may need several changes, with something for each family member. Review check list notes, complete them, and hammer out the priorities.

Home Value

"Home Improvement" doesn't always mean remodeling. Some basics relate to maintaining the value of your home.

Maintaining value means maintaining the house itself and includes everything from keeping out termites to putting on a new roof, or applying new paint. Don't lose sight of the need to *maintain* your house value.

The Final Rating

Keep in mind the theme about total worth. Spending dollars wisely is a balance between economic value and the return in satisfaction.

Example sheets in Chapter 1 show a partial check list from a make-believe house — included to show you how to make changes work in *your* case. My "Interior Space" example sheet indicates the *highest* priority items, which include:

1. a. Re-doing the kitchen
   b. Relocating and enlarging the pantry
   c. Adding a powder room
2. Adding a study

Lower priority items include:

3. Re-lighting the dining area and adding a snack bar in the new kitchen.

Priority items are firm objectives. They would be the major part of a remodeling scheme for my make-believe house. If you have not already done so, use the following procedure to establish your own priority ratings.

LIST YOUR PRIORITIES

By now, you should have read the chapters about areas for which you have a concern. If you did not fill out the check lists at the end of these chapters, please do so.

Copy or remove the completed check lists from each chapter and go to the master list in Chapter 1. This is the summary check list which contains all of the spaces and features in your home. Transfer the information from the various chapters to the master check list.

STARTING TO PLAN

Whether you do the final planning yourself, or hire an architect, you are way ahead of the game. In completing the check lists you know *what* has to be done. It's now a matter of arranging alterations and additions on paper.

Two basic methods for putting on paper the plans and final design are: (1) hire a professional or (2) do it yourself. Let's first discuss doing it yourself. The discussion to follow begins with design and planning — through complete construction — for the do-it-yourselfer.

Doing it Yourself

In deciding *what changes to make in your home*, you have achieved the major objective of this book. Let's go further now, with guidelines to help you *get it all done*!

In Chapter 13, I discussed hiring a professional to help in planning, design, and construction drawings. Basically, it should be done when a project exceeds a certain size, complexity, or cost. In the planning stage, the point at which to retain help varies with each person's experience, skill and natural talent. But, some situations should be considered likely candidates for professional involvement. Such changes include: almost any addition or exterior change, or substantial interior changes such as complete kitchen redesign or enlargement. Retain help with any change affecting the structure, such as foundations or altering any part of walls,

Check List
— Interior Space/General Areas —

Interior Space	Existing Yes/No	Quality and Size of Space	New Features, Alterations and Additions Desired	Importance of Change to this Space	Priority Rating for Total Project	Remarks
Entry	Yes	Too small	Increase size	2	4	Increase inside area or add entrance court
Family Room	Yes	OK - dark at fireplace end	Add natural light	3	4	Skylights probably best
Den/Study	No	—	Add study built-in shelving	2	2	
Living Room	No	—	None	—	—	Re-do spare bedroom? Add entr. court/glass door
Dining Room/ Area	Yes	Too dark	Improve with better fixtures	2	3	
Kitchen	Yes	Too small poor layout	More counter & cabs; new layout/lighting	1		
Breakfast	No					

Example of How to Use the Check List

Sample

Note: You may wish to remove or copy the check list sheets for more convenient use.

beams, floor, or roof. Also, an obvious time to call for help is when you have tried, but cannot develop a concept or solution.

Of course, there are hundreds of remodeling projects good for *doing-it-yourself.* Let's look at ways and means of getting them done!

Planning and Design

COST EFFICIENCY

The concept of this book includes getting the *most value* for the money spent. Good planning, efficient use of space, and wise materials selection are all part of that process. Planning considerations include: (1) multi-purpose space; (2) flexible space for future changes in family size or lifestyle; (3) space constructed with standard, cost competitive materials.

Planning and design is a matter of arranging your ideas on paper. Taken step by step, you can approach it with confidence.

Chapter 1 explained how to draw the plan of your house as it now exists (before alterations). Now, use that "as-built" plan to begin the rough sketches for remodeling.

VISUALIZE THE SPACE

Rough sketching is easier if you can visualize what the space would be like to sit in, walk through, and live with. Following is an exercise to help visualize your floor plan in three dimensions.

Look at the as-built plan and imagine yourself in different locations within the rooms. For example, you may be sitting on a sofa looking at a fireplace. (Draw furniture to scale using the same method you used to draw the existing plan.) Then imagine (still looking at the plan) getting up and walking to the kitchen. Think about your path of travel — what you do and see as you walk. Follow similar procedures until you feel familiar with

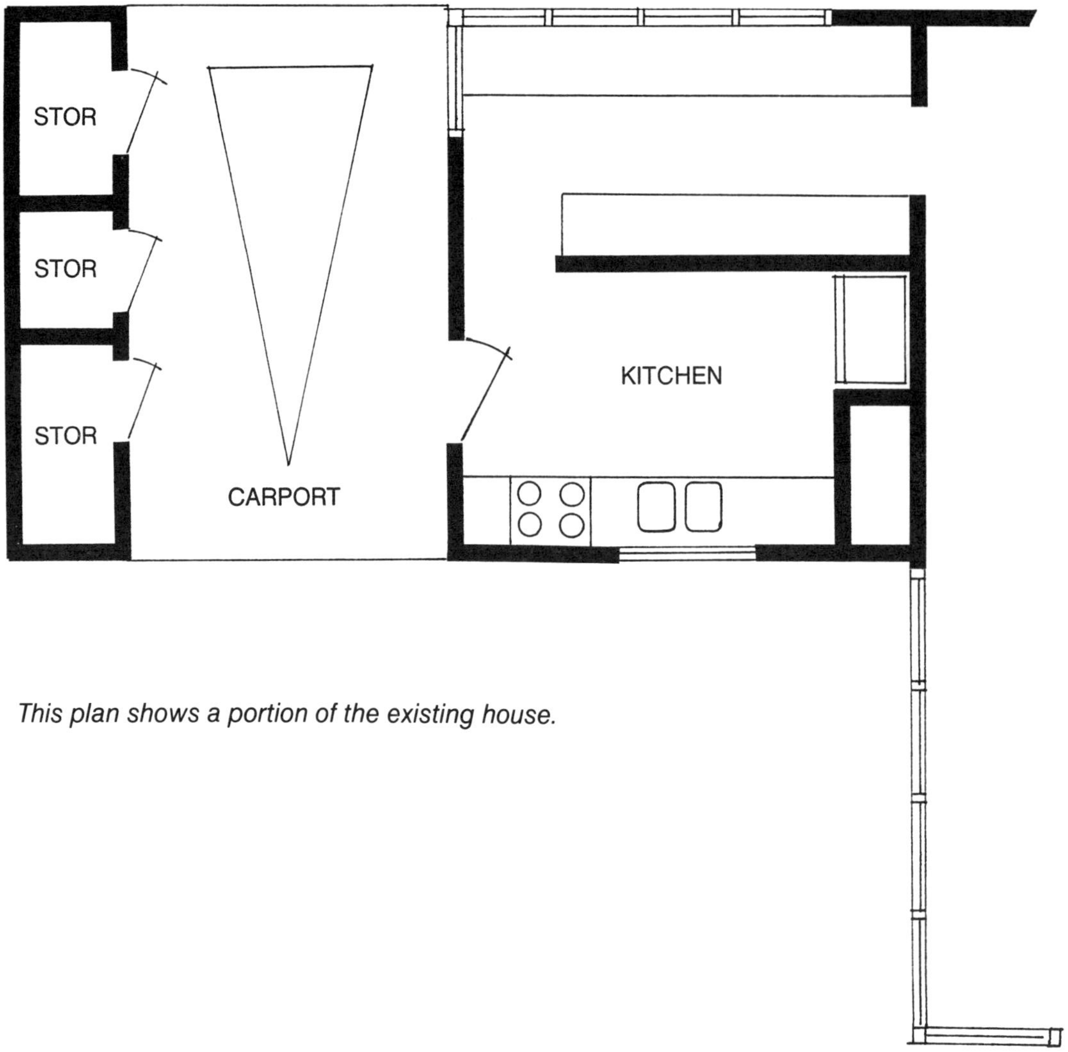

STOR

STOR

STOR

CARPORT

KITCHEN

This plan shows a portion of the existing house.

The existing plan is drawn in circles.

First circle sketch. This scheme requires cutting a passage from kitchen to den. No view from kitchen to front yard. Laundry location is bad. The decision is made to move storage to the other end of the house.

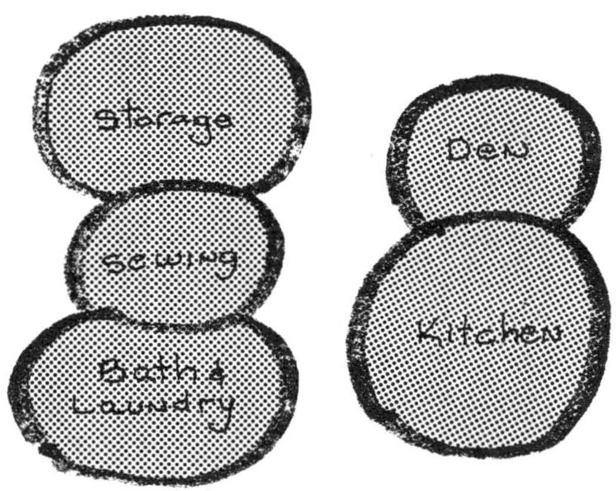

the space. Go on to other areas and rooms in a like manner.

Think about traffic patterns and how they affect areas for work, or for quiet. Where is the sunlight coming from and is there enough in the right places? How do furnishings affect traffic and function, etc.?

Once familiar with your house in this way, you are better able to begin rough sketching of your *ideas for changes*.

ROUGH SKETCHING

First ideas can be shown by rough sketching done *over* your *existing floor plan*. Lay tracing paper (the same kind used to draw the existing house plan) over the as-built plan. Doing that helps keep the sketching to scale. Also, looking through the tracing paper you see how changes might effect existing conditions, such as walls or plumbing.

For instance, suppose you want to enlarge a room or rearrange the kitchen. By working directly over the as-built plan, you can tell how your ideas affect what is in place.

Before sketching, make copies of the as-built plan. Use a copy to work with and put the original drawing away. Also, buy a quantity of tracing paper. One sheet won't do it!

When rough sketching on tracing paper, remember that paper is cheap and easier to come by than ideas! Don't hesitate to sketch any idea that comes into your head.

Don't try for a finished drawing with the first sketch. Let first sketches be rough and loose. Lay down more clean tracing paper and sketch again — and again — changing or refining each time.

If you reach a point where no new ideas develop and you're still not satisfied, stop for a while. Leave it for a day. It's not realistic to expect to solve remodeling planning and design in one sitting!

Various methods can speed your initial sketching ideas. Some people use a grouping of circles to represent spaces and rooms. This has the advantage of keeping ideas focused on general planning rather than details. Any

Second Sketch — Better access from kitchen and outside. Better laundry location. Try to improve access from front and make better use of rear yard and patio location.

Spaces are in their best relationship to each other. Den location best for access and rear yard view.

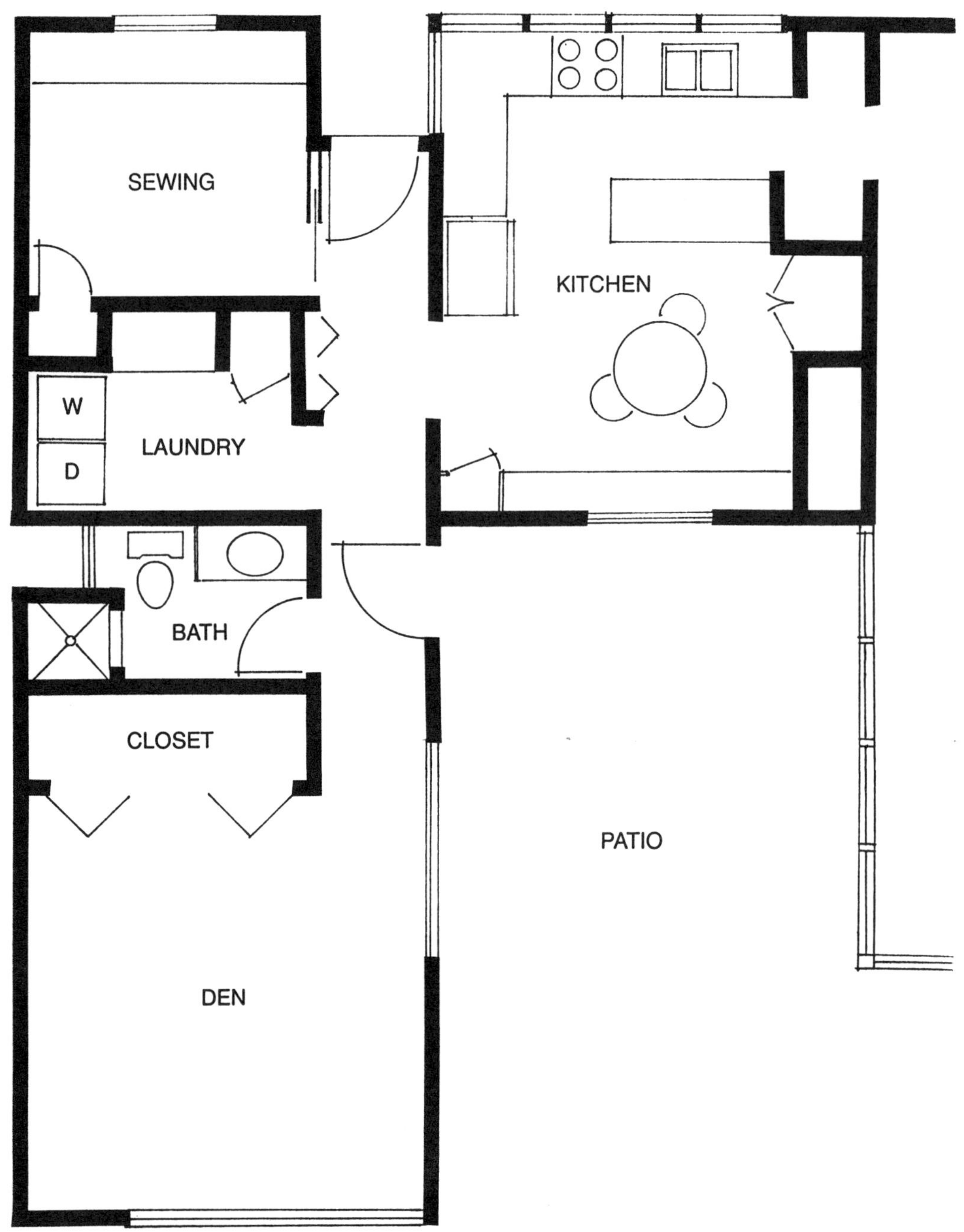

AFTER *The finished remodeling plan, developed to scale.*

method is OK. The important thing is to *stay loose* in your thinking at this stage. Put ideas down in rough form and don't worry about details.

STRUCTURE

If remodeling involves altering walls, floors, or roofs, you may have a structural change.

The structure of your home is that which holds it all together. Some you can see, like exposed beams, and some are hidden from view. Before planning your changes, you should become familiar with your house structure.

Know which walls are bearing and nonbearing. Determine what is holding up the floors and roof. Regardless of the size and shape of your home, *never guess* which walls are load bearing. A visual inspection of floor and roof joists, trusses, rafters, beams, etc., must be made. You can do this, but I strongly advise that you hire a consultant to assist you.

A construction expert can, at nominal cost, verify the size and location of structural elements. Like an x-ray of the body, the skeleton of the house must be revealed — at least that portion of the house affected by remodeling.

Bearing Walls and Partitions

You should assume that, at least, half the exterior walls are weight bearing walls. In some cases, they are all weight bearing. (Weight bearing or load bearing mean the same thing. Where the word *bearing* is used, in this book, it means weight bearing or load bearing.)

Interior partitions are another matter. You may have an assortment of bearing and nonbearing interior partitions. There are ways to find out which is which.

If the floor and roof structure is not visible, either from basement, attic, access panels in the ceiling, or crawl space under floors, then observation holes will have to be cut. A competent consultant can help decide where to make openings to get a clear picture of the existing structure.

Bearing walls are usually (but not always) at right angles to the trusses, joists, or beams. If the roof system is trusses, there may be enough visibility in the space above the ceiling to observe which walls are bearing.

With a flat roof, or a floor joist system, there usually is no space to see beyond the next joist or beam. In this case, many observation holes may have to be cut to know which walls carry the load.

Often, bearing will not occur over an entire partition, but only at one point where a beam is resting. At that point, there might be a supporting column inside the partition. Always verify.

NOTE: It's also possible that a partition is supporting part of a roof or floor load even though it was not originally intended to do so! That happens when joists or beams deflect (sag) enough to rest part of their weight on a partition below.

As you can see, possibilities with load bearing, and the house structure in general, are endless. Consult a professional.

MARK THE PLAN

Have a consultant mark a copy of your existing floor plan showing all bearing walls and partitions. It's a good idea to color them in red, to easily see through the tracing paper. Now, as you sketch, you will know immediately if you are affecting a bearing partition.

REMOVING A BEARING WALL OR PARTITION

If you must remove all, or part of, a bearing partition or outside wall, have it checked by a structural engineer. Ask for

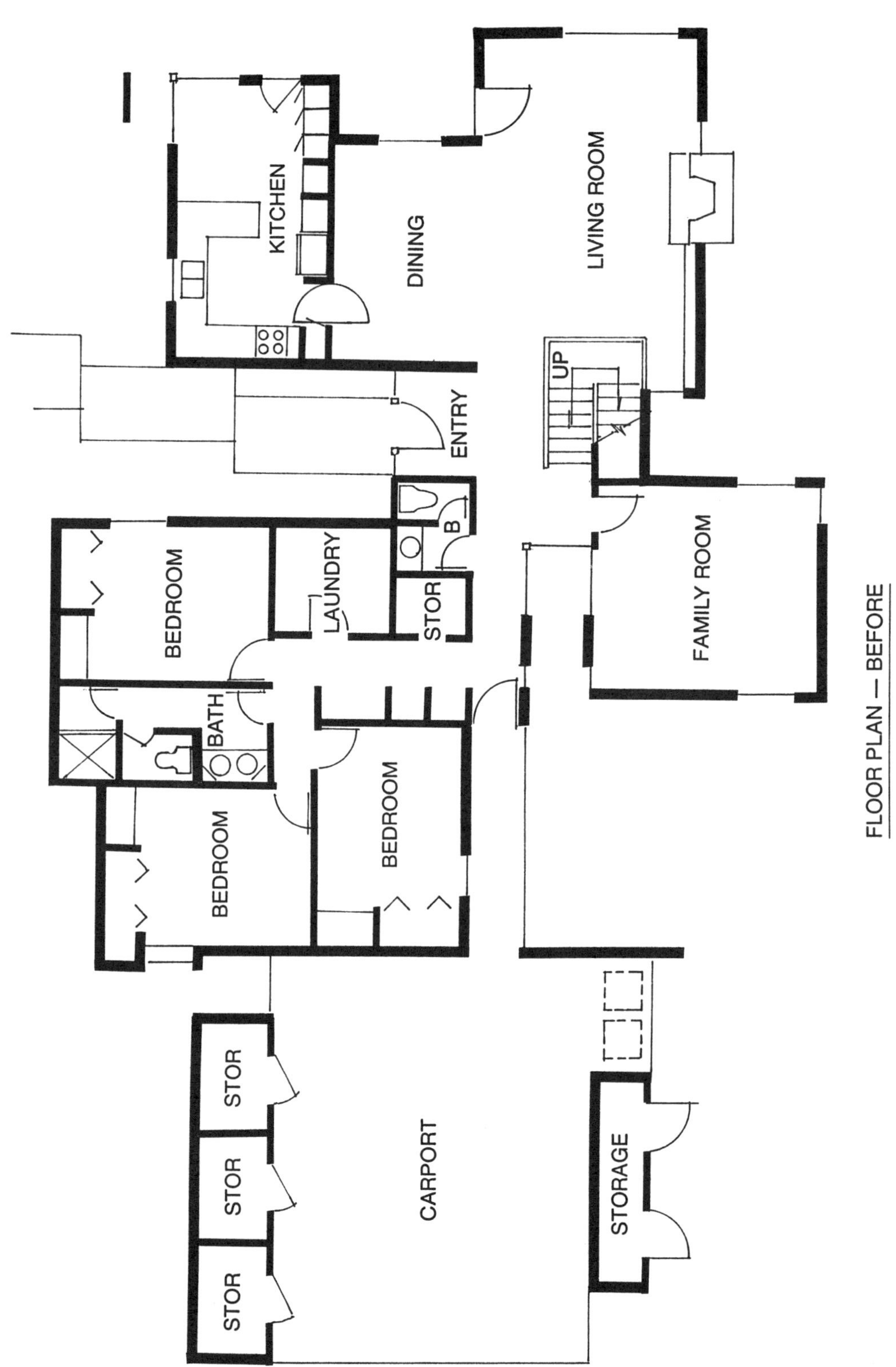

FLOOR PLAN — BEFORE

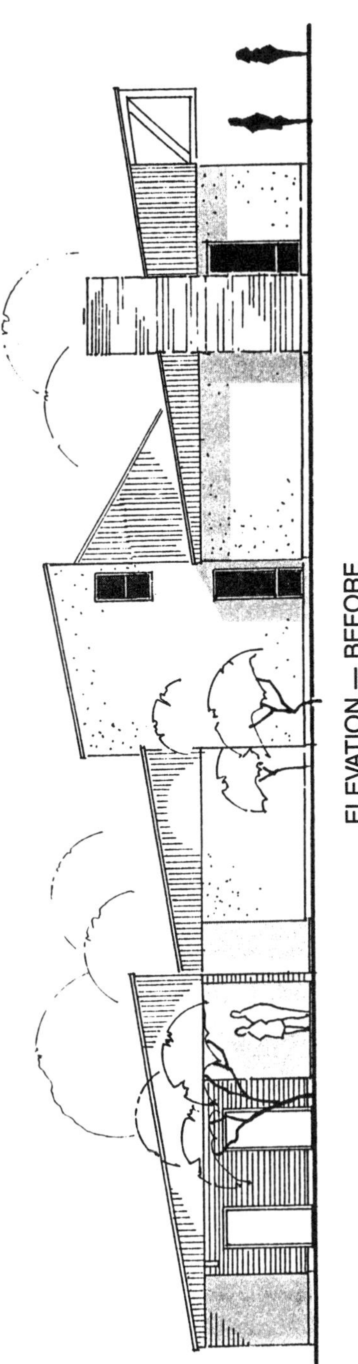

This plan and elevation of the house represent the home before remodeling was considered.

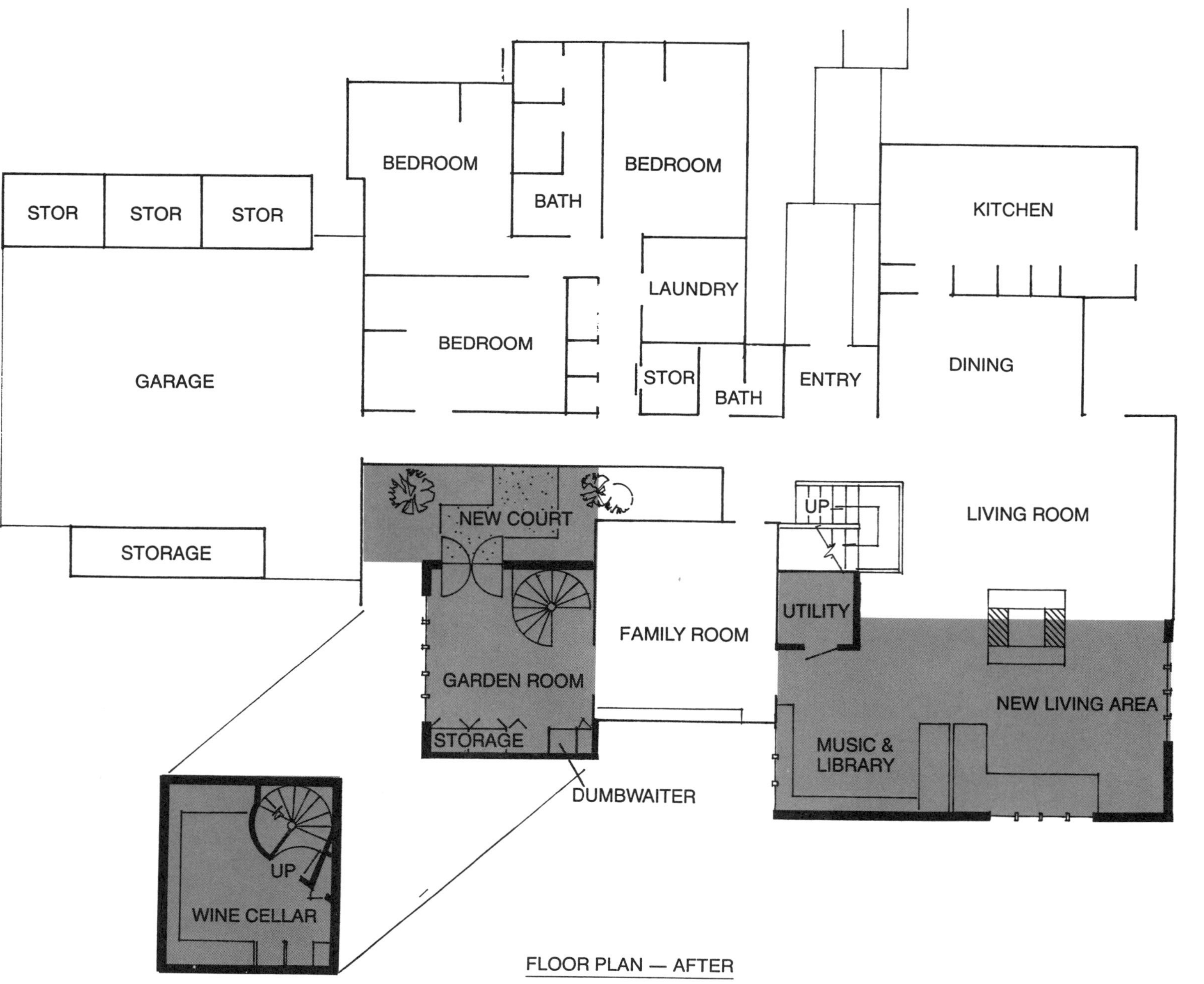
STOR
STOR
STOR
BEDROOM
BATH
BEDROOM
KITCHEN
LAUNDRY
BEDROOM
GARAGE
STOR
BATH
ENTRY
DINING
UP
NEW COURT
LIVING ROOM
STORAGE
UTILITY
FAMILY ROOM
GARDEN ROOM
NEW LIVING AREA
STORAGE
MUSIC &
LIBRARY
DUMBWAITER
UP
WINE CELLAR
FLOOR PLAN — AFTER

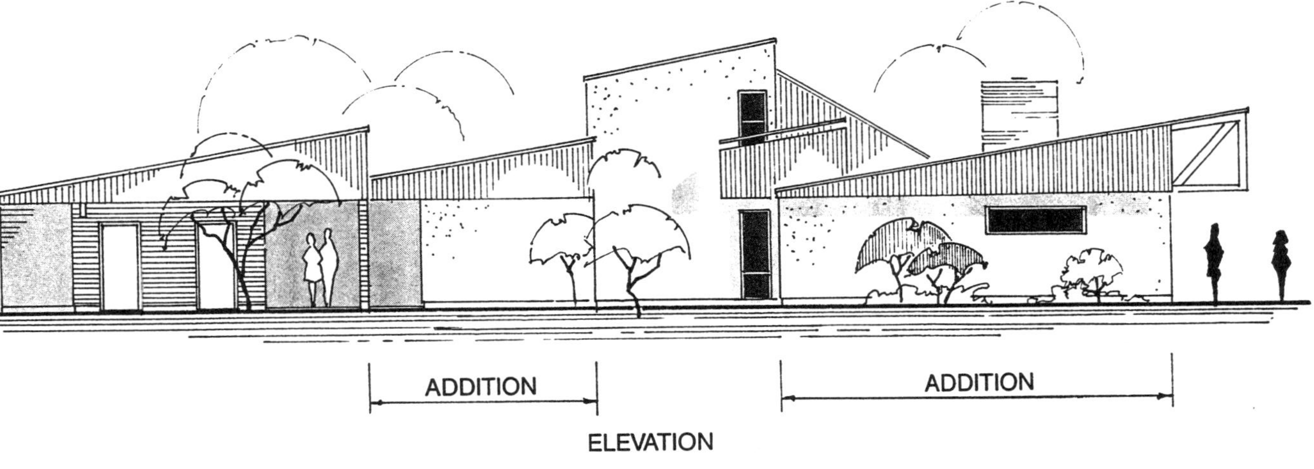

The owner's priorities for renovation were:

1. An addition to the living room space for free flow of large gatherings of people.

2. A wine cellar.

3. A smaller social space, near the wine cellar, for a small group of people.

The finished renovation plan and elevation shows that the architectural style was carried from the existing home to the addition.

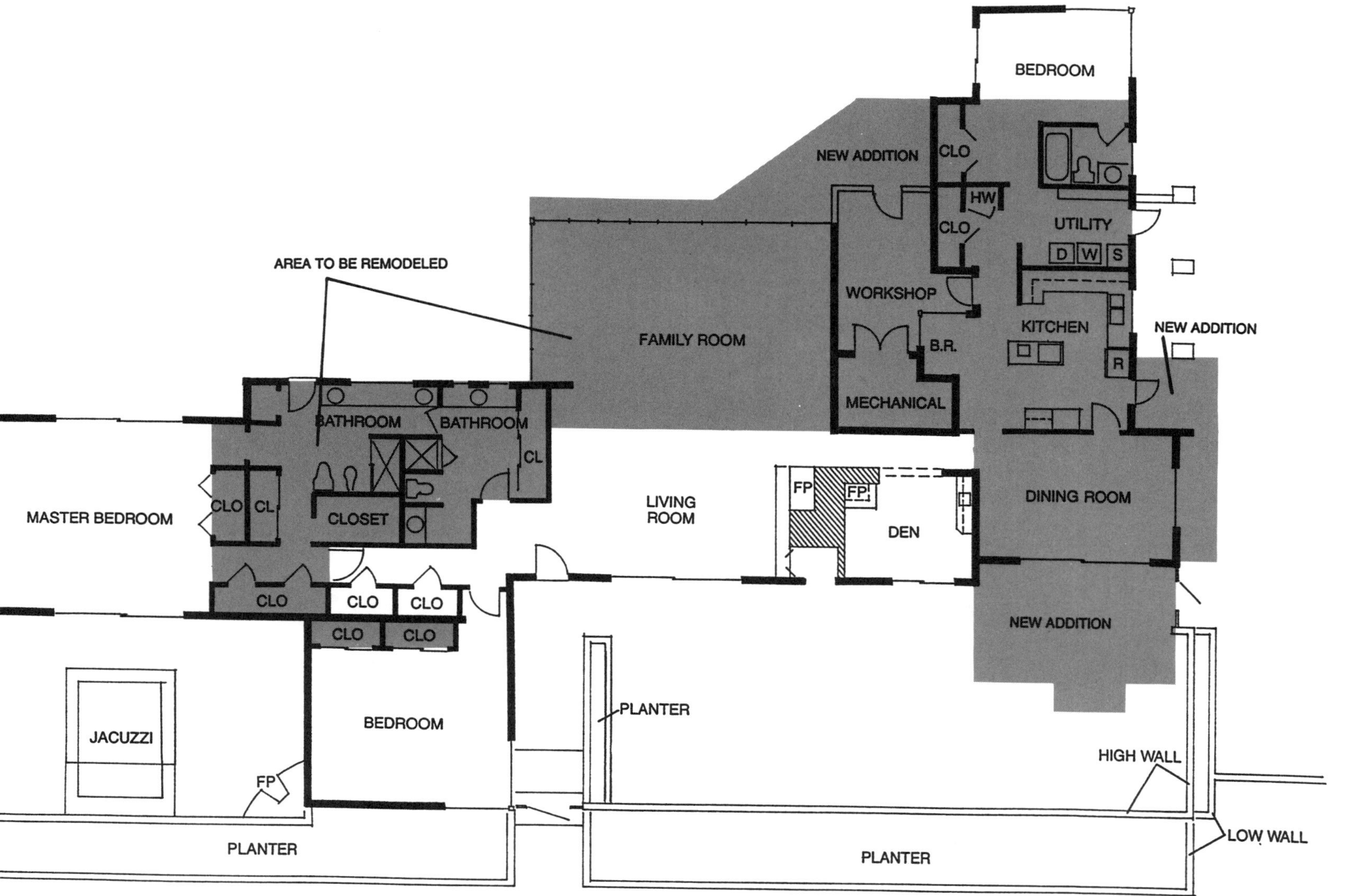

BEFORE *This existing house was the victim of a poorly done previous alteration.*

The mechanical equipment room and workshop separated the kitchen from family activity. The kitchen view was the carport.

Combined family and living area was large but there was no space available for separate activities. Also, the added-on family room had a ceiling height of 7 feet!

The master bath had no tub and was partly shared with bedroom no. 1. The closet arrangement was poor.

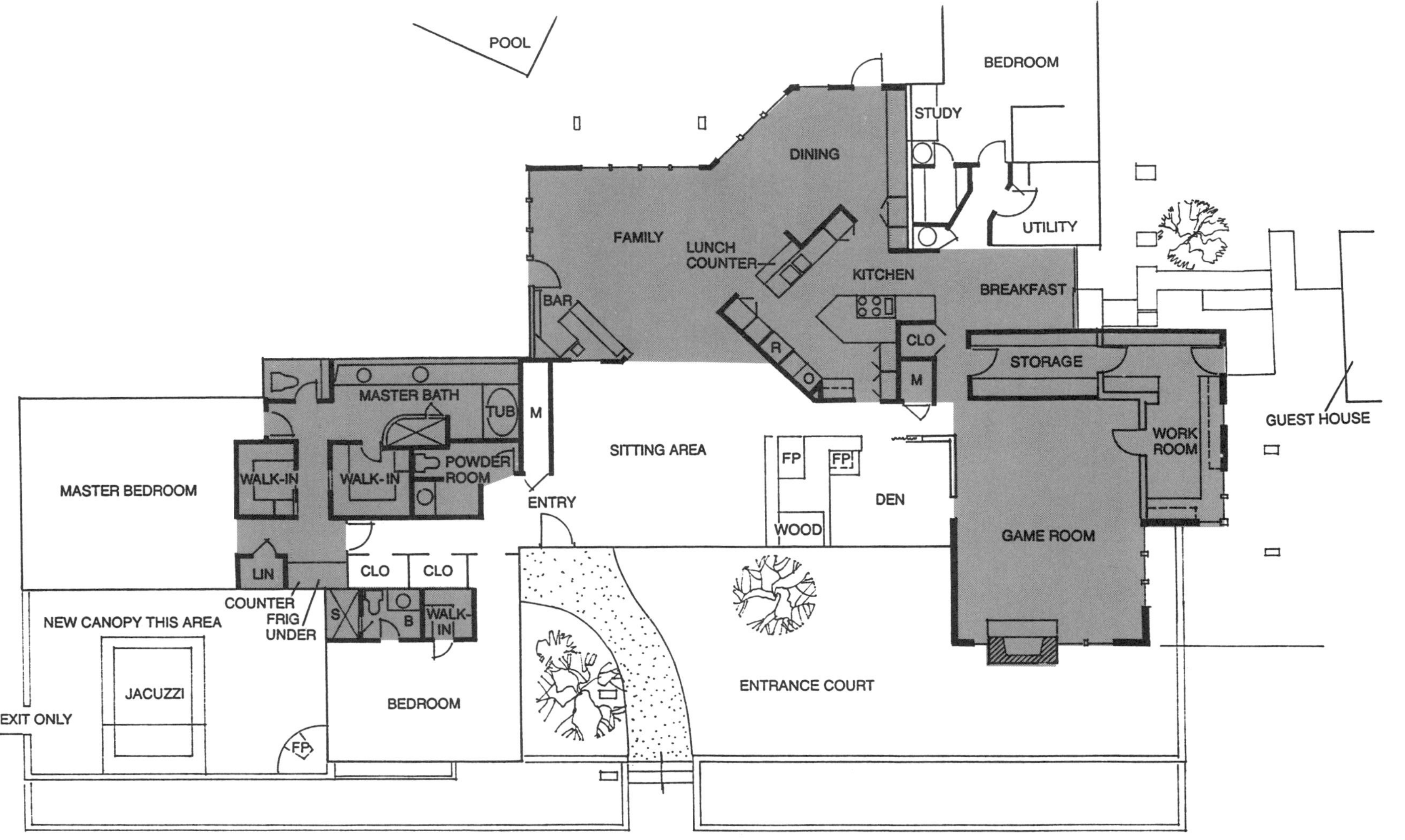

AFTER *The new kitchen is centrally located, looking across the family room to outside activities. A new dining area is adjacent. The new breakfast room looks out on a patio where the carport used to be. The master bath is re-done, a powder room was added, and new bath installed for Bedroom No. 1. A new game room, central storage room, and work/hobby room were added.*

This would be called a major *alteration project. Most areas of the house were affected.*

recommendations and the approximate expense to make the structural changes.

EXISTING UTILITIES

Find all existing utility locations. Water and sewer, electric wiring, and heating or air conditioning lines are likely occupants inside the walls. Electrical work may be little problem or expense, unless you change the service to the house or relocate panel boxes. If plumbing is involved, get cost estimates for the changes. Will it affect the operation of the water system? Ask if re-routing plumbing will mean removing part of the floor or ceiling. Getting answers early may influence your planning. Knowing the cost in advance helps to decide if it is good value, relative to the whole project.

MAKING THE CHOICE

Whenever possible try to make changes without affecting the structure. Improving your house without removing *any* partitions is, of course, the easiest. Next in line, is to remove only nonbearing partitions. Choice is affected by appearance, expense, complications, and overall value to the remodeling. If, to achieve what you want, you must replace structural elements with another structural system, retain a professional.

ADDITIONS

Chapter 9 is devoted to additions and should be reviewed if you plan to expand.

For most additions, I recommend you retain a professional. The value is many fold: (a) To verify and calculate the structure; (b) To help insure aesthetic success. (An addition should either retain or improve the appearance of the house); (c) To assist in more efficient use of your funds.

THE FOUNDATION

Much remodeling does not affect the foundation. Changes that do affect the foundation include: adding bearing walls or columns, adding an underground space, or enlarging the house.

Foundation work has its own special concerns, such as: check the soil condition, verify site drainage, calculate load bearing weight, and others. Seek expert advice with foundations.

COST CONTROL

Keys to cost control in remodeling are: (1) *know exactly where you're going before starting construction*; (2) *get good, firm bids and material prices*; (3) *avoid changes and "extras" during construction.* Simple as the above sounds, often the opposite happens on all three points.

Saving Money with Construction Drawings

The *value* of complete construction drawings is that the project is *first constructed on paper.* On paper is the place to develop the work, step by step, showing what has to be done. On paper is the place to make changes and refine ideas in the process. Changes made during actual construction can be *expensive*!

COMPLETE DRAWINGS MEAN BETTER BIDS

With complete drawings and specifications, a contractor can provide a bid for total cost. Without such drawings, a good contractor is reluctant to give a firm bid. He may prefer, instead, to work on a "cost plus" basis.

"Cost plus" means that you pay the contractor for labor and materials as costs occur, plus a fee for coordinating the work. "Cost plus" is really an open-ended agreement. You will not know the cost until the final bill arrives. It is not impossible for that amount to be double what you "guessed" it might cost!

If a contractor agrees to give you a guaranteed cost, without plans, it's based on his best guess. Built into the guess will be a substantial amount for unknown conditions that *might* occur during construction. He can't be blamed for trying to protect himself — but that's hardly a way to get the most for your money.

In addition, without plans both you and the contractor are relying on memory of conversations, or a brief written agreement describing the work to be done. These brief agreements seldom include everything. That leaves you open for disputes about the extent of the work to be done for the price quoted.

Disputes can occur about things unthought of. For instance, the type of door hardware (price varies greatly), door material (wood or metal), door type (hollow core or solid core). You may have assumed he would use 6″ or 8″ of insulation in a roof addition, but he assumed 4″. He might furnish silver colored aluminum windows and you wanted bronze colored. The list goes on.

Misplaced assumptions can cause problems. You may assume the contractor will do everything exactly as was done with the existing construction. The contractor may not observe all existing conditions, or may simply do what is less costly. The possible areas for conflict are endless. They can include: windows (double or single glazed), pipe (metal or plastic), thickness of materials, types of plumbing and electrical fixtures, finish materials for floor, walls, and ceiling, changes to the heating or air conditioning system for optimum comfort and efficiency, etc., etc.

Even *with* drawings and specifications, dispute is possible. Without them, the possibilities are vast.

DOING THE BUILDING YOURSELF

If you plan to do the construction yourself, drawings are equally important. An experienced builder will know how to plan the job and anticipate what is coming next. You won't have that advantage, and without drawings to guide you, time and money are wasted.

Beginning the Construction Drawings

When satisfied that your rough sketches represent what you want, it's time to begin accurate drawings for construction.

Construction drawings are accomplished many ways: Doing them yourself, hiring a draftsman to assist you, or, as I recommend, retaining a professional. Let's first explore doing-it-yourself.

DOING THEM YOURSELF

Doing the drawings for construction is a step-by-step process and you should not be in a hurry. You will need tracing paper and a few tools such as a triangle, drafting tape, leadholder, straight edge (T square or parallel rule), and an architectural scale. (An architectural scale is like a ruler with divisions in feet and inches for drawing to proper dimensions.) Don't forget erasers! A blue-print shop or art supply store has these materials.

The complete learning process for drawing plans and construction details is a book in itself. Many have been published. They can be found in your public library or book store. A superficial explanation here would be of little benefit.

Another learning source is a school, such as a community college. Reading books and taking courses in construction drafting is a beginning for the learning process.

The discussion here assumes you have gained sufficient knowledge of construction and drafting to produce the drawings.

DON'T BE IN A RUSH

Remember, the drawings for construction are detailed instructions to the builder.

Make them as complete as possible. Think through all parts of the construction affected by a remodeling change.

For example, when you remove an interior wall it affects both floor and ceiling finish. That portion of the disturbed floor and ceiling will have to match the rest. Often, it means redoing the entire area. Instructions are so given on the drawings.

Think about finish surfaces. Should you touch-up or repair and repaint the entire space? In fact, while the work is being done, you may want to repaint the whole house. Make the decision a part of the instructions on the drawings — to be included in the bid and construction contract.

REMEMBER DESIGN

As you progress with construction drawings, remember that the final product, when built, should function well *and look good.* Don't count on the builder for that. His job is to build, not to decide what to build.

Be specific in naming electrical and plumbing fixtures. Select them for appearance, function, and cost. If you want a color other than the standard, make note of that so you won't face an add-on charge.

USE CHECK LISTS

When doing the drawings, keep notes on things to include. If you think of something for a different part of the job, write it down for later reference.

Refer to the chapter check lists for items to include on the drawings. For instance, you could forget to add a light in a certain area or special storage cubicle in the kitchen.

A thorough set of drawings is your best friend through the construction process.

ECONOMY WITH STANDARD MATERIALS

When planning room sizes and materials, keep in mind that most panel type materials come in a standard 4-feet by 8-feet.

Drafting equipment and supplies.

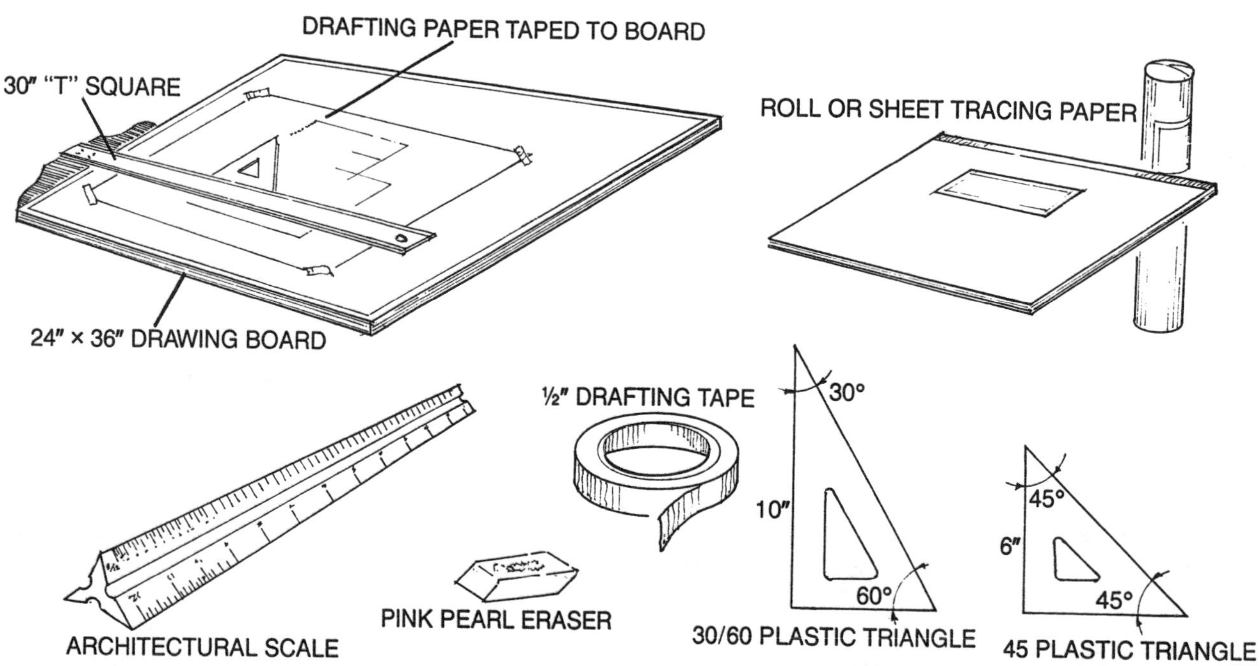

Gypsum board (drywall), masonite, plywood (rough and finish paneling) are some of these materials. Many materials for ceilings and floors are made to be compatible with those dimensions.

However, don't cling to modular sizes as being *a requirement,* if they don't meet your needs. Panel materials are available in other sizes. Most material can be cut to fit any condition. Windows and doors are custom made to virtually any size. It's all a matter of *relative* economy.

Building economy relates to *material* quantity and *installation* time. The larger the project, the more savings realized when planning with standard, or modular, material sizes. With a small renovation relative savings realized by strict adherence to modular building materials is less.

CONSTRUCTION TERMINOLOGY

Become familiar with construction symbols and terminology. If you do the drawings yourself, you will use them. If someone else does the drawings, it will help you understand them better.

Choosing Materials

Materials that you plan to use should be chosen early. Those affecting appearance should be chosen while completing the design. Others can be selected as construction drawings progress.

COMPATIBILITY

Make a survey of *existing* finish materials. Check windows, doors, and hardware as well as the floor, wall, ceiling, and exterior finishes. Select new materials for compatibility with

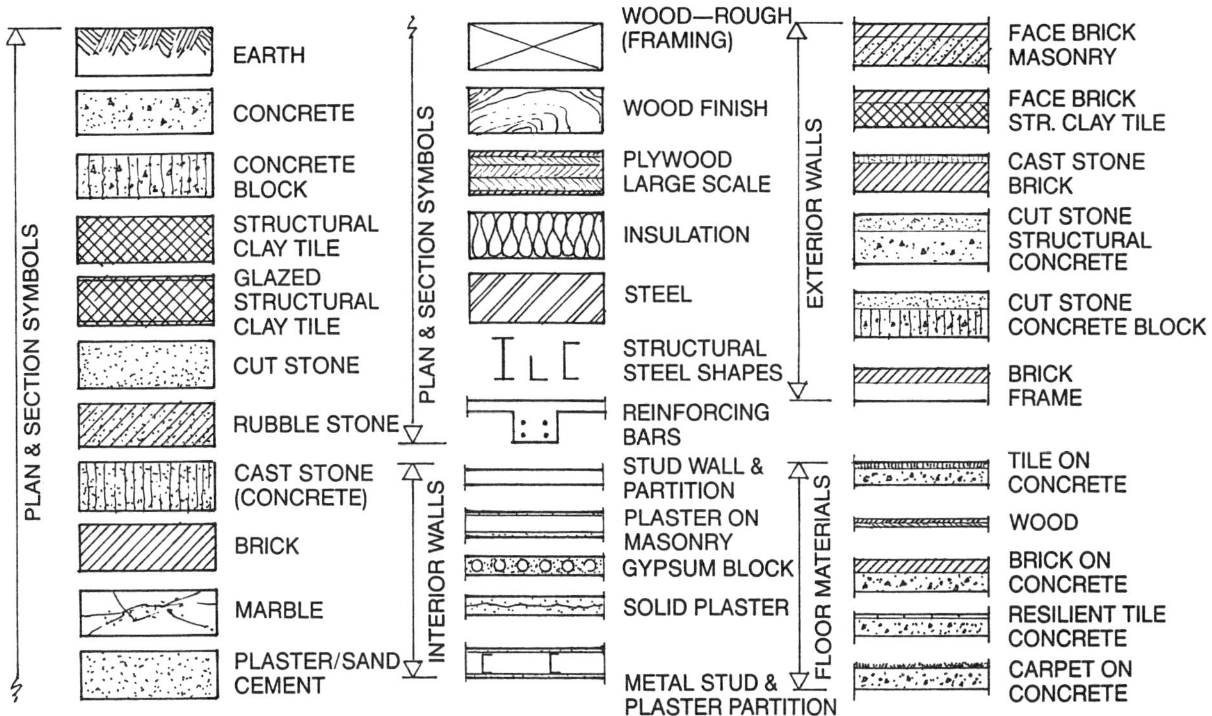

ARCHITECTURAL SYMBOLS
PLAN & SECTION MATERIAL SYMBOLS

the remodeling scheme *and* the existing home. Materials foreign to those existing will stick out like a sore thumb and be immediately recognized as a remodel job or add-on.

Don't let your renovation jump out and say, "Hi, I'm the new addition!"

Compatibility doesn't mean you should avoid innovations in materials and methods. On the contrary, use them, when practical, but select new shapes, textures, and colors to be comfortable with the old.

Interior Surface Materials

When choosing materials, your own experience is the natural point of departure. But don't stop there. Look around and ask questions.

If you see an interesting material in another home, ask about it. Check building supply stores for product information. Every surface has its own special criteria for selection.

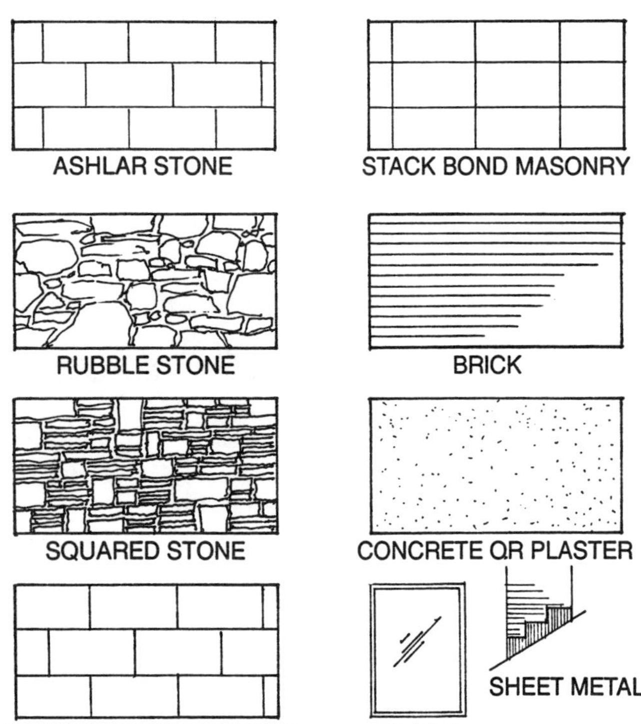

ARCHITECTURAL SYMBOLS
ELEVATION MATERIAL REPRESENTATIONS

Lived-in areas need good looking finishes that will last. Floors receive everything from stone to plush carpeting. Wall materials include: textured drywall for painting, smooth drywall covered with paper or fabric, wood products, ceramics, mirrors, and many others. Ceiling materials include wood, metal, drywall, and tile.

Kitchen surfaces are made for appearance, durability, and easy maintenance. Your choices are many.

Quality control varies. Check with previous product users. Know the pros and cons before making a selection.

Cost is a factor, but weigh *relative value* to achieve a balance between separate materials cost and total cost. Labor installation costs are so high that *using materials of marginal quality is not cost effective.*

Labor costs vary widely for installation of different materials on the same surface. *Check installation costs before selecting materials.*

The following pages contain guidelines for selection of various materials.

Flooring Materials

A good floor finish complements the space while satisfying your taste, work habits, and life style.

RESILIENT FLOORING

Resilient flooring is the most common, and least expensive of all applied finishes. It's often used in kitchen, bath, utility, and work/hobby areas.

CHOICES: The economical choice is the 12 inch square tile. A more expensive choice is sheet vinyl, which has a softer feel and usually requires little maintenance.

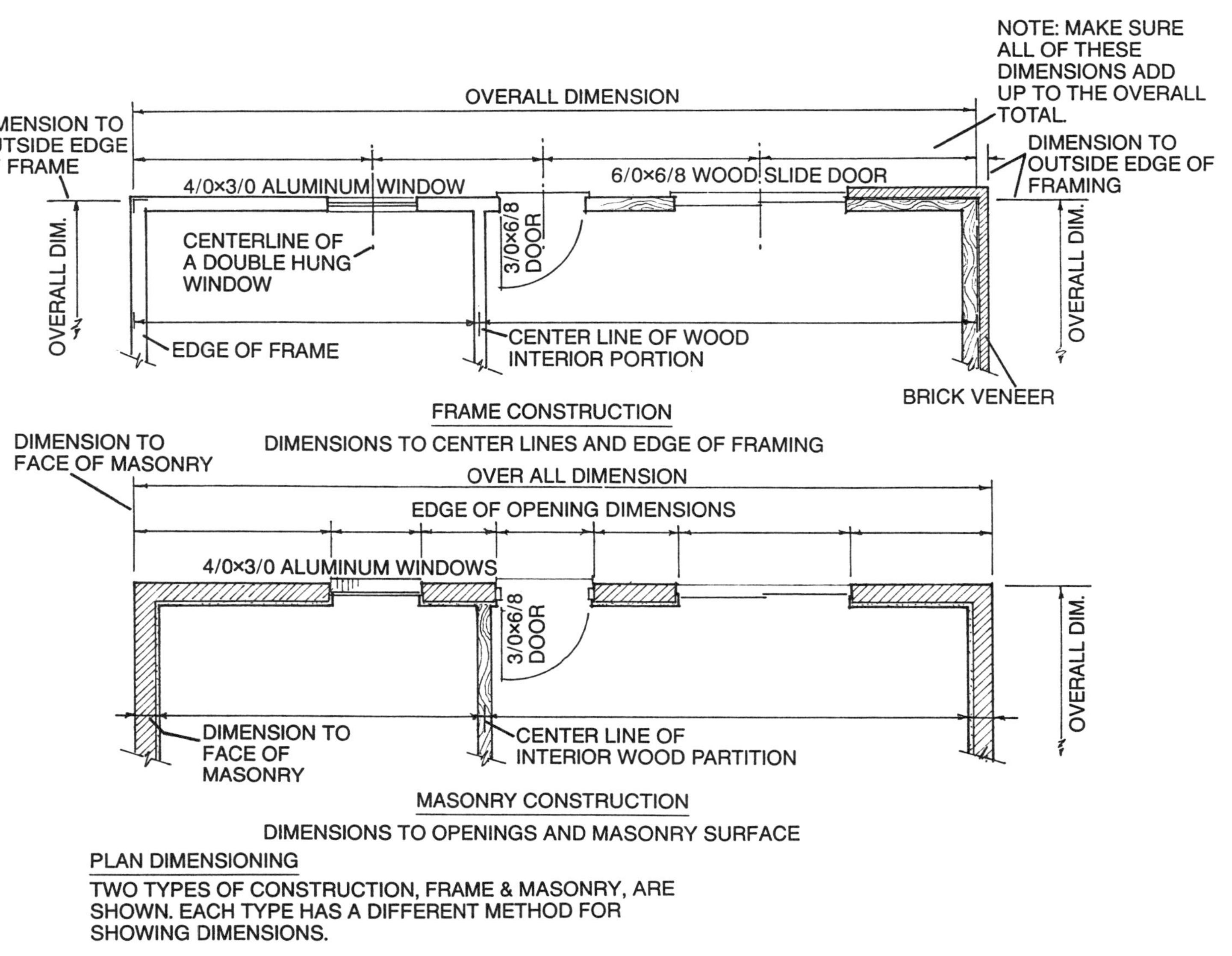

PLAN DIMENSIONING

TWO TYPES OF CONSTRUCTION, FRAME & MASONRY, ARE SHOWN. EACH TYPE HAS A DIFFERENT METHOD FOR SHOWING DIMENSIONS.

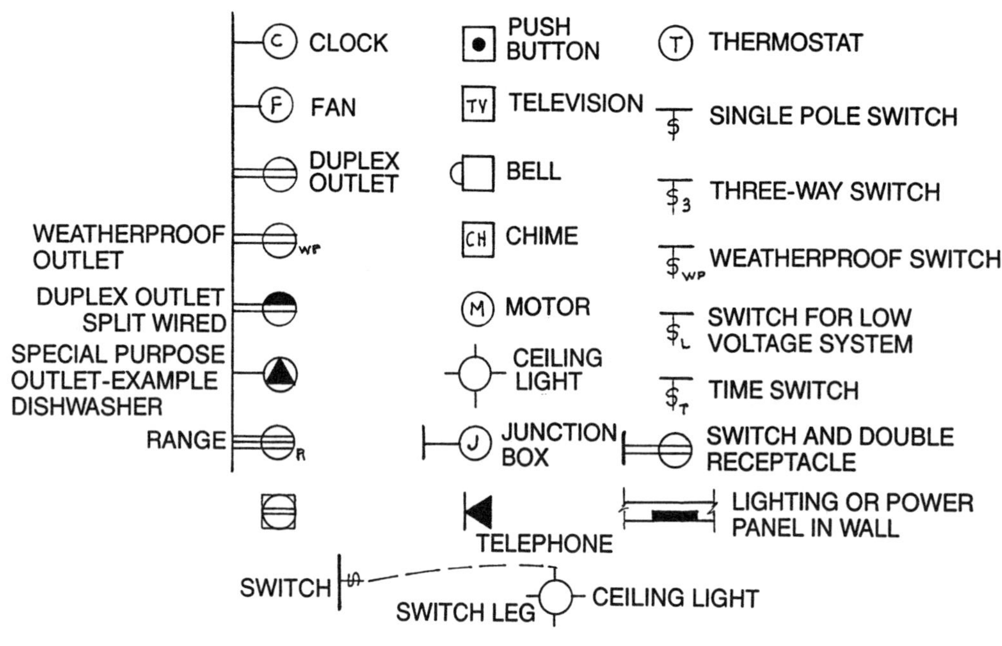

ELECTRICAL PLAN SYMBOLS

INSTALLATION: Typically, the 12 inch square resilient tiles install easily. Purchase a few extra tiles for replacement in case of future damage. Sheet vinyl requires careful planning to install properly.

MAINTENANCE: Sheet vinyl, which has fewer seams, is normally easiest to maintain. The coved base (turning the flooring up the wall) simplifies cleaning at the junction of floor and wall.

COLOR SELECTION: Manufacturers frequently add or drop colors to meet changing consumer demands. It may require a search to get beyond bland colors and designs.

CERAMIC TILE

Ceramic tile comes in a matte (unglazed) finish or a glazed finish. It resists stains, burns, and marring. Glazed tile does not require finishing. Color selection is good.

That's the good news. The bad news is higher cost and low level of comfort. Standing on it for some time can be tiring. Also, a breakable object dropped on this floor will probably do just that . . . break! Ceramic floors are cold to the touch in winter.

BRICK AND STONE

Brick and stone, like ceramic tile, provide a good looking surface, but share the same disadvantages of hardness and expense. They do not clean as easily. Consult a specialist regarding the sealing and maintenance of the material chosen.

WOOD

Wood floors create a nice feeling. With careful selection and good maintenance, they can be used in most areas. Wood flooring was once used in all areas of many early American homes.

Some question the practicality of wood flooring in the kitchen. Its durability is increased by the use of a chemical sealer. Sealers increase resistance to water and staining, but, being a surface finish, they can scratch. The appearance of chemically sealed

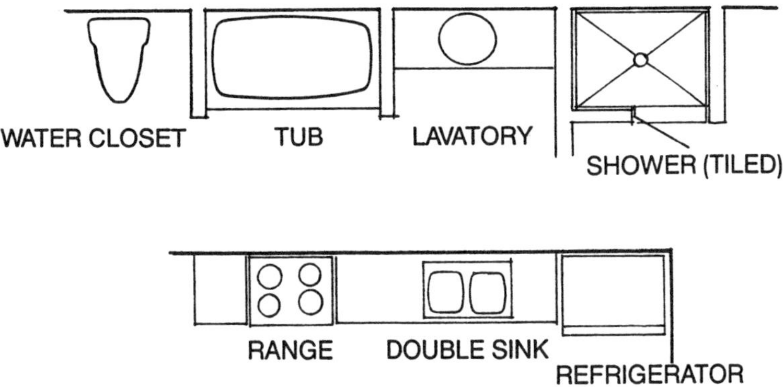

PLUMBING AND APPLIANCE SYMBOLS

wood will be different than wood finished with a natural penetrating seal and stain. See samples of each before deciding on the finish.

CARPETING

Carpeting is the most common floor finish for living areas. It offers the greatest choice of colors and textures and provides a feeling of comfort at a reasonable price.

Select carpet for economic balance with the house. A modest home can receive a modestly priced carpet that is good looking and well made. A high-priced home may have carpeting costing ten times as much. This wide cost range, not available in most other flooring materials, is partly responsible for the universal appeal of carpeting.

ACOUSTICS: Airborne-sound absorption is another valuable quality. Carpeting can be laboratory tested for sound absorption and assigned a Noise Reduction Coefficient (NRC) rating. For instance: Most carpet (without cushion underneath) with a 1/8″ pile has an NRC of about .15. Carpets with 7/16″ pile can have an NRC of about .40. Pile height does make a big difference. A cushion, or pad, also adds to sound absorption.

IN THE KITCHEN

Carpet in the kitchen provides warmth and quiet and is easy on the feet. It comes in rolls or carpet tiles. If stains and wear spots are a concern, consider carpet tiles, which are replaceable. For durability and maintenance, limit selection to short pile, one-level carpet.

CARPET FIBERS

Many fibers are used, some of which are listed below. Be aware that fiber properties are relative and the information listed here is not true in all cases at all times. In addition, changes and innovations are constantly being made. See a reputable dealer for the latest accurate information on carpeting and fibers.

WOOL: The oldest popular carpet fiber seems to be wool. It's the one fiber in wide use which is a natural material. Known for its appearance, durability, and cleanability, it's available with built-in anti-static properties and moth-proofing.

ACRYLIC: Acrylic fibers have high resistance to soil and stains, easy cleanability, good color fastness, and resiliency. The fibers are excellent in taking dyes in a wide spectrum of color with deep brilliancy. (In my view, that

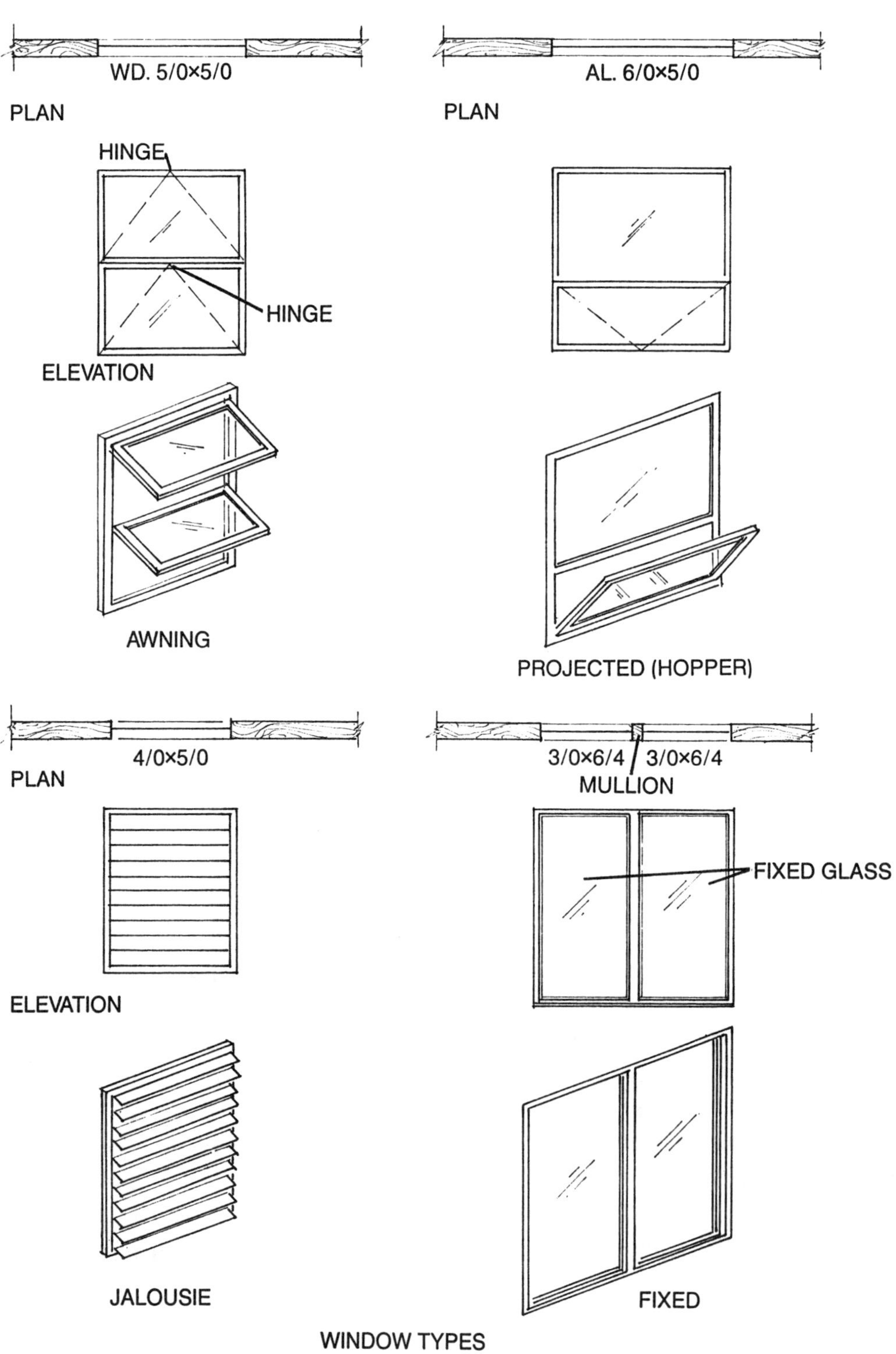

WINDOW TYPES

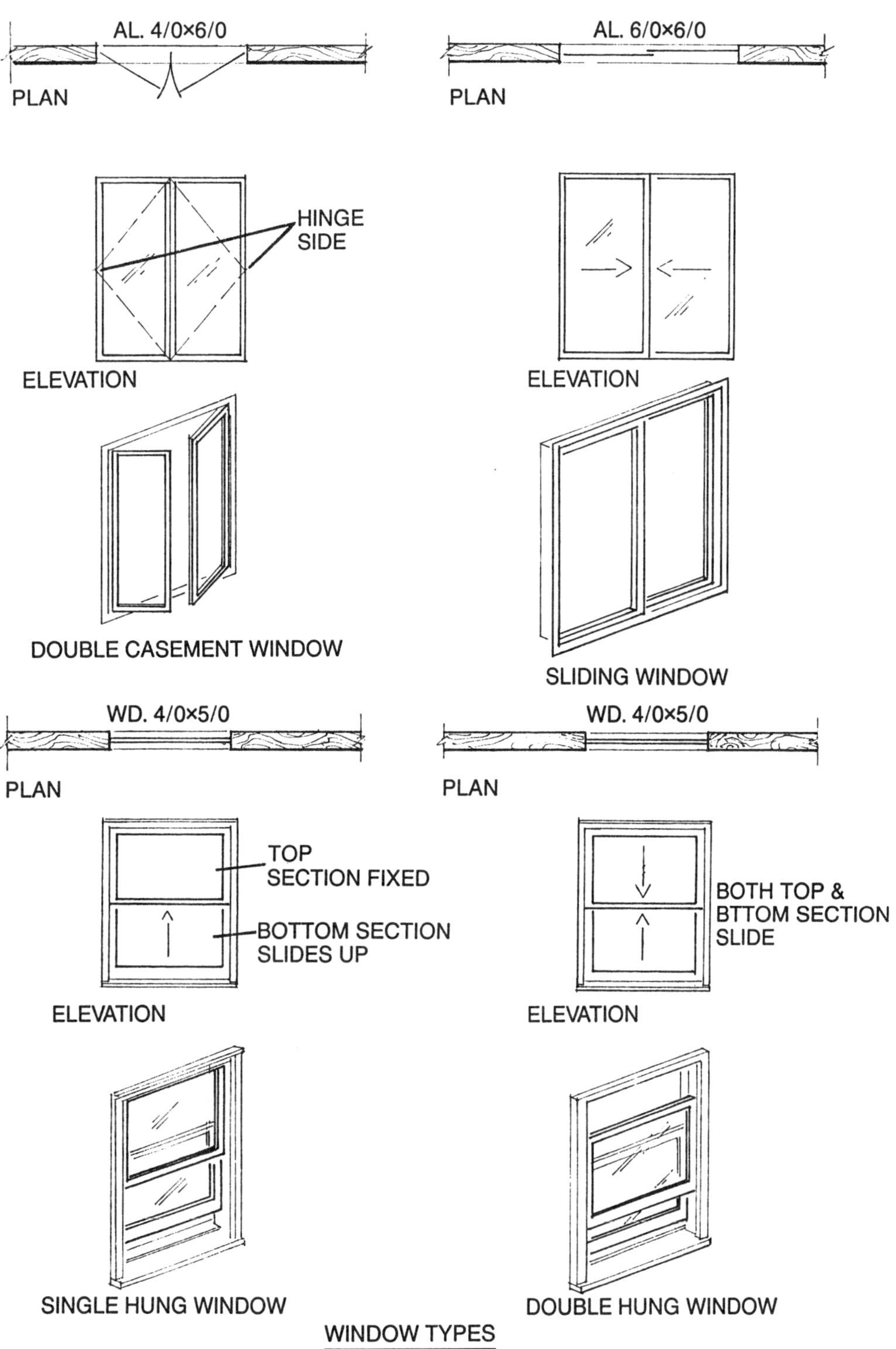

WINDOW TYPES

has been a consistent trait with acrylic fibers.) Industry claims are: non-allergenic, mildew-proof and mothproof.

NYLON: Nylon is considered the most abrasion resistant. It has high resistance to crushing. Other factors include: cleanability, dye-ability, stain resistance, soil hiding properties, and color-retention. Industry claims are: non-allergenic and mothproof.

Counter and Vanity Tops

There is no "perfect" counter top material. That is, if you define perfect as: "Resistant to all forms of abuse, resistant to extremes of temperature, resilient, non-absorptive, economical, and beautiful to look at."

There are, however, several good "imperfect" counter top materials.

LAMINATED PLASTIC

Laminated plastic is by far the most popular counter top. It's economical, durable, attractive, and resistant to moisture and most mild chemicals. Laminates are bonded to a wood subsurface which provides more resiliency than ceramic tile or marble. Color selection is good. Disadvantages, with most, are susceptibility to scratching and damage caused by heat. Counter inserts are available for cutting, chopping, and hot pot parking.

CERAMIC TILE

Ceramic tile offers high resistance to general abuse and heat. Color selection is good. The overall appearance is a customized look.

Disadvantages are higher cost, the hard surface, and higher maintenance with the grout joints. Glass breakage is more likely and the noise level, working on the surface, is high.

MARBLE AND OTHER PRODUCTS

Real marble is an elegant material, but is easily stained and scratched.

Synthetic marble is not quite the same look, but is more stain-resistant and practical. It's often used in bathrooms, but serves in some kitchens. Other durable synthetics are available in the market place and should be reviewed carefully in relation to your needs.

WOOD

Wood counters have a comfortable look and are appropriate for many kitchens. Be aware that burn, stain, and cut marks will change the counter's appearance in time. Maintenance is required. Hygiene is a consideration about which you should satisfy yourself.

Your Final Selection

Physical characteristics, cost, and ease of cleaning are factors in your final selection. Beyond that, think about the character of the material as it relates to other materials in the room and adjacent spaces.

Sound Control

Porous, thick, soft, and rough describe materials used for sound absorption. Dense, thin, hard, and smooth describe materials that bounce sound around a room.

ROOM SHAPES AFFECT SOUND

A small square room with smooth, hard surfaces may produce sound reverberation even with normal conversations.

Varying dimensions and wall angles will help prevent sound waves from bouncing back and forth.

Exterior Surface Materials

An exterior surface is normally more expensive to refinish than a like inside area. Changing the color with new paint is one thing, but to change the surface material itself can be costly. Weigh the value received against the cost.

WALLS

Some changes are high-yield. For instance, if you have masonry walls you never liked, they can be covered with stucco. Or, conversely, a plaster finish over existing brick walls can be sand blasted away to create a handsome masonry wall.

ROOFING

Similar examples exist with roofing. Other factors come into play, however, such as the weight of a new material.

Materials affecting the weight on a roof structure include roofing, ceiling, and equipment such as air conditioning, heating, plumbing, and electrical. Installing a heavier material can over stress the roof structure.

For example, to change from a lightweight composition roof shingle to clay tile is a substantial addition in weight. Have a structural engineer check the roof structure before making such a change.

Cost of roofing materials varies widely. A composition shingle roof can be less than half the cost of a tile or wood shingle roof.

FLAT ROOFS

Resurfacing on a so-called flat roof (many "flat roofs" have a pitch of 1/4 inch to 1/2 inch per foot) is done commonly to prevent leaking, or to improve energy conservation. Consult a roofing expert for recommendations.

If you live in a hot climate, ask about a finish coating to increase sun reflection. Some roofing materials will substantially increase the insulation value.

ADDITIONS

Special considerations apply when you add-on. Additions influence the aesthetic appearance of your home. Please review Chapter 9, ADDITIONS, if you do plan to enlarge your home.

Listing the Materials

As you progress with drawings, keep a list of all materials selected. If you hire a contractor, a materials list helps: (1) In cost estimating to provide an accurate bid; (2) To avoid disagreements during construction about materials included in the guaranteed bid.

HOW TO LIST MATERIALS AND SPECIFY THEIR USE

There are two common methods to list materials and describe their use: (1) on the drawings, include as much information as practical; (2) provide a separate list and specify, if necessary, how materials should be used.

ON THE DRAWINGS

Assume you are adding on and the drawings include a cross section view of the addition. (A cross section is a vertically cut view showing how the structure is assembled, from foundation to roof.) It will show all materials, such as: concrete footings, wood floors, outside and inside wall construction, ceiling material, roof rafters, sheathing, and finish roofing materials. Each item is be noted on the drawing to indicate:

a. Type of material (i.e., random length oak hardwood flooring).
b. Size of material (i.e., 3/4" thick by 3 1/4" wide).
c. How the material is attached (i.e., type of nails, fasteners, glue, etc.)

A SEPARATE LIST

It's often cumbersome to include *all* verbal information on the drawings. Separate documents make it easier to specify remaining materials and their use. The information

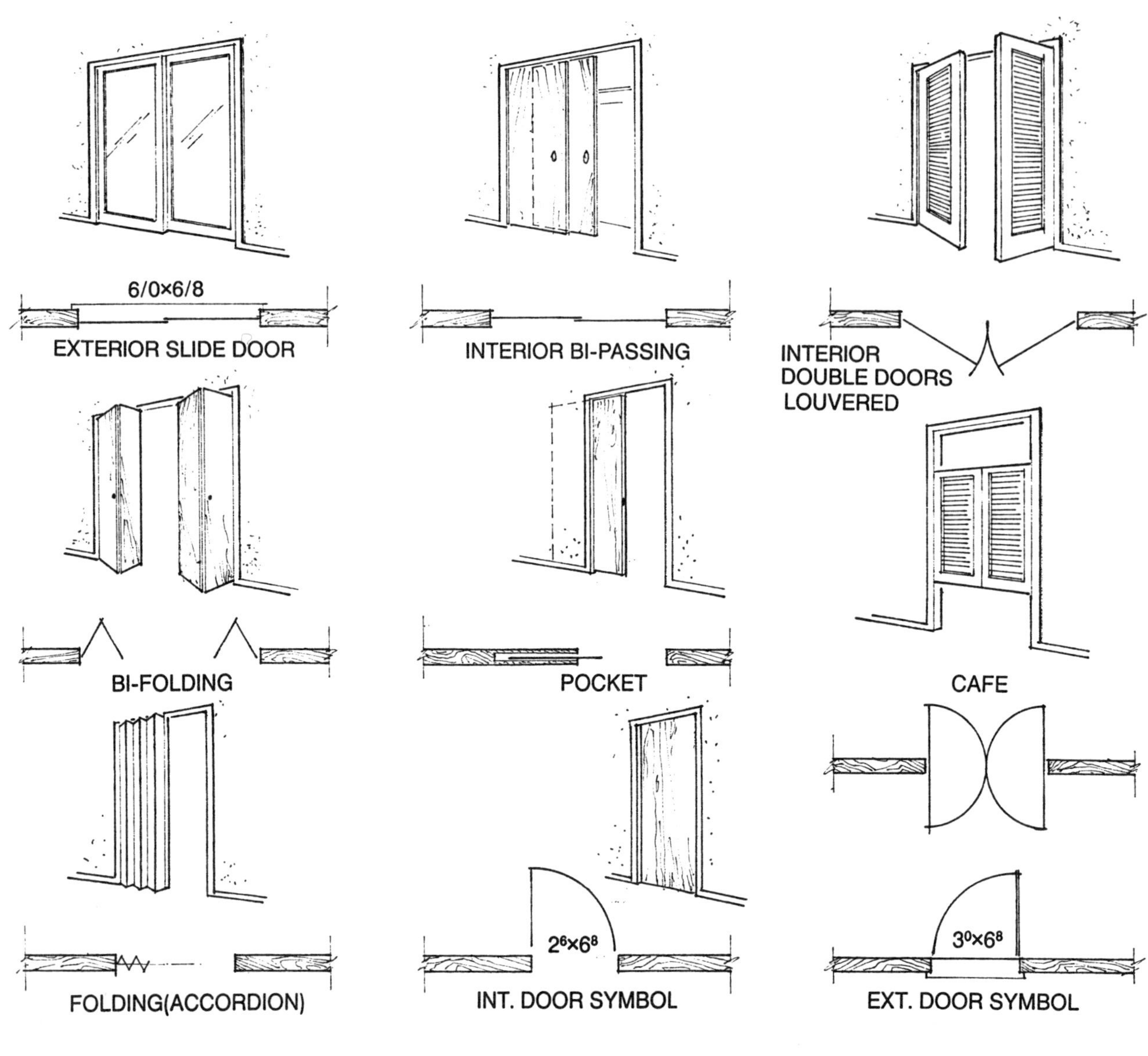

DOOR SYMBOLS

and instructions become a supplement to and binding part of the drawings.

Below is a sample list. Add to it as required for your project. Printed "materials and specifications" forms should be available at your local home builder's association or FHA office.

Example Specification and Materials List

NOTE: *The following are not intended to be a complete list or instructions. They are examples only.* Remember, the list is to include all information not shown on the drawings.

1. Demolition Work: Note material, fixtures or appliances to be saved or salvaged by the contractor.
2. Foundation and Earth Work: Call for termite treatment, ask for weed free top soil, etc.
3. Asphalt Paving: Call for minimum thickness — usually 2″ asphalt on top of 4″ aggregate base course. Describe surface finish.
4. Concrete: Describe thickness, strength, texture, color, etc.
5. Masonry: What kind, what color, what texture, etc.
6. Miscellaneous Metal: Call for materials, such as copper, aluminum, etc. Describe their location, such as fireplace hood, metal gutters, etc.
7. Carpentry and Millwork: Describe types of wood for various applications (i.e.: exterior finish wood at edge of roof, window sills, and jambs, etc.) If you want clear wood of a certain species, specify it. Interior wood trim can range from white pine to oak. Wood floor cost varies with wood type, thickness, and pattern. Call for grade and thickness.
8. Cabinets: Describe what you want.
9. Insulation: What kind, where, and how much. Specify the "R" value. "R" value is a measure of materials resistance to heat flow.
10. Roofing: What kind, color, brand, etc.
11. Caulking and Sealants: Specify that you want all joints and intersections of materials to be tightly caulked and sealed for weather protection. Find the best type available and call for it.
12. Doors: Specify the material, thickness, design, and finish.
13. Hardware: For doors and cabinetry. Cost varies widely, so specify what you want.
14. Glass: For windows and doors. Do you want single glazed, double or triple glazed? It can be solar gray, bronze, reflective, etc. Tempered safety glass should be used as required by local and Uniform Building Codes. I recommend its use throughout.
15. Plaster and Stucco: Check out various systems available in your area. Specify thickness, texture, and color. Color can be painted on or mixed in with the plaster.
16. Interior Finishes for ceilings, walls, baseboards, floors, etc. What materials, thickness, textures, colors, etc.
17. Painting: Type of paint, how many coats, colors, etc.
18. Appliances: Select early for exact size, color, etc.
19. Electrical: Type and finish of fixtures, switches, etc.
20. Plumbing: Type and finish of fixtures. Type of pipe (copper, for instance), size of hot water tank, etc.
21. Heating, Ventilating, and Air Conditioning (HVAC): Specify type and size of equipment to be in the bid price. Drawings to show separate zones or thermostats.

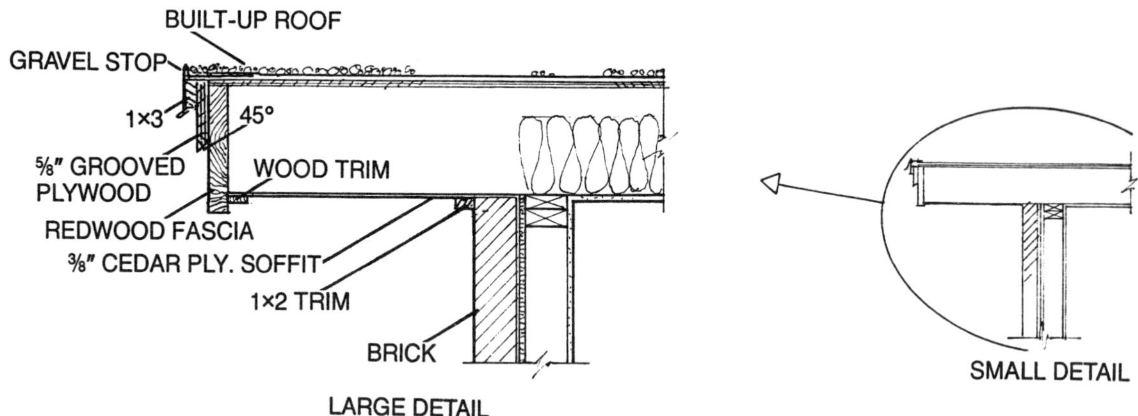

Larger details permit more accurate notation and allow easier reading of how maerials go together.

A BONUS FOR YOUR EFFORTS

The list of materials and specifications is a good double check for the completeness of the drawings.

For instance, suppose you want to specify the type of fascia material (the edge of the roof) such as redwood, hemlock, sheet metal, etc. and the soffit (underside of the roof overhang) such as plaster, plywood, etc. When you look at the drawings to check this condition you might find it was forgotten and not shown at all!

Another place easy to forget items is on the electrical lighting plan. A complete list of all fixtures, by name, will help to avoid omissions.

Remember, items not on the drawings or in the materials list and specifications, won't be in the bid. They could become expensive "extras" during the job!

NOTE: Somewhere in the drawings or specifications you should note who is responsible (you or the contractor) for obtaining and paying for all fees and permits required for construction.

Bidding and Construction

Bidding the work and building the project is done many ways. Three ways are mentioned here: (1) Ask several contractors to bid the work and select one for the job. (2) Be your own contractor. Bid the work yourself and coordinate the work of the subcontractors through construction. (3) Get prices on materials and do the construction work yourself.

If you proceed with method number (3), doing it yourself, you probably have construction experience. If not, I suggest you get some training prior to starting construction.

Should you proceed with method number (2), acting as your own contractor, the guidelines given here should be helpful.

Let's review procedures used to pursue method number (1), that is, to have several contractors bid the work and select one.

Selecting Bidders

Don't be content to "let your fingers do the walking" in the yellow pages. Spend time to select the most qualified bidders.

PITFALLS

There are many good builders, but "rip-off artists" do exist, so beware. Consumer Affairs departments of various government agencies continue to verify that point. Surveys taken reveal wide disparity in bids and contracts for the same job. In fact, remodelers estimating the same work can vary in price by as much as *three hundred percent*! Projected completion dates vary from three weeks to three months.

If pressure tactics are used — back away. If a remodeler tells you it takes only a half hour to evaluate the drawings and specifications for an estimate — beware! If a builder doesn't use understandable language, look elsewhere.

REFERENCES ARE IMPORTANT

Ask the contractor how long he's been in business. Verify that with the registrar of contractors, county clerk, or state licensing board.

Ask for owner references on his last several jobs. (Be sure they aren't brothers-in-law or cousins.) Look at the completed work.

Ask the references if the contractor did the following:

Start on time.
Finish on time.
Cooperate with homeowner and family during construction.
Keep the construction area tidy and clean up at completion.
Was the boss (the one you are now dealing with) on the job site.
Is workmanship good — any problems since and, if so, did the contractor respond quickly and take care of them?

GETTING A GOOD ONE

Ask neighbors and friends. Usually they have nothing to gain from a recommendation and you can easily check the contractor's work.

Other sources for recommendations are impartial local professionals and professional organizations.

Ask the Better Business Bureau and consumer protection agencies about complaints against any one on your list. How were complaints resolved? None of this is fail-safe, but is worth doing.

Never feel awkward about interviewing prospective contractors at length before construction bidding.

BID LIST SIZE

More than one bidder is advisable for a competitive price. Bid list size depends upon the project. A small project should have a smaller number of bidders, say two to four. Home remodeling projects are generally small projects.

It takes time to bid any project. The larger the list of bidders, the less the odds of any one bidder getting the job. Therefore, a large list of bidders might scare away the one contractor you really want.

BIDDERS SHOULD BE SIMILAR

Select builders of comparable quality. To include one bidder of marginal quality will erode the serious intent of good builders. They may assume that the lower quality bidder will plan to cut corners to become low bidder. Therefore, they might not spend the time required to give you a competitive bid.

The Bidding Process

After selecting bidders, give each two copies of the plans and materials list and specifications. Normally, you furnish these free of charge. If a bidder wants more copies, he can buy them at the cost of making them.

QUESTIONS AND ANSWERS

Even with a good set of drawings and specifications, questions come up during bidding. A bidder may want to do something different than as shown on the drawings. Also, it's rare to have a "perfect" set of drawings and he will ask for clarification.

A bidder might want to substitute products or materials at variance from the drawings and specifications. *Always* get independent verification about quality of substitutions, or don't allow them. Beware of exaggerated claims.

Write down any change agreed upon. Let other bidders know about the changes so all are bidding on the same thing. To prevent dispute during or after construction, each of you should have a written copy of all changes. Have all bids submitted to you *on the same date.*

Awarding the Contract for Construction

It's not always clear cut as to whom you will select. Here are things to look for:

If the low bidder is far lower than the next lowest bidder (say 15% or more), be cautious. There may be no problem, but review (with him) the drawings and specifications. Satisfy yourself that he did not forget something. You want the best price, but your purpose is to benefit from his expertise, not his mistakes.

If the bids are higher than your budget, here are several possible reasons: (a) Your budget is unrealistically low; (b) All bidders, for whatever reason, didn't estimate carefully for the lowest possible cost; (c) Drawings and specifications might not be complete enough for accurate estimating.

Regarding items (b) and (c), talk to the bidders. Satisfy yourself as to their position. Discuss the completeness and clarity of the drawings and specifications.

The culprit may be item (a), too much work for the budget. Discuss this with the low bidder. Ask where building costs can be cut. Rethink your priorities to see what you can eliminate. Another option, of course, is to remodel in stages.

If you decide to remodel in stages, I advise consulting an architect who does this sort of work. Spending money efficiently, when building in stages, is sometimes difficult. Also, you must avoid having a half finished project that looks half finished!

Item (b) is rare, but, if it appears evident, select new bidders. Question them about their work load. Ask if they really want the work and will bid competitively.

If item (c) is apparent, work with the lowest bidder. Decide if the drawings must be added to or clarified to help obtain better bids.

It is not uncommon that a combination of the above reasons is the cause of high bids. An important point: It is seldom necessary to give up a project. You can usually get what you need, or find a way to compromise and be content with the result.

Holding the Price

It's contract-signing time and the price suddenly takes a jump! If the reasons given are that materials costs have risen or the work will take more time, consider going back to the next lowest bidder.

Starting Construction

Be business-like in your approach to construction. There are many considerations. A few reminders are listed below.

INSURANCE

Your contractor should carry proper insurance. That includes liability insurance (employees, comprehensive, and auto). His subcontractors should carry similar insurance. Have your agent check all coverage for proper limits and completeness.

In addition, he and his subs should carry workman's compensation insurance. Have the contractor furnish proof of all coverage and review it with your agent. Ask an attorney to review all facets of your contract.

HOMEOWNER COVERAGE

You need extra insurance during construction. Work with your agent. Be sure your liability and fire coverage are adequate.

WARRANTY

Does your contractor provide a written warranty on workmanship? Some states require it. A minimum of one year is in line.

THE CONTRACT

Always have a written agreement with a contractor, even for small jobs. Take part in drawing it up. Let the contractor know you will be active and interested.

Consult your attorney before signing. The contract doesn't have to be long, or filled with legally hard-to-understand jargon. It should *state exactly what is to be done and for how much.*

NOTE: I am not an attorney and the following should not be considered legal advice. Every situation is different. Items listed below are a few general reminders of things to consider for your contract.

1. An itemized list of all drawings, materials list, and specifications.
2. Describe additional work or changes agreed upon.
3. Total cost of the job and the method of paying the contractor. *There is seldom a good reason to pay any money before work is done.* I advise against it! (It is common practice to reserve 10% of each payment as a final payment to be made when all work is completed and checked.)
4. Have a clause whereby you withhold final payment for at least a week after job completion. This gives you time to thoroughly inspect the work. Job completion is not a fact until all municipal building inspectors have checked and approved the work.
5. It's wise to call for a signed lien waiver (from the contractor, subcontractors, and major suppliers) when you pay the contractor. Check with your attorney on this provision.
6. As added protection, the contractor may furnish a performance bond for assurance of job completion. This is not always practical for small jobs and it adds a small cost to the contract price. Ask your attorney.
7. Include the starting date and approximate completion date. The contractor should be close to these dates or have a good reason why not.
8. Before construction starts, the contractor should obtain and post building permits. You need one to comply with local building codes. Also, without one, the proper inspections by city or county inspectors will not be made. They check to see that the work meets building code standards.
9. Have your attorney check the contract before signing.

The Construction Process

As with most business arrangements, the basics apply. Common sense, and the attitude of being reasonable, go a long way toward success. Try, early on, to establish the posture between you and the builder, of mutual fairness.

Following are some points to keep in mind:

1. Inspect the work, but don't interfere with the work in progress. A good time to inspect the job is before or after the work day, but while it's still daylight.
2. Hire consultants to check something you have doubts about, such as mechanical equipment, electrical, plumbing, or structural work.
3. If you initiate a change during construction discuss, with the builder, the least expensive way to make it. The cost is passed on to you. Make changes in writing, with the cost noted.
4. Don't give directions to subcontractors. Always go to the general contractor. He must maintain control of the job, and the subs.
5. Be available. Be prompt with answers and decisions.
6. Keep the agreed completion date in mind. Have periodic meetings with the builder about the progress. Let him know of your interest to finish on time.
7. If you are supplying various appliances, fixtures, or special materials during construction, pursue the ordering and arrival of same.
8. The contractor must furnish many items for your renovation. Contractors can forget things, too, so it's OK to ask if they have been ordered.
9. A job taking several months to complete requires monthly progress payments to the contractor. Payment requests should contain a trade-by-trade breakdown of labor and materials in place. Check the construction before making payments.
10. When nearing completion, carefully check the work. Avoid approving construction with a hurried inspection. Be sure all is done according to the terms of the contract.
11. If construction is being monitored by local authorities, don't make final payment until all work has been approved and you have received their certificates of approval.

Doing it Yourself is Not for Everyone

Regardless of the details, home remodeling should be fun. Throughout the book we discussed options for planning, design, and construction. Select the best approach for *your* situation. Some of you want to do it all yourself, including construction. Others will prefer to work with consultants throughout the project.

Please Note

As earlier stated, I do recommend that you retain the advice and services of professionals. That recommendation includes: planning and design through completion of construction (architect); site work (civil engineer); the structural system (structural engineer); insurance, contracts, etc. (insurance agent and attorney, knowledgeable about construction).

Retaining a Professional

Review the previous chapter if you choose to retain an architect. It covers their selection and participation with you in the stages of the work. Following is a brief review of those stages:

CHOOSING AND RETAINING THE CONSULTANT

How do you find a good one? Ask and look. Find completed projects you like and ask who was responsible. When you speak with consultants, get references and a list of completed projects. Talk with their former clients. Methods of retainer vary greatly. Guidelines given in Chapter 13 should be helpful.

THE PLANNING AND DESIGN PHASE

Once retained, give your architect *all* the information you have, including the budget for remodeling. The architect is the last person to be coy with about available funds. No one is in a better position to help you spend it wisely. To misrepresent the amount you will spend, means wasted effort and final results less than they could have been.

Other information to provide the architect includes: Your likes and dislikes *about everything*, including: finish building materials, colors, textures, lighting, etc.

It's not necessary to attempt rough planning and design sketches on your own. Good designers are able to come up with ideas and develop complete remodeling plans based on your priorities and desires. It's better not to become attached to an early attempt of your own. To do so, might inhibit your ability to accept a good, but completely different, scheme presented by the architect.

THE CONSTRUCTION DRAWINGS AND SPECIFICATIONS

Once you're satisfied with the final design, the architect begins work on construction drawings and specifications.

During this time you may be answering questions presented by the architect. They might pertain to things like kitchen appliance selection, final choice on finish materials, plumbing fixture selection, lighting, etc. It's also a time to line up your financing, if you haven't done so.

The more input you give the architect during initial meetings, prior to and during the planning phase, the smoother things should go as construction drawings progress.

BIDDING THE WORK

Work together with the architect to develop a list of contractors to bid your remodeling. (Selecting and working with bidders is discussed earlier in this chapter under "Doing-It-Yourself.")

The amount of bidding time depends upon the complexity of your project, but is typically two or three weeks. During that time the architect works with the bidders, answering questions, and generally trying to obtain the best possible bids.

SELECTING THE CONTRACTOR

If you have selected bidders wisely, you normally accept the lowest bid. Your architect and attorney can provide assistance in contractor selection and awarding the contract.

CONSTRUCTION

During this final phase of your "Dream House" project, your professional consultant can carry the ball. Among other things, this allows you to enjoy improvements as they emerge, without worrying about details.

In Summary — Choices for Success

You will make many decisions throughout your remodeling project. Choices include methods and materials. They relate to cost, function and aesthetics. How should you do it — this way or that way?

I have a philosophy about ideas in any form, which includes this premise: You can always scale down from a design with big ideas — scale it down to meet your budget. But, without any big ideas to start with, there is nothing to build on. "Big ideas" defined, includes words like *far-reaching* (but *not grandiose*). So, open your mind and let it roam free.

Remember a basic thought expressed throughout this book: When possible, make decisions based on the directions that will best enhance your desired lifestyle. Attempt always to increase the quality of your environment and the pleasure derived from your home.

Glossary

ABUT — Join one end of a material to another material.

ACCENT LIGHTING — Directional lighting to emphasize a particular object.

ACOUSTICAL — Material with sound absorbing qualities.

ANCHOR BOLT — Threaded steel rod inserted in a masonry wall or concrete footing to anchor ledgers or plates.

BACKFILL — Replacing excavated earth, usually against foundation or stem wall, or in a ditch.

BALUSTER — Any of the small posts under a railing in a staircase.

BASEBOARD (Base) — Trim or finish material at intersection of floor and wall.

BATTEN — Strip of wood, usually vertical, covering a joint or used in a series as part of a design.

BEAM — Horizontal member, structurally supporting a load.

BEARING PARTITION — Interior wall which supports a load.

BOARD FOOT — Unit of measurement for wood quantity, 1″ thick, 12″ wide and 12″ long.

BRACE — Stabilizing member used to stiffen a portion of a structure.

BRICK VENEER — Brick facing.

BRIDGING — Cross bracing used between joists.

BTU — British Thermal Unit, a unit for measuring heat.

BUILT-UP-ROOF — Layers of roofing felts and asphaltic compound.

CANT — Angular member used under finish roofing, normally to eliminate right angle at intersection of roof and wall.

CANTILEVER — A beam secured at one end, extending over and projecting from a support.

CASEMENT — A window frame that opens from hinges on the side.

CAULKING — Compound used to seal or waterproof joints or cracks.

CENTER TO CENTER — Also noted as C.C., measurement from center of one member to center of another.

CLERESTORY — (Clearstory) The upper portion of a building (space) with windows above adjacent roofs.

COLUMN — A vertical structural member supporting a load.

CONTROL JOINT — A linear space separating areas of material that helps to control the location of cracking due to expansion and contraction.

COPING — The capping or covering to a wall.

CORBEL — Portion of building material projecting from a wall, sometimes used for support.

COUNTERSINK — Recessing the head of a screw, nail or bolt.

COVE LIGHTING — Lighting shielded by a horizontal ledge or recess, distributing light on upper wall and ceiling.

CRAWL SPACE — Shallow access space, usually between ground and floor framing.

CRICKET — Pitch in roof to divert water.

DIRECT LIGHTING — At lease 90% of emitted light is directed toward the surface to be illuminated.

DORMER — A window in a sloping roof.

DOUBLE HUNG — Describes a window divided horizontally, both top and bottom sections of which operate up and down.

DOWNLIGHT — A small, direct light fixture — recessed, surface mounted, or suspended.

DOWNSPOUT — A pipe, usually metal or plastic, which carries water from gutters or roof drains to the ground.

DRY WALL — (Gypsum board) sheets of paper covered plaster.

DUCT — A tube or conduit which conveys and distributes air for heating or air conditioning. Also refers to a wire conduit.

EASEMENT — A right which one has in the land of another; as a right of way, access to water, power, etc.

EAVES — The lower part of a roof projecting beyond the face of the wall.

ELEVATION — The surface or face of something (building, interior wall, etc.) viewed straight on, without perspective.

FACADE — The elevation or main face of a building.

FASCIA — A vertical band, usually with a small projection, at the edge of a roof.

FLASHING — Metal or other sheet material used in wall or roof construction to keep out moisture.

FOOTING — A thickened section of concrete, wider than the foundation wall or column it supports.

FOUNDATION — The supporting part of a structure, below the floor system and below grade.

FURRING — Wood or metal strips fastened to wall or ceiling over which a finish material will be placed.

GABLE — The sloping ends of a ridged roof and the triangular segment of wall they enclose.

GLAZING — Glass set into window frames or openings.

GROUT — A thinned mortar used to fill voids and cavities in masonry.

GYPSUM BOARD — (Dry wall) Sheets of paper covered plaster.

HARDWARE — Exposed metal parts of a house, such as doorknobs and locks, door and window hinges, levers, cabinet hinges, drawer pulls, etc.

HEAD — Horizontal section at the top of a wall opening (i.e., top section of a door or window).

HIPPED ROOF — Roof sloping on four sides.

HOSE BIBB — End of water pipe, threaded for hose connection, on an outside wall.

INCANDESCENT LAMP — Normal light bulb in every day use.

INDIRECT LIGHTING — The greater percentage of light is emitted upward.

INSULATION — A material with high resistance to transmission of heat or cold.

JALOUSIE — Narrow glass slats in windows, usually operable.

JAMB — Sides of door and window.

JOIST — Member, in a series of members, used to support floor, ceiling, or roof.

KEYSTONE — The central stone of a semicircular arch.

LAG SCREW — Square or hexagonal headed wood screw, normally used for heavy duty.

LAMINATE — Layers of material bonded together.

LANDING — A platform at the end of a flight of stairs or between flights of stairs.

LEDGER — Wood member anchored to wall, used for supporting end of joist.

LIEN WAIVER — In construction, a document attesting that a party has been paid for labor and materials.

LINTEL — Horizontal structural member spanning an opening.

LOAD BEARING WALL — Wall supporting a load.

MANSARD — A four sided roof with two slopes each side, the lower slope being steeper than the upper.

MECHANICAL EQUIPMENT — Heating, ventilating, and air conditioning equipment.

MILLWORK — Finished wood work and products that usually require refinement and attention to detail. Items include door and window frames, trim, moldings, paneling, balusters, and hand rails.

MODULAR — Repeated units of divisible measurement.

MOLDING — A linear trim material, usually with a curved surface, used for decoration or to cover a joint.

MULLION — Vertical member separating two or more windows.

NONBEARING PARTITION — An interior wall supporting its own weight, but no other load.

NONBEARING WALL — A wall supporting its own weight and no other load.

PARAPET — A wall projecting above the roof.

PARTITION — Interior dividing wall.

PENNY — Refers to nail length. For instance, a 10 penny nail is 3 inches long.

PIER — A mass of masonry, as distinct from a column, used for structural support.

PITCH — Slope in a roof.

PLATE — Horizontal member, usually wood, directly under wall studs, joists, or roof trusses.

PLUMB — Vertically level or true.

POINTING — To mortar fill crevices or voids in the joints of a masonry wall.

PROGRAM — A written description of requirements for a building or project. Requirements are based on needs and desires of building occupants.

RAFTER — Normally a roof timber that extends from the ridge to the eaves.

REBAR — Abbreviation for steel reinforcing bar used in concrete or grouted masonry walls to provide tensile strength.

RESILIENT — Ability to return to original shape.

RIDGE — Apex of a sloping roof, running from end to end.

RISER — The vertical portion of a step, between treads.

RUSTICATION — Masonry or stonework with roughened surfaces and recessed joints.

SCALE — The proportion that the building in a drawing bears to the real building it represents (i.e., ¼ inch equals one foot).

SCUTTLE — An opening in ceiling or roof for access.

SET BACK — The required distance for separating building construction from a property line.

SHAKE — Wood shingles, hand split.

SHEATHING — Material covering joists, rafters, or studs, used under the finished material.

SHIM — A wedge or filler.

SOFFIT — Underside of exterior overhang.

SOLE — Flat horizontal member under studs.

SPECIFICATIONS — Written instructions and description of building materials, methods and installation.

STUDS — Vertical members in wall framing.

SUB FLOOR — Material under the finish floor.

TOE NAIL — Nail driven in at an angle.

TONGUE-AND-GROOVE JOINT — A joint in which the tongue of one board fits into the groove of another.

TREAD — The horizontal portion of a stair.

TRUSS — A rigid framework of members for supporting the roof, usually bearing on outside walls.

VAPOR BARRIER — A water resistant membrane.

VENT — A pipe or opening which allows flow of air.

WEATHERSTRIP — Sealing material used at doors and windows.

Index

A

Accent lighting, 261
Acoustics, 205
Additions, 167-189
  as aesthetic compliments to existing house, 171-3
  check list, 188-9
  drainage considerations, 167-8
  effect on market value, 178
  effect on outside space, 167
  not always cost-effective, 178
  planning/preparation, 167-8
  property line considerations, 167
  property lines, 169-170
  protecting existing interior space, 168-9
  second floor, 174-5
  site considerations, 167
  site plan, 169
  suggestions for location, 167-8
Advice, expert, when to solicit, 156-7
Aesthetic considerations, 21
Appliances, kitchen, 30
Architect, 15, 223-9
  construction drawings and specifications, 225
  design sketches, 224
  determining the fee, 223-4
  how to select, 223
  planning and design, 224
  role in remodeling design, 15
  when to employ, 228-9
  working with, 223-6
Architectural draftsman, 16
Art and accessories, 207
  where to buy, 207
Attic, 60-2
  as children's play area, 62
  remodeling options, 60-2
Attorney, when to consult, 257
Awarding construction contract, 256

B

Basement, remodeling options, 62-3
Basement storage, 110
Bath and bedroom, 87-104
Bathroom storage, 109
Bathrooms, 98-101
  subdividing, 98-9
Bearing partition, 261
Bearing wall, 233-4
  removing, 233-4
Bed designs, 92-4
Bed, platform, 94
Bedrooms, 87-9, 91-2, 94, 96, 97
  children's, 91-2
  dressing area, 96
  furnishings and accessories, 92
  guest, 87-9
  lighting, 97
  planning the layout, 94
  storage, accessories, 97
  storage, closets, 96
Bedroom and bath, 87-104, 102-3
  check list, 102-3
Bedroom locations, 87
Bedroom storage, 94-6, 108-9
  adults, 96
  children's, 94-5
Bidders, selecting, 254-5
Bidding process, 255
Bidding the work, 225, 254-6
Bids, from contractors, 240-1, 254-6
"Big Idea", 219, 259
Budget planning, 219-21
  cost and design factors, 220-1
  cost effective, 219-21
  exterior walls, 220
  financing, 221-2
  flooring, 220
  heating/cooling equipment, 220
  remodeling in stages, 221
  roofing, 220
Budget, 19, 219-222
  factors to consider, 219
  remodeling, 19
  remodeling/renovation, 219-222
Building inspectors, 257
Building permits, 257
Built-in furniture, 206
Built-ins, 54, 156
  family room, 54
  vacuum system, 156

C
Cantilever, 261
Carpet and floor coverings, 205-6
Carpet and floor coverings, where to buy, 205-6
Carpets, varieties of, 247-250
CHECK LISTS
  Additions, 188-9
  Bedroom and bath, 102-3
  Exterior space/general areas, 26-7
  Family room/living spaces, 72-3
  Furnishings, exterior, 216-7
  Furnishings, interior, 214-5
  Indoor recreation/hobby, 82-3
  Interior space/general areas, 24-5
  Kitchen and dining/general design, 48-9
  Kitchen features, 50-1
  Kitchen, 30
  Landscaping, 200-1
  Lighting, exterior, 152-3
  Lighting, interior, 150-1
  Maintenance and repair, 198-9
  Outdoor recreation/hobby, 84-5
  Special purpose, exterior, 164-5
  Special purpose, interior, 162-3
  Storage spaces, 116-7
  Work/utility/storage, 118-9
Check lists, 22-3, 242
  as reference tools, 242
  filling in, 22-3
Children's bedroom/play room suite, 91
Children's bedrooms, 91-2
Clerestory, 262
Color selections, 22
Construction drawings and specifications, 225, 240, 241-2
  as cost control tools, 240
  doing them yourself, 241-2
  important for do-it-yourself project, 241
Construction process, 257-8
Construction terminology, 243
Construction, 21, 225-6
  phasing, 21
  responsibilities of parties involved, 225-6
  starting the, 256-7
Consultants, choosing and retaining, 258-9
Contract, remodeling, 257
Contract for construction, awarding the, 256
Contractor, selecting the, 225, 259
Contractor's warranty, 257
Contractors, references, importance of, 255
Contractors' bids, 240-1, 254-6
Corbel, 262
Cost control, 240
"Cost Plus", meaning of, 16
Costs, estimating, 16
Counter and vanity tops, 250
Cove lighting, 262
Cricket, 262

D
Darkroom, 160-1
Den and study, 59-60
  location of, 60
Design, good, 13
Design program, 14, 219
  importance of, 14
Design sketches, 224
Design solutions, preconceived, 14
Dining and kitchen, 29-51
Dining spaces, 39-40
  options, 39-40
Do-it-Yourself projects, 16, 19
Doing it yourself, not for everyone, 258
Draftsman, architectural, 16
Drawings, construction, as cost control tools, 240
Drawings, value of, 15-6
Dressing area, bedroom, 96

E
Easement, 262
Electrician, when to consult, 138
Entrance to home, 197
Entrance, creating a, 21
Expert advice, when to solicit, 156-7
Exterior improvements, 194
  landscaping, 194
  storage, 194
Exterior improvements and landscaping, 191-201
  cosmetic, 191-2
Exterior lighting, 144-7
  pre-planning, 144-5
  security and safety, 145
Exterior maintenance, 191-2
Exterior surface materials, 250-1

F
Family room, 53-78
  built-ins, 54
  multipurpose, 53
  open planning, 58
  openness from kitchen, 58
Family room and living spaces, 53-73
Family room/living spaces, check list, 72-3
Fascia, 262
Financing the project, 221-2
  lenders' fees, 222
  personal borrowing, 222
  refinancing, 221-2
  second mortgage, 221
Finish materials, 21-2
  floor, 21-2
  walls and ceilings, 22
Fireplace, 64-6
  adding, 64-6
  designs, 64-6
  location of, 66
Floor materials, 21-2
Floor plan, 16-9, 20
  as planning tool, 16-9
  dimensions added, 18
  existing, sketch of, 17
  redrawn to scale, 20
Flooring materials, 244-250
Function, improving, 21
Furnishings, 22, 203-217
  compatible with owners' personality, 203
  exterior, check list, 216-7
  interior, check list, 214-5
  layout, 207-211

Furniture, 108, 206
built-in, 206
used for storage, 108
Furniture selection, 203, 206-7
budget, 206-7
cost control, 203
danger of over-furnishing, 204
planning, 204-5

G
Garage storage, 110
Garage/carport conversions, 62
Garden, indoor, 159-160
Gardening room, 160
Getting it done, 243-259
Getting started, 13-27
Glossary, 261-5
Good design, 13
Graph paper, 19
Greenhouse, 155, 160
Guest bedroom, 87-9
Gymnasium, 155

H
Habit patterns, 14
Habit trap, 14
Heating, ventilating, and air conditioning equipment (HVAC), 253
Hobby and recreation areas, 75-85
Hobby space, 75-6
electrical needs, 76
equipment needs, 76
multipurpose, 75
objectives, 75-6
Home, 15
as economic venture, 15
as personal sanctuary, 15
Home entrance, 197
Home office, 155
HVAC, 253

I
Improvements, best investment return on, 15
Indirect lighting, 263
Indoor garden, 159-161
Indoor recreation space, 76-9
children's needs, 78-9
room arrangements, 77
storage space, 77-8
Indoor recreation/hobby, check list, 82-3
Inside storage, 105-9
Inspecting the work, 258
Inspectors, building, 257
Insurance, 256-7
contractor's, 256-7
homeowner's, 257
Intercom system, 156
Interior surface materials, 244
Investment in pleasure, 155

K
Keystone, 263
Kitchen, 30-3, 35, 37, 38, 41, 42-7, 30-2
cabinet drawings, detailed, 43
cabinets, 41
dishwasher location, 37
lighting, 42
microwave location, 38
oven location, 38
planning considerations, 43-7
planning, detailed, 42-7
sink location, 37
storage needs, 33, 35
surface materials, 41
walls and ceilings, 42
work area, 30-1
work triangle, 31-2
Kitchen and dining, 29-51
Kitchen and dining/general design, check list, 48-9
Kitchen cosmetics, 30
Kitchen efficiency, 30
Kitchen features, checklist, 50-1
Kitchen layout, sample, 34
Kitchen layouts, variations, 37
Kitchen plans, basic, 33
Kitchen remodeling, 29-38
appliances, 30
construction costs, 30
danger of overimprovement, 29
personal priorities, 29
planning, 36
style and decor, 30
Kitchen storage, 105-6

L
Landscaping check list, 200-1
Landscaping, 194, 196
as energy efficiency factor, 194
as part of overall exterior plan, 194
cost control, 194
design harmony, 196
Laundry appliances, 113-4
Laundry storage, 113
Library, 64
Lien waiver, 263
Light and color, 142-3
Light and texture, 144-5
Light fixtures and mirrors, 136
Lighting, 22, 97, 121-53, 205, 261, 262, 263
accent, 261
bedroom, 97
cove, 262
design flexibility, 125-6
dimmer switches, 139
effect on aesthetics, 125-6
exterior, 144-7
check list, 152-3
pre-planning, 145
security and safety, 145
indirect, 263
check list, 150-1
low voltage, 138-9
exterior, 138
interior, 138
master switching, 145
Natural and Artificial, 121-153
psychological effects, 122
Lighting and color, 137
Lighting considerations, summary, 148-9
Lighting effects, 121
Lighting needs/requirements, 124-5
Lighting placement, importance of experimentation, 136-7
Lighting plan, 254
Lights, multiple-switching, 123
"Living needs", 53
Living spaces and family rooms, 53-73

Luxury, affordable, 156

M
Maintenance and repair, check list, 198-9
Maintenance, exterior, 191-2
Mansard, 263
Market values in area, importance of, 15
Master bedroom location, 87
Master bedroom/bath suite, 88-90
Master switching, 145
Materials and specifications, sample list, 253
Materials, 243-4, 251-2
  finishing, importance of compatibility, 243-4
  selection of, 251-2
Millwork, 263
Mud room, 114
Multiple-switching lights, 123-4
Music room, 156

N
Nonbearing partition, 264

O
Office, at home, 155
Open planning, 58-9
  effect on heating/cooling costs, 58-9
  family room, 58
Outdoor dining, 40
Outdoor recreation, 79-81
  planning, 79
  transition space, 79
Outdoor recreation/hobby, check list, 84-5
Outside storage, 109-112
Overimprovement, 14-5, 29
  as result of poor design, 15
  danger of, 14-5
  kitchen remodeling, 29

P
Pantry storage, 33
Parapet, 264
Partition, 233-4, 240, 264
  nonbearing, 264
  removing, 233-4
Patterns, habit, 14
Permits, building, 257
Phasing construction, 21
Planning, 2280240
  considerations involved, 229-240
  final, 228
    doing it yourself, 228
    hiring a professional, 228
  importance of early rough sketches, 231-2
Plans, value of, 15-6
Platform bed, 94
Preconceptions, how to avoid, 14
Price, holding the, 256
Priorities, 227, 228
  deciding, 227, 228
  listing, 228
  wants vs. needs, 227
Priority ratings, 23
Privacy, needs for, 53-4, 58
  space for, 58
Professional, consulting for safety reasons, 223
Professionals, when to consult/retain, 258
Program, 264
Property deed restrictions, 175
Property line considerations, additions, 167
Property lines, relationship to planning of additions, 170-1

R
Recreation space, 76-81
  indoor, 76-9
    children's needs, 78-9
    converting space, 78
    room arrangements, 77
    storage space, 77-8
  outdoor, 79-81
    planning, 79
Remodeling, 19, 22, 29-38
  as family affair, 22
  budget, 19
  family involvement in, 19
  kitchen, 29-38
Remodeling contract, 257
Remodeling/renovation budget, 219-222
Restrictions, property deed, 175
Return on remodeling investment, economic, 228
Return on remodeling investment, personal satisfaction, 228
Roofing, 251
Roofing materials, 193
Rustication, 264

S
Sauna, 155, 156
Second floor, as addition, 174-5
Security alarm system, 156
Selecting the contractor, 225
Site considerations, additions, 167
Site plan, for planning of addition, 169
Skylights, 140-2
  for nighttime, 140-1
  for ventilation, 140
  orientation and heat gain, 140
  stained glass, 141-2
Solar equipment, 114-5
Sound, as affected by room shapes, 250
Special purpose spaces, 155-165
Special purpose, exterior, check list, 164-5
Special purpose, interior, check list, 162-3
Specifications, 264
Stained glass, 121
Standard materials, use of to save money, 242-3
Starting the construction, 256-7
Storage, 54, 94-6, 105-13
  basement, 110
  bathroom, 109
  bedroom, 94-6, 108-9
    accessories, 97
    closets, 96
  exterior, 194
  family room, 54
  garage, 110
  in furniture, 108

(Storage, continued)
inside, 105-9
kitchen, 105-6
laundry, 113
outside, 109-112
Storage and utility spaces, 105-119
Storage closet, large, importance of, 105
Storage needs, 33, 35
kitchen, 33, 35
pantry, 33
Storage spaces, check list, 116-7
Storage wall, family room, 54
Structural engineer, when to consult, 193
Studio, 155
Study and den, 59-60
Surface materials, 244, 250-1
exterior, 250-1
interior, 244
Surveyor, when to employ, 171
Swimming pool, 155

T
Terminology, construction, 243
Tiffany lamp, 142
Trap, habit, 14

U
Urban housing, remodeling, 15
Utility and storage spaces, 105-119
Utility locations, determining in early planning, 240

V
Vacuum system, built-in, 156
Vanity and counter tops, 250
Versatility, remodeling to provide, 67-71
Versatility, space, pre-planned, 54
Video theater, 156

W
Wall and ceiling materials, 22
Wall, bearing, 233
Warranty, contractor's, 257
Wet bar, family room, 55-7
Wine cellar, 156, 157-9
Work area, kitchen, 30-1
Work triangle, kitchen, 31-2
Work/utility/storage check list, 118-9
Working with an architect, 223-6

Z
Zoning laws, 175